Main

D0629684

African Children's and Youth Literature

Osayimwense Osa

Clark Atlanta University

Twayne Publishers
An Imprint of Simon & Schuster Macmillan
New York

Prentice Hall International
London Mexico City New Delhi Singapore Sydney Toronto

African Children's and Youth Literature
Osayimwense Osa

Copyright © 1995 by Twayne Publishers

Twayne Publishers
An Imprint of Simon & Schuster Macmillan
866 Third Avenue
New York, NY 10022

Library of Congress Cataloging-in-Publication Data

Osa, Osayimwense.
    African children's and youth literature / Osayimwense Osa.
        p.   cm.—(Twayne world authors series; TWAS 853)
    Includes bibliographical references and index.
    ISBN 0-8057-4524-6
    1. Children's literature, African (English)—History and criticism. 2. Young adult literature, African (English)—History and criticism. I. Title. II. Series.
PR9344.08   1995   94-44450
820.9'9282'096—dc20   CIP

10 9 8 7 6 5 4 3 2 1

Printed in the United States of America

To the evergreen memory of
My father, Pa Johnson Nagbare Osa, and my mother, Mama Osaruyi Osa,
who loved, inspired, and energized me in my infancy,
childhood, youth, and adulthood, igniting my imagination and
spirit of inquiry

Contents

Preface   ix
Acknowledgments   xv
Chronology   xvii
Introduction: A Farewell to Neglect   xix

Chapter One
Cyprian Ekwensi: Pioneer African Writer for Children and
Young Adults   1

Chapter Two
The Bride Price: A Masterpiece of African Youth Literature   25

Chapter Three
African Young Adult Love and Marriage   47

Chapter Four
Material Wealth, Greed, Corruption, and the African Young
Adult   66

Chapter Five
A Quest for Utopia: *A Paradise for the Masses* and African Youth
Activism   93

Chapter Six
African Children's and Youth Fiction about War   110

Chapter Seven
Reaching African Children and Youth and "Thinking
Multicultural"   136

Notes and References   143
Selected Bibliography   151
Index   159

Preface

The approach of this work is critical; it is a study of African children's authors and their works, intended to fill that yawning gap in the criticism of African literature—children's literature. It does so through a study of selected African literary works for children and young adults, focusing on Anglophone African countries—Nigeria, Ghana, Sierra Leone, Gambia, Kenya, Uganda, Tanzania, Malawi, Zimbabwe, and South Africa. In a work like this, certain geographical areas may be skirted primarily as a result of their low output in children's literature. For example, Sierra Leone has a strong oral tradition, but not much is now being done to keep it alive.[1] Virtually the same situation exists in Gambia, Tanzania, Uganda, Lesotho, Zambia, and Malawi. Andrée-Jeanne Tötemeyer opined that black protest writers, of which there were a considerable number, both in South Africa and in exile from that country, perhaps considered the writing of juvenile literature a luxury in the tense atmosphere of struggle they experienced.[2] After the death of apartheid, indications in the "new" South Africa are that the shaping of a common South African cultural identity by means of juvenile literature is gaining momentum.[3] Because the bulk of children's and youth literature is being written in Nigeria, the discussion of the children's and youth literature from this country is longer than that of the others.

The focus on Anglophone African countries is primarily for convenience and perspective. The children's literature in Francophone or Portuguese-speaking Africa is not very different because the political boundaries that made them Anglophone or Francophone or Portuguese-speaking took no real cognizance of tribal kingdoms or differences. An artificial political boundary divides Gambia and Senegal through the Wolof tribe territory. This is an artificial "division" of the same people. In fact, griots and storytellers in Gambia and Senegal are the same. Similarly the Ewe tribe is divided between Ghana and Togo. But it is still the same family. Some sections of Western Cameroon were a part of Nigeria. There are Yorubas in Dahomey (present-day Republic of Benin), a Francophone territory, as well as in Nigeria, an Anglophone territory. Folk tales from Anglophone, Francophone, or Portuguese-speaking Africa are very similar because their roots are in their indigenous culture and they were originally told in their indigenous tongues. And, of course, it is when they are told in these tongues that the thrust and impact of the tales are fully realized.

This being the first volume in the Twayne's World Authors Series to be devoted to African children's literature, it is necessary that a brief introduction to the origins or roots of African children's literature be given. Some space in this regard will be given to folk tale—the universal oral tradition of all, young and old.[4] Although folk tales abound on the African continent, only *An African Night's Entertainment* is discussed because it is an excellent example of a literary retelling of a traditional folk tale, and it has been very popular with African children and youth since its publication in 1962. It is discussed in Chapter 1 as one of Cyprian Ekwensi's works for children and youth.

This book's main focus is on the African youth novel, which is a very popular genre in contemporary African children's literature. The novels selected for discussion are the most outstanding ones addressing children and young adults and their interests and developmental tasks. *The Bride Price* is so rich that it receives a chapter of discussion to itself. Drama, biography, autobiography, short story, and the African school story that are not as substantive as the prose fiction are discussed only briefly.

Illustrated books and picture storybooks are not really dealt with in this study because they are not yet substantive enough to merit serious critical analysis. Nonetheless, it is significant to note that Meshach Asare's *The Brassman's Secret* (1981) epitomizes the Africanization of the children's literature based on the cultural heritage of the past. It was the first children's book that won the 1982 Noma Award Prize for publishing in Africa. It was cited by the Award Jury as "an exciting and unusual children's story, beautifully and imaginatively illustrated to bring out important aspects of Asante culture, particularly the crafting of the famous goldweights, and traditional Asante architecture." Like *The Brassman's Secret*, Buchi Emecheta's *Titch the Cat* (1979), illustrated by Thomas Joseph, and *Nowhere to Play* (1980) are not really dealt with. I do hope that picture books and illustrated books in African children's literature, African folk tales for children, and the pedagogical concern of African children's literature and its use for reading promotion will form interesting subjects of scholarship elsewhere.

This work does not, however, completely insulate itself from nonliterary scholars. The literary critic, the educator, and the librarian have much to learn from one another. As Anne Scott MacLeod says, "It is no one's benefit to divide the world of children's literature into a series of airtight compartments. All of us must resist isolation, no matter how specialized our interests."[5] In fact, children's literature is enriched by contributions from other disciplines, and such contribution is desired. This is reflected in the recent comment by U. C. Knoepflmacher that

> the time may not be far away when universities and colleges institute cross-curricular programs devoted to studies in childhood. Such programs would enlist the expertise of child psychologists, anthropologists, folklorists, sociologists, social historians, art historians, theologians, film and theater experts, as well as teachers of literature who might be called on to play a central role by offering their well established courses as core studies.[6]

The texts worth discussing here are either the most successful ones by the writers in question or major ones that provide the scholar with a composite picture of African children's and youth literature, including an impression of the quality of African children's writers' art in general. As in any literary corpus, there is certainly an apparent disparity in quality among the African children's and youth literature I discuss here. Because many of the texts have been neglected in criticism and because they may be hard to obtain, I have given useful plot summaries. As a book with a critical bias and not a historical one, this study concentrates primarily on works that I believe have substance and are highly significant. One overriding commonality among contemporary African children's literature is that it is preponderantly didactic. A didactic or moral stance has always been an integral part of African literature for juveniles.[7] Most of the writers of African children's literature derive their inspiration from traditional values in a strong desire to mold children along acceptable African way of life. This is why most African children's novels have a didactic bias. Chinua Achebe recently stated that

> our responsibility as Nigerians (or as Africans) of this generation is to strive to realize the potential good and avoid the ill. Clearly, children are central in all this, for it is their legacy and patrimony that we are talking about. If Nigeria (or Africa) is to become a united and humane society in the future, her children (and all other African children) must now be brought up on common vocabulary for the heroic and the cowardly, the just and the unjust. Which means preserving and refurbishing the landscape of the imagination and the domain of stories, and not—as our leaders seem to think—a verbal bombardment of patriotic exhortation and daily recitations of the National pledge and anthem.[8]

While stories are for entertainment, they are also seen as moral guides. Though geared toward children and the young adult audience, the primary works in this study can be equally enjoyable reading for adults. None of the writers are themselves children or young adults, but they capture the characteristics, predicament, and nuances of childhood and young adulthood so successfully that one can assert that childhood and young adulthood are alive in them. As Robert Cormier has said, "Most of us carry the baggage of that adolescence with us all our lives. And I think that's why a lot of young adult novels jump over the border of the genre and can be read by other people."[9] For Eleanor Cameron, "childhood is the enchanted cauldron out of which so much arises that there is far more than can be used."[10] Similarly, Virginia Hamilton recently said in her 1992 Hans Christian Andersen Award acceptance speech, "I hold in common with most authors of youth literature, a high degree of near-photographic memory from my own childhood. . . . I still keep inside me that curious six-year-old, that ten-year-old lover of pranks and jokes and the defiant thirteen–fourteen-year-old."[11] The works in this study primarily reflect the world of African children and youth. They also give African children and young adults a window through which they can view their world and integrate themselves into it. A comparative study of young adult literature of two or more countries (Western or non-Western), so as to see if adolescence is basically the same everywhere, is academically worthwhile.

Like many Africans I am bilingual. In addition to our indigenous tongues, we have, in a variety of degrees, mastery of the colonial language that our respective countries adopted as their official language as well as their language of instruction in schools. As one steeped in Edo culture of Benin City, Nigeria, where I was born and bred, I have included some Edo traditional expressions pertinent especially to children and have provided their English translations. Undoubtedly, African children's literature also needs to be expressed in African tongues. As Akinwumi Isola has rightly stated,

> Normally the society that structures the physical and cultural surroundings of children also provides them with their first language, which is the seminal foundation for literature. Sadly however, the debate over the most appropriate language for African writers suggests that some disaster has befallen African society—a disaster that has either rendered it incapable of supplying its citizens with their first language or made it impossible for that language to support the production of written literature.[12]

Isola concludes that "if these [African] children are ever to enjoy a relevant information and an acute sense of their own identity, they need to
be exposed to literature that has been written in their own mother
tongue" (26).

No disaster has really rendered African society incapable of supplying
its citizens with their first language(s) or made it impossible for their languages to support the production of their written literature. The numerous first languages of Africans can vitally support the production of
written literature. G. A. Gundu, a native speaker of Tiv, said in 1989
that "with the steady rise of serious studies of African languages it is
hoped that criticism of children's literature in these tongues will be genuinely addressed."[13] Such a study will obviously complement this one in
English.

Drawing from various segments of African culture, this study seeks to
illuminate African cultural assumptions, especially those about love and
marriage and other aspects of social conduct that non-Africans may find
strange. Furthermore, it also helps to elucidate that although Africa has
regional or cultural similarities, it is not a homogenous country but a
vibrant, heterogenous continent. Just as there is no language called
"African," so also there is really no one culture that cuts across the whole
continent. While the bride price on young adult girls may be quite high
in some African communities, it is minimal and demanded only by tradition or custom in others. While some African communities encourage
their youth to marry within their extended family—that is, marriage
between cousins, nieces, and other relations—others do not. In the latter category of communities, the slightest indication of any blood relationship between a young man and his fiancée is enough grounds to end
an amorous relationship or any marriage negotiation. This diversity is
reflected in this work.

Sociocultural connections with African America and the Caribbean
are quite strong in African literature and criticism. African children's and
youth literature is a major and significant part of the children's literature
of the black world (Africa, African America, and the Caribbean), which
merits scholarly attention. I hope this book will be an inroad to such
endeavor.

Acknowledgments

I am indebted to Dr. Ruth MacDonald of Bay Path College for her meticulous guidance and suggestions throughout the preparation of this work. I sincerely acknowledge all the assistance and support I have received over the years from Dr. Nancy J. Schmidt of Indiana who has been my special mentor in African children's literature. I wish to express my gratitude to the following: Dr. Hugh Keenan of Georgia State University for his helpful advice; Dr. Richard F. Abrahamson who introduced me to scholarship in children's literature at the University of Houston; Dr. David Dorsey of Clark Atlanta University for his insightful comments; the Twayne editors Anne Kiefer, Lesley Poliner, and Barbara Sutton for their diligent editorial work; Mr. John Nix and Mrs. Kemie Nix, Founder and Executive Director of Children's Literature for Children in Atlanta for their multifaceted assistance during the writing of this work; Mr. Robert M. Quarles, the Interlibrary Loans Coordinator of the Atlanta University Center's Robert W. Woodruff Library, who located for me materials in various libraries. I also gratefully acknowledge the financial assistance of the Clark Atlanta University Faculty Development Program, which enabled me to complete the typing of the manuscript. My thanks to my family—Justina Osa, Osaguona, Osazuwa, Ewere, and Etin-Osa, whom I physically missed for a long time during my writing of this book.

I thank the following publishers for permission to quote from their works: Macmillan Press, Ltd., Paperback Publishers, African Universities Press, Ravan Press (South Africa), Evans, Heinemann Educational Books, Cambridge University Press, and George Braziller, Inc., Publishers.

Chronology

1973   University of Ife (now Obafemi Awolowo University) hosts the conference on Publishing and Book Development, giving significant attention to children's literature.

1976   International Seminar on the Writing and Production of Literature for Children is held at the University of Ghana, Legon, under the auspices of UNESCO.

1977   The Children's Literature Association of Nigeria (CLAN) is founded. Macmillan begins publication of its young adult novels in its "Pacesetters" series.

1978   The Children's Literature Foundation (CLF) is founded in Ghana.

1979   Nigeria English Studies Association devotes its annual conference in Lagos to Junior Literature in English as part of its celebration of the International Year of the Child.

1980   Zimbabwe (former Southern Rhodesia) gains political independence after bloody struggle.

1981   Nancy J. Schmidt's *Children's Fiction about Africa in English* is published by *Conch Magazine* in New York.

1983   The seminar "Creative Writing and Publishing for Children in Africa Today" is held in Freetown, Sierra Leone.

1984   The Nineteenth Congress of the International Board on Books for Young People, devoted to "Children's Book Production and Distribution in Developing Countries," is held in Nicosia, Cyprus.

1985   Agbo Areo publishes *A Paradise for the Masses*, his work on African youth activism.

1986   The International Youth Library in Munich and the German Commission for UNESCO hold a conference on African youth literature at Schloss Blutenburg in Munich.

1987   South Africa's first national symposium on children's literature, "Towards Understanding . . . Children's Books for all South Africa's Children," is held; it results in the eventual creation of the Children's Book Forum (CBF). Zimbabwe hosts International Book Fair devoted to children's literature in Africa.

1988   The International Youth Library in Munich hosts its first international conference—"Children's Literature Research: International Resources and Exchange"— 5–7 April.

1989   *Journal of African Children's Literature* (now *Journal of African Children's and Youth Literature*) is founded at the Bendel State University (now the Edo State University) in Ekpoma, Nigeria.

1990   Nelson Mandela is released from jail after 27 years. Namibia gains independence. Georgia State University's English Department offers a seminar course in African children's literature (summer).

1991   University of Calabar, Nigeria, devotes its eleventh annual conference on English language and literature to "Children and Literature in Africa." Clark Atlanta University School of Library and Information Studies offers a graduate course in African children's literature.

1992   The course Africana Children's Literature is offered at Clark Atlanta University's English Department. South Africa is admitted as member nation of the International Board on Books for Young People.

1993   As part of its thirtieth-anniversary celebration Kennesaw State College, Atlanta, includes "Children's Literature in Africa" in its 1993 Conference on Children's Literature, "Illuminating Young Minds."

Introduction: A Farewell to Neglect

In scholarly works on the history of African literature, children's literature has been given little or no attention. A. W. Kayper Mensah and Horst Wolff's *Ghanaian Writing*[1] and Martin Tucker's *Africa in Modern Literature: A Survey of Contemporary Writing*[2] neglect children's literature as a genre. C. L. Innes's 1990 work, *Chinua Achebe*, does not discuss Chinua Achebe's writing for children—a discussion that would have undoubtedly enriched the book. And as Shaun F. D. Hughes remarks, more could have been made of Achebe's juvenile fiction to determine how it fits into his idea of a curriculum for African children and to investigate the traditional values he chooses to emphasize in the texts as well as the narrative strategies he finds appropriate for this kind of writing.[3] Adrian Roscoe's *Mother Is Gold: A Study of West African Literature*[4] makes brief mention of children's literature, devoting 11 pages to describing folklore of several Nigerian authors. Ernest Emenyonu discusses briefly Cyprian Ekwensi's children's writing in *Cyprian Ekwensi*.[5]

The recent book *Nigerian Female Writers: A Critical Perspective*[6] devotes its fourth section to children's literature. The section attempts to look at all the children's works—both successful and unsuccessful—of 12 female Nigerian writers, but only the names and biographical information of such writers as Helen Ovbiagele, Charry Ada Onwu, and Anji Ossai are given, and nothing about their works. Despite this shortcoming, the inclusion of female children's writers in *Nigerian Female Writers: A Critical Perspective* is an exemplary step, considering that they have been sadly neglected for too long. As J. O. J. Nwachuku-Agbada rightly notes in his review of that volume, however, "Only one or two of the essays in this section focus upon the problem of what constitutes successful children's literature." Furthermore, he states that "all too often the critics rehash the plots of various texts and make little effort to assail their authors' thematic and artistic flaws vis-à-vis the needs of their young audience readers."[7] The critics seem to "rehash" the plots of some texts because they are ephemeral. The critics cannot intellectually manufacture what is not there. As a matter of fact, only works of value and significance in children's and young adult literature can equally elicit a rich scholarly discourse.

I have elsewhere maintained that a substantive body of works for African children and youth now exists to merit scholarly attention;[8] and even then it is mainly the successful ones that can fruitfully engage the literary critic's attention. There are, of course, some problems in such a study. According to Nancy J. Schmidt, who has developed a keen interest in research in African children's literature since the 1960s, "Children's literature about Africa is an uncharted universe. It is written in English, French, German, and other European languages, as well as in Hausa, Swahili, Twi, Yoruba and other African languages. There is no bibliography which thoroughly covers children's literature about Africa in one European or African language."[9] It is interesting to note that this problem of bibliography is not peculiar to Africa. As Anne Scott MacLeod has noted, "The lack of comprehensive bibliographical systems internationally as well as nationally, has been a major frustration for those working in the field" (MacLeod, 217).

The works in this study are written in English by authors from various tribal backgrounds in Africa and these works reflect this fact.[10] For example, the phenomenon of "Magun" in *A Paradise for the Masses* is mainly in the Yoruba community, and the author of this novel is Agbo Areo, who is a Yoruba. The *osu* tradition in *The Bride Price* is mainly among the Igbo, and Buchi Emecheta, the author of this work, is an Igbo. Their works that have some tribal differences as well as similarities can be regarded as national because they are Nigerian. It is the same pattern in other African countries. Certainly, there are shared characteristics in African children's literature—from the rich heritage of African oral literature through contemporary realistic fiction for children and young adults.

Three detailed studies of African children's literature provide useful information on the new field. All three are written by scholars who have a particular interest in children's literature, and they help to establish the genre as a relatively new field worthy of serious scholarly attention.[11] Nancy J. Schmidt's *Children's Fiction about Africa in English* (1981) is not strictly literary criticism of children's fiction but a combination of anthropological and literary approaches—an expansion of her 1975 bibliographic project, *Children's Books on Africa and Their Authors: An Annotated Bibliography*. Essentially a sociocultural critical work, it deals with the children's literature available in the United States—542 works written before 1977. With its wide coverage, Schmidt's book surpasses in scope and depth John Rowe Townsend's *Written for Children*,[12] which generalizes about African children's literature from a sample of about 50 books, and Dorothy Broderick's *Image of the Black in Children's Fiction*,[13] which primarily deals with blacks in America.

Schmidt's book is a major introductory work on children's literature in Africa. Especially in its study of the cultural background and content of African children's literature, her work is now a powerful reference point for scholarly works in African children's literature.[14] Schmidt's work provides useful and illuminating insight by a scholar who has a consuming interest in Africa. This scholarly bent essentially stems from her 1966 doctoral dissertation, "An Anthropological Analysis of Nigerian Fiction in English." Quite a number of her scholarly essays on African children's literature are tinged with some anthropological flavor. There is, of course, nothing wrong with the anthropological and literary approach that Schmidt adopts in her scholarly writings. African children's literature has long deserved the serious attention Schmidt's efforts reflect.

But there are other approaches as well. For example, in addition to the work of John Rowe Townsend and Dorothy Broderick already mentioned, there is a small but growing body of other studies. Gulten Wagner addresses African children's literature from its oral roots through the early Christian missionary contributions, establishment of indigenous publishing of children's books, a reappraisal of the curriculum to make it more relevant to African children's needs, and the librarian's role in promoting children's books through book reviews and the compiling of annotated bibliographies (Wagner, 231–36).[15] Biola Odejide primarily uses the reader-response approach in her 1986 doctoral dissertation, "Visions of Contemporary Society in Nigerian Children's Realistic Fiction." According to her, this approach was dictated by a conviction that awareness of the target audience is integral to the criticism of juvenile literature. Also in 1986 Osaze Fayose completed her dissertation, "Nigerian Children's Prose Fiction." Asenath Odaga has written a critical survey of segments of Kenya's children's literature using a cultural and historical approach, and my *Nigerian Youth Literature* (1987) suggests a pedagogical rationale for including Nigerian authors' fiction in the secondary or high school curriculum. *Foundation: Essays in Children's Literature and Youth Literature*[16] is a collection of my previously published articles on the subject.

Besides doctoral dissertations and the small body of published works, there have been significant fruitful gatherings of enthusiasts at conferences and exhibitions from the late 1960s through the present day, within and outside Africa. The Nigeria English Studies Association devoted its first conference to junior literature in English in 1979, and the proceedings of that conference have been published as *Junior Literature in English* (1981). In October 1984 the International Board on Books for Young People (IBBY) devoted its Nineteenth Congress in Nicosia, Cyprus, to "Children's Book Production and Distribution in Developing Countries—Africa, Asia, and Latin America," where children's literature in Africa was given significant attention. Concluding his paper "The Production and Distribution of Children's Literature in Africa: A Diagnostic Survey" at this seminar, Francis Nyarko stated, "It has taken the 1970's to awaken interest in children's literature on the continent. By the end of the 1980's Africa will have a much better story to tell in the production and distribution of children's literature."[17]

This statement could not be more prophetic. Book Development Councils have been formed in some African countries to give the book industry direction. The Children's Literature Association of Nigeria (CLAN) was formed in Nigeria in 1977, and the Children's Literature Foundation (CLF) was formed in Ghana in 1978. IBBY national sections are being established in various African countries to strengthen African children's literature in all its ramifications.

While South Africa works its way toward a more sensible and equitable government, the Southern African Children's Book Forum has got quietly with the business of supporting the cause of children's literature. The enthusiasm raised at South Africa's first ever National Symposium on Children's Literature (1987), appropriately entitled "Towards Understanding . . . Children's Books for All South Africa's Children," resulted in the creation of the Children's Book Forum (CBF). The CBF now has regional branches in all South African provinces, including several of the so-called black homelands, and an affiliated branch in Southwest Africa (soon to become independent Namibia).[18] South Africa is today the newest member country of the IBBY, and its CBF is actively encouraging awareness of the potential of children's literature.

At the Schloss Blutenburg in Munich, Germany, in March 1986 an international symposium on African youth literature was attended by more than 40 experts from nine African and European countries. Main concerns were the historical development, special preconditions, and the actual state of African children's and youth literature, as well as chances for further encouragement of this literature. This symposium was tremendously significant in the sense that it was held at and organized by the Internationale Jugendbibliothek (International Youth Library)—

an associated project of UNESCO and the only library in the world devoted to the systematic collection of the world's children's literature—and it attracted scholars outside the African continent.

That European scholars—Gerda Streit, Frank Ruprecht, Elfriede Hillers, Birgit Dankert, and Jurgen Martini—enthusiastically attended the symposium and presented various papers on African children's and youth literature indicates the international interest the genre is attracting, particularly among academics. It is gratifying to note that the proceedings of this symposium have been jointly published by the German Commission for UNESCO in Bonn and the International Youth Library in a beautiful volume, *African Youth Literature Today and Tomorrow* (1988). Its publication obviously adds to the growing volume of scholarly works in the field. It is not too much to say that this symposium partly served as an impetus for the Zimbabwe International Book Fair, "Writing and Publishing for Children in Africa and the Third World," held the next year in Harare, Zimbabwe.

The Zimbabwe International Book Fair has been the most ambitious of all the conferences so far devoted to children's literature on the African continent. An academic and international flavor was lent to the fair by the presence of children's literature specialists from Europe, the United States, and Africa, and by the presence of distinguished African writers and their active participation in the children's literature workshop. Prominent among them were Anne Pellowski, director of the information Center of Children's Culture in New York; key IBBY members; Nancy Schmidt of the African Studies Program of Indiana University, who is the leading authority on African children's literature today; and Chinua Achebe and Cyprian Ekwensi.

At the opening of the book fair's workshop on "Children's Literature in Africa and the Third World" Chinua Achebe condemned imported foreign children's and youth books that African children find difficult to relate to and called on all serious African writers to write wholesome books for children. Nancy Schmidt called for the establishment of a journal of African children's literature that would include information about the criticism of children's literature. She rightly observed that such a journal would both mark the maturing of African children's literature and contribute to its future growth and development. She also suggested that the foundation of an African Center on Children's Books could provide a repository of children's literature from all nations in all languages that would permanently record the history of African children's literature and provide a resource center for research about all aspects of the creation, production, criticism, and audience response to African children's literature.[19]

In 1989 the *Journal of African Children's Literature* (now the *Journal of African Children's and Youth Literature*) was established; before this no periodical exclusively devoted to criticism and review of African children's literature existed. This is why the *African Book Publishing Record*, which is under European editorial control in Oxford, England, described the maiden issue of *Journal of African Children's Literature* as "a most welcome debut in its field." The theme of the eleventh annual University of Calabar International Conference on African Literature and the English Language in the spring of 1991 was "Children and Literature in Africa."

With the various local and international conferences, the incontrovertible brilliance of some works of African children's literature, and the establishment of the *Journal of African Children's and Youth Literature*, African children's literature can no longer be denied its rightful place in university departments. Still, like any relatively new field, some problems remain.

Critics of African children's literature are still a rare species, and the teaching of the literature itself in many cases has been strongly individual effort on the part of those passionately interested in it. Bendel State University (now Edo State University), the University of Ibadan, the University of Nigeria, Nsukka, the University of Ghana, and the University of Stellenbosch in South Africa teach African children's literature to their students. Coppin State College in Baltimore, Maryland, has an African children's literature component in the course Children's Literature: An International Perspective. In the summer of 1990 Georgia State University's English Department offered a seminar in African children's literature. In the summer of 1991 the Clark Atlanta University School of Library and Information Studies offered a summer graduate course in African children's literature, and in the spring of 1992 the Clark Atlanta University English Department offered the course Africana Children's Literature, which essentially explores the sociocultural link between the juvenile literature of Africa and African America.

At the University of Bayreuth in Germany, Jurgen Martini, Eckhard Breitinger, and Joachim Schultz have African children's literature as their research territory. Martini has developed a strong research interest in Anglophone African children's literature and has made quite a number of trips to Africa, especially Nigeria, as regards his calling, and has produced quite a number of scholarly papers on the field. Breitinger has also produced incisive papers in the field as well. Schultz's area is Francophone African children's literature, where he has equally contributed. In Australia, Sophie Masson is engaged in scholarship in African children's literature.[20]

The junior novel for African children is, however, a relatively recent phenomenon. Macmillan Press Ltd. started in the late 1970s a new series of novels—"Pacesetters"—directed at the African youth audience. Today the series has more than 70 titles. All the novels in the series are written in English by African authors, and all of them have mainly an African setting. With the exception of Cyprian Ekwensi, Buchi Emecheta, Chinua Achebe, and David Maillu, some of the authors in this study are almost unknown to the literary critic. This is primarily because criticism of juvenile literature is in its formative stages. But not all the novels in the Macmillan Pacesetters series qualify as adolescent or young adult novels because some of their protagonists are not youths and some of the novels do not capitalize on their interests and characteristics. Such works in the Pacesetters series are excluded from this study. Some are only briefly mentioned to illuminate a particular issue under discussion.

Although some novels like Buchi Emecheta's *The Bride Price, Naira Power*, and *A Kind of Marriage* deal to some extent with idiosyncrasies of African adults, their impact on youth is paramount. The world of the adult depicted in a limited way in some of the novels can be understood by children and young adults. The youthful mind is immensely adaptable, "taking the lowest when it is there" but capable of any feat if required.[21]

European and American readers who have an established tradition of children's literature may tend to apply their own concept of childhood and young adulthood to these stories about African youth. Having lived in both African and Western cultures, I can definitively stress that any simplistic, superficial tendency on the part of Westerners or Americans to look at African youth like their own youth should be discarded. Although the Western youth and the African youth may be of the same chronological age, they live in two different worlds. While age boundaries are helpful for comparative purposes, they can also create some distortion. In various cultures of Africa a man and a woman are not considered adults until they have a child of their own.

One feature that is notable for its absence from more than 50 African-published children's books examined by John Rowe Townsend is

preoccupation with race or racism (Townsend, 290). In any near racially
homogeneous world like black Africa, racism is not an issue of any significance. In South Africa, where there are blacks, whites, and coloreds,
elements of racism do exist in youth fiction. Racism is subtly hinted at in
Ezekiel Mpahlele's *Father Come Home*. What comes near to the spirit of
racism but manifests itself in a different form in Africa is tribalism,
because of its multilingualism. But racism (or tribalism) is not a preoccupation of African children's and youth literature. Where it surfaces at
all, as it does in Efua Sutherland's play for children, *Foriwa*, it is its positive side—working together for unity—that is highlighted.

According to a UNESCO study on youth in Angophone Africa, "The
African youth emerges from the womb of a colonial past. The burden of
African history is particularly heavy on the African youth, for it is a history of social trauma and catastrophic disruption, whose character and
scale is unimaginable if we attempt to understand them from the perspective of the situation of the youth in advanced Western countries."[22]
The concerns of the European or American youth can differ from those
of the African youth. For example, American youths can sometimes
work and pay their own bills, but for economic reasons in African countries, this is rare; traditional African culture does not encourage high
school teenagers to have girlfriends or boyfriends, and it frowns on dat-
ing among them. The culture does, however, consider courtship normal
for older young adults as it is usually seen as part of the marriage
process. Unmarried teenagers or boyfriends and girlfriends do not live
together, and there is nothing like commonlaw marriage. Unlike
Western culture, where some healthy couples may decide not to have
children, in Africa a marriage is not considered fulfilled until a child,
especially a male, is produced. Childlessness is enough grounds for a
marriage breakdown or divorce. The special primacy of the child or children in marriage is unquestioned.

Romantic love is the most ubiquitous theme of the Western novel,
but it is a comparatively rare concern in African fiction. The African
novel, for various historical and aesthetic reasons, is a far more public
and socially and politically oriented literary form than its European
counterpart.[23] These are a part of the African culture constraints that
affect the African youth novel. The central theme of African children's
and youth literature is the rites of passage or initiation into adulthood,
and young Africans may experience exhilaration, various crises, and dis-
illusionment in this passage or initiation. It is this Sturm und Drang of

the passage or initiation to adulthood that is vividly captured especially in realistic fiction for African young people. The African children's and youth novel, and the folk tale as well, are expected to influence young Africans' perceptions of the world while subtly preparing them for adulthood.

Chapter One

Cyprian Ekwensi: Pioneer African Writer for Children and Young Adults

Awarded the Dag Hammarskjöld International Prize in Literature in 1968, Cyprian Ekwensi, who was born in 1921, is unique among African creative writers because he has written for both children and adults throughout his prolific career. Today his works have made quite a significant mark on the emerging children's literature of Africa. Ekwensi's children's writing has been the subject of literary criticism because of its importance in his oeuvre.[1]

In 1979 the Nigerian English Studies Association invited Ekwensi to be keynote speaker at its tenth annual conference, devoted to junior literature in English, as part of the country's celebration of the International Year of the Child. He was invited in that capacity because he is a strong pioneer in the writing of African children's literature. Between the novels *People of the City* (1954) and *Burning Grass* (1962) Ekwensi turned to the "tale" and engaged in the writing of children's literature. Perhaps he wanted to try his hand at a different kind of fiction and assess the response of readers and critics, or maybe he had a different type of message suited only for the teenager. Whatever the case, Ekwensi could not have made a better choice, for his children's readers or books rank among his most successful writings (Emenyonu, 46).

Ekwensi stated in his keynote address, "The development of an independent country struggling to get a place in the world community of nations has robbed many a family of the leisure so necessary for telling the folktale, and gradually that direct touch between parent and child is being lost in the whirlwind of industrialization, urbanization and flyover. . . . [F]or this reason, if for no other, books must be produced to replace the family gathering under the moonlight tree."[2] This reasoning has guided Ekwensi in his production of works for children. His long folk tale *An African Night's Entertainment* and his novella *The Passport of Mallam Ilia* are two attempts to capture that direct touch "which is being lost" between parent or adults and children in contemporary life. Children are a part of the storyteller's audience in *An African Night's Entertainment*, and a youth, Hassan, is the old storyteller Mallam Ilia's audience in *The Passport of Mallam Ilia*. The oral quality of both works is very prominent.

An African Night's Entertainment

Ekwensi wrote in 1950, "While I was writing *Ikolo the Wrestler*, I was lucky enough to meet an aged Hausa Mallam who told me a single folk-tale of book length. Amused by the short tales which I was collecting, he asked me if I would care for one which would keep my readers awake all night. Thus was born my *African Night's Entertainment*, which is still to be published."[3]

Twelve years later *An African Night's Entertainment* was published and has become, indeed, a folk tale now committed to the permanence of print. Ekwensi has not categorically said that he wrote *An African Night's Entertainment* for children, but this long folk tale has remained very popular with African children since its publication in a children's edition in 1962. African children who had hitherto been fed with a literature from Europe and North America now had something substantively within their cultural milieu. When repatriation of school syllabuses was advocated after regions of Africa gained political independence from Britain in the 1960s, suitable African texts for African children were scant. The African Universities Press in Nigeria was set up to meet this problem (Roscoe 1971), and *An African Night's Entertainment* opened its African Readers Library Series and has become a classic of African children's literature.

An African Night's Entertainment distills all the ingredients of the traditional African's yarn-spinning session. One would obviously expect some rich oral literature tradition in the written folk tale and fiction of cultures where the printed word is less important than the spoken word. Oral literature is part of African culture, and a countless number of stories for children abound on the continent. Literature must be popularized so that reading experience is based primarily on enjoyment reading rather than on the achievement of reading itself. For the traditional African who typically has not derived his enjoyment from the printed word and has been raised on oral materials, a work that can sustain reading interest must be carefully designed. Such a work is *An African Night's Entertainment*. As a long folk tale in print, it is quite a good transitional reading material. It begins with an evocation of a traditional storytelling scene:

> "Put your money on this sheepskin," said the old man, "and if, by the time I finish my tale, there is one of you awake, that man shall claim everything we have collected."
> Young men, old men, children, women, they all put some money on the sheepskin beside the story-teller. He waited till they had sat down. He himself settled comfortably on the *catifa* and smiled.
> "It is a long tale of vengeance, adventure and love. We shall sit here until the moon pales and still it will not have been told. It is enough entertainment for a whole night."

This opening passage will have an immediate impact on a large number of readers in Nigeria as well as in other parts of Africa. African children instantly see what they do in most evenings. It belongs to their lives. They gain an intimate contact that is often denied them in European and North American literature.

The communal flavor of traditional African life-style is quite apparent in the opening of *An African Night's Entertainment*. The storyteller directs the affairs of the storytelling session, and by virtue of his position some measure of authority is conferred on him. If there is any interruption of the storyteller's narrative, it must be with permission, and it is in most cases to clarify a point in the story for the listener to understand the plot development. The storyteller is usually gifted in all the antics of narrating strategy. The delivery by a dull storyteller, unlike the delivery of the old man in *An African Night's Entertainment*, is likely to lure Africans to sleep, especially in the evening. At the end of this long folk tale the mood of communalism or comradeship that characterizes its beginning resurfaces:

> He glanced round at his listeners. They squatted like little cones of white, their heads between their knees. Quietly he rose and reached for the glistening coins on the sheep skin. Had he not warned them that they would all be asleep?
> The coins chinked, and a voice said: "Old man, don't do that. Have you won the bet?" He started. One by one the cones took the shape of bright-eyed men who suddenly roared with laughter. The old man had no alternative. He, too, laughed. (*African Night*, 94)

This is a powerful story of love, marriage, and vengeance. Mallam Shehu, a wealthy man who lacks a child, has a very frightening dream in which he sees a horse he really wants. With his wealth, he outbids another buyer, buys the horse, and takes it home. The horse later produces a foal, and when the foal is old enough, Shehu mounts and rides it. The foal stumbles, throws Shehu, and runs away, leaving Shehu with a broken arm and broken leg. The nightmarish dream shakes him out of sleep. Severely distressed, Shehu summons Mallam Sambo, the dream expert of the community, to interpret his dream.

Sambo interprets the dream as a warning to him of a marriage that will produce a son who would be a curse to him. Sambo goes on to admonish him to forget marriage, but Shehu refuses. Soon after his dream Shehu finds a young woman, Zainobe, whom he admires. With his wealth and a secret and alluring perfume prepared by Sambo, Shehu steals Zainobe from Abu Bakir, her fiancé. Soon after smearing the charmed perfume on herself, Zainobe's mind gradually turns against Abu. Her mother uses some of the perfume and she too starts hating Abu. Shehu tells Zainobe, "Remember, . . . that Abu is a poor man. If you marry me, you will be free from want. Your parents will have everything that money can buy" (*African Night*, 18).

Zainobe falls for the trap. It is money that really swings her to Shehu. She confides in her mother, "If Mallam Shehu marries me, none of you will ever want for anything in this world again; you won't have to smoke yourself in the kitchen or wear rags" (*African Night*, 21). Mallam Shehu completes his ignoble snatching of Zainobe from Abu by distributing money to Zainobe's relatives and sending a lot of money to the greedy king of the land. Captivated by Shehu's lavish gift, the king takes it upon himself to do the marriage preparation—a duty that rightfully belongs not to him but to Zainobe's father. But Zainobe's father, Mallam Audu, is totally against the idea of his daughter married to anyone but Abu. In his dogged stance, he is completely alone. He tells the greedy but powerful king who tries to persuade him to see the wisdom in his daughter marrying the man she really loves: "If you are using your power as king of this land to force me to accept your views in this matter . . . that is a different thing; but as long as I live, Abu is the man to marry Zainobe" (*African Night*, 28). In his abuse of power, the king, besides handling the marriage perfume, sends the bride price on Zainobe to Abu Bakir in repayment of whatever money he might have deposited with her parents. But Abu Bakir rejects it. Through possession and wealth personified in Mallam Shehu, and power personified in the king, Abu Bakir's betrothed is robbed from him in broad daylight. Cheated, Abu swears vengeance, and a substantial part of the tale is about his suffering, tribulations, and his final success at getting a magic potion from a faraway "enchanted forest of death," Kurmin Rukiki, which he administers to Kyauta, the son product of the union of Shehu and his erstwhile love, Zainobe. In his unquenchable thirst for vengeance, he keeps himself in a very evil and negative emotional state. During his long search for one who knows how to wreak vengeance, he is destroyed physically: he loses one of his eyes and one of his ears; he is psychologically wounded; he is wrongly imprisoned as a thief. When he finally succeeds and returns with his magic potion, and a black talisman that makes him invisible, his people do not recognize him until he explains to them in detail his identity. He shows his agitation by putting an evil spell on the innocent Kyauta, who subsequently goes mad.

As predicted by Sambo, Kyauta becomes a curse on Shehu and Zainobe. Under Abu's spell he becomes a liar, a truant in school, and later a hardened thief. In one of his robberies he kills his father, and Abu's spell loses its potency. Kyauta's sanity returns, and Zainobe tells him her old dream that Abu put a spell on him. Abu is later killed by Kyauta, who then goes mad again, "eating wild fruits, hunting game, sleeping in the rain and in the sun," and after a year he comes back to his heartbroken mother to live out his last days with her. The storyteller ends with a moral: "One must not take it upon oneself to inflict vengeance. But you can see the moral for yourselves" (*African Night*, 94). Everybody suffers in the story.

One can visualize at the beginning the physical setting of the oral performance. The picture of the old storyteller sitting comfortably on the *catifa* and smiling is inviting, and this is what an oral storytelling session is supposed to do. He really succeeds in entertaining the audience before him throughout the night. Toward the end of the old man's narration, "the moon was still shining . . . but there was not even a glow in the fire." The image of the moon especially recalls that the long story has been narrated by moonlight—a traditional setting for African stories. The mention of no glow in the fire seems to be the only realistic weakness of *An African Night's Entertainment*. Nowhere in the beginning of the story is it mentioned that a fire was nearby for the storyteller and the listener to warm themselves. After all, money, sheepskin, and *catifa* are details mentioned at the beginning. Nevertheless, the image contained in "there was not even a glow in the fire" conveys the passing of time when a glowing fire normally dies out. It also suggests the end of the tale and helps to recall the bet between the story-teller and his audience at the beginning of the story—"if by the time I finish my tale, there is one of you awake, that man shall claim everything [the money], we have collected." Thinking the listeners are asleep after glancing around at them, the old man rises from his *catifa* and reaches for the glisten-ing coins on the sheepskin. The chinking of the coins suggests the music that has been absent from the traditional narrative. But the listeners are not asleep, and a voice reminds the old man that he has not won the bet.

The description of the listeners as "squatted like little cones of white, their heads between their knees," is very picturesque. Most Hausa Muslims wear white dresses and white turbans. Sitting in the dim moon-light they look like white cones. These "cones" take the shape of bright-eyed men who "suddenly roared with laughter." All along they have been alert. They are all awake and collectively win the bet. The vividness reflected in the storytelling setting is also mirrored in some powerful proverbs that spice the tale.

"A woman is like a cloth in the marketplace" and "women are like streams and like horses" are like Shakespeare's "frailty thy name is woman." They are significant in the structure of the story and in African culture itself. They give prominence or emphasis to the unpredictability of the future. We can see the freshness and effectiveness of the proverbs couched in African sociocultural milieu. The traditional African market is not like a Western mall, store, or grocery store. What comes close to it is the flea market in America. Even then the African market is still different.

There are no price tags on the items for sale. The customer and the trad-er or merchant can spend quite a good deal of time in haggling over the price of an item like the cloth. The trader wants good money or good gain on his merchandise, and the customer wants a good deal or bargain. The haggling is often a friendly one and also a communal one. (Today, however, the love of money has destroyed the friendship and spirit of bargaining. Traders are quite short-tempered now and do not want to waste time hag-gling over prices.) It is against this backdrop that Zainobe tells Abu, "When a trader has got hold of some good cloth and has taken it to the market, at least ten bidders will price it before he sells it to the highest bidder . . . *a girl who has not been married is like a cloth in the marketplace.* You are only the first person to demand my hand in marriage. Do you imagine that means that you are definitely going to be my husband?" (*African Night*, 22, 24).

As soon as Abu begins to suspect Zainobe's loss of interest in him, he tells her, "Women are like water, because you cross a stream in the dry season and when you return in the rains the same stream will drown you. If you love a horse very much and you feed her, when you come to ride her, she'll throw you down and break your backbone. So is a woman's love. Dry today like the ebb tide; high tomorrow like a flood" (*African Night*, 14). There are basically two seasons in most of sub-Saharan Africa, especially West Africa—the rainy season, which begins about April and ends roughly around September–October, and the dry season, which begins around October–November and ends in March. As their names imply, the rainy season is characterized by heavy rains that can flood rivers and streams, but the dry season (the *harmattan*) is hot and dusty and dries up some streams.

Abu uses the image of water in flooded streams, and no water in dry stream, and the image of loving a horse and later riding it to break one's backbone, to illustrate the promise and disappointment that can characterize love affairs. In their own case, nothing is further from the truth. Zainobe as a cloth in the marketplace is bought by the rich man, Mallam Shehu. In essence the Shehu-Zainobe marriage is determined by money and material goods and not by genuine love. In terms of a horse, Zainobe breaks Abu Bakir's backbone. The marriage ride comes to naught. It is interesting to recall that the foal Shehu loves dearly throws him down and breaks his leg and arm in his dream.

That two young adults can put a lot into their messages in traditional African proverbs indicates the strength of the oral or verbal art. Throughout this long folk tale the living voice and living language are discernible; no character is fully realized, and there is no deep probing into the psyches of the characters. The story is told in a well-controlled language within the African child's comprehension. The precise and vital language can hardly be faulted.

When we consider that Ekwensi had only once heard the story of *An African Night's Entertainment*, from an aged Hausa mallam, his print rendition of this oral tale seems remarkable. Without this printed form, perhaps this story would have passed into oblivion by now. In 1934, 18 years before the publication of *An African Night's Entertainment*, a Hausa booklet entitled *Jiki Magayi* was published; its content is similar to the material of *An African Night's Entertainment*. It had been published for the Literature Bureau, Zaria, by West African Publicity, Lagos, and was written by Rupert East, superintendent of the Literature Bureau, and Malam J. Tafida Zaria. In fact, the plots of *Jiki Magayi* and *An African Night's Entertainment* are to an overwhelming extent fundamentally the same. Because Ekwensi earlier admitted hearing the tale from an aged Hausa mallam and because the publication of *Jiki Magayi* predates *An African Night's Entertainment* and they have a common plot, there is enough ground for speculating strongly that Ekwensi took much from *Jiki Magayi*.[4] But he did not plagiarize it, as some have illogically charged, for, as he has argued in defense, no one can own a folk tale. Literary works can be copyrighted; oral tales cannot. To treat oral tales as copyrightable reduces their universality and accessibility to any writer.[5]

It is a credit to Ekwensi that he is able to blow life into this ancient Hausa folk tale, tucking into it some timeless, innate human problems that cause strife. The structure of the tale is an interesting one. It begins in the unknown world of dream and ends in the realistic world. The events in Shehu's dream foreshadow the impending events in real life. Shehu reveals his selfishness and power by snatching a betrothed young girl from Abu Bakir with his money. He exclaims, "Will Allah indeed let me see a son of my own? . . . If so I do not care how much I suffer after that" (*African Night*, 10). He does not care who gets hurt in his search for a child of his own. Abu Bakir's quest for vengeance becomes an obsession. He seeks vengeance to retrieve the image of himself Shehu has destroyed by stealing Zainobe.

Two human elements of war—possession and power—are illustrated in the tale. Betrothed for a long time, Abu Bakir regards Zainobe as his, but he lacks the wealth to really make her committed to him as a wife. It is such monetary possession that Shehu uses to take her away from Abu. Abu considers Shehu's act not only a theft of his beloved but, through Shehu's ostentatious display of wealth and power, a theft of his own power and self-esteem. Regaining his self-esteem and power becomes Abu's single-minded quest—an obsession with vengeance that he eventually attains. It is clear that the display of wealth and power is a part of human nature that can be abused. Such a desire is not exclusively African, even though the African folk tale illustrates it. Folk tales belong to no one country, "they are part of the common stock of humanity and are closer to mankind than any written word. They are the delight of our childhood and they are part of our unconscious thought."[6] The entrusting yarn-spinning spirit of *An African Night's Entertainment* is continued in *The Passport of Mallam Ilia*.

The Passport of Mallam Ilia

Unlike *An African Night's Entertainment*, whose listening audience consist of children, teenagers, and adults, *The Passport of Mallam Ilia* consists of only one listener, a high school boy, Hassan. Ekwensi clearly meant *The Passport of Mallam Ilia* for children. In the framework he contrives, 60-year-old Mallam Ilia tells his story to Hassan. What makes *Passport* interesting is essentially its thrilling action from the first page to the last. Old Mallam Ilia recalls his youth as one of excitement: "As a youth my life was wild, and there was nothing I loved better than a good fight, or a hard race on horseback."[7] It is this youthful energy that he carries into the deadly game called *shanci*. Certainly only the brave could take part in *shanci*. How Ilia finds himself in *shanci* is quite intriguing.

While Ilia is relaxing and sharing stories with his friends around a campfire outside his father's house one evening as most Africans are wont to do, a company of Arab traders on horseback from the Sahara canter up and draw rein. When Ilia asks if they can be of any help, Kanemi, the leader of the group, tells him, "You can be of the greatest help, if you are not *cowards*" (*Passport*, 14). To young Ilia the word *coward* is offensive, and he reacts by instinctively springing to his feet drawing his sword to fight. There is no indication in the novella that Kanemi and the Arab traders came to fight. It is Ilia's youthful nature that spurs him into ready action when there is really no visible threat of attack. His other friends do the same though not as much as Ilia does. Ekwensi's attention to detail in the meeting between Ilia and his friends and Kanemi and the Arab traders is quite fascinating, and it helps to set the novella's tone of action:

> "Greetings while you rest!" they hailed.
> "You are welcome," I answered. "How is it with you? Can we be of any help?"
> "Yes," sneered the leader of the group. "You can be of the greatest help, if you are not *cowards*. . . ."
> At the mention of that word "coward," my sword-blade flashed out. The firelight, catching against it as I sprang at the speaker's horse, made it glisten dangerously. The great man reared backwards, and, with a simple movement of his riding whip, flicked the weapon clean out of my hand, and roared with laughter.
> "A brave lad, truly. Ha, ha! A brave lad. How would you like to win the hand of my daughter Zarah?"
> My companions, who had also sprung to their feet at the mention of that obnoxious word, paused and regarded my fallen sword with a surprise no less than mine. It was the first time I had ever been disarmed by anyone; so easily too—*and* in the presence of my friends and hero-worshippers.
> "Get out of here!" I roared. "You and your daughter." (*Passport*, 14–15)

Diction in the above excerpt is a distillation of agility—*flashed, sprang, flicked, disarmed,* and *roared.*

It is Ilia's show of bravery that draws Kanemi into inviting him to take part in the *shanci* game where he might win a prize—his own daughter Zarah as a wife. The game of *shanci* is intriguing but very deadly. The winner is not necessarily the bravest but "the lucky one," as Ilia would say. In olden days the bravest of the young men who won *shanci* games and married did not really marry out of love. For many men to die in a bloody contest over a young girl was not really worth it. Looking back to those days, Ilia tells Hassan, "I had heard of *shanci* before Kanemi explained it to us, but never before had I imagined that I should play it, and for such high stakes. In a way I am glad the British came to Kano so soon after and stamped out such dreadful customs" (*Passport,* 19). In the above excerpt is glimpsed some ancient custom that a rational mind like Mallam Ilia knew would not last forever.

Besides stopping this traditional deadly game, the British helped in the early construction of railways primarily for commercial reasons. This is why there were probably more goods trains than passenger trains during the British colonial days. Nevertheless, the railway accelerated the interaction between the people of the northern part of Nigeria and the people of the southern part. As a matter of fact, "the action begins in a train travelling to Northern Nigeria but flashes back into the history of Hausaland before the British conquest, the Hausa wars, and the German campaigns in the Cameroon in 1916 . . . moves through French Equatorial Africa to Mecca via the Sahara. From Mecca we are taken to East Africa at the time of the second World War and the final action takes place again in a train" (Emenyonu 1974, 54). In essence, then, *The Passport of Mallam Ilia* is a mixture of exciting elements of the past and the present.

The prologue of *The Passport of Mallam Ilia* establishes Hassan as a curious and good listener and Ilia as a good storyteller. The epilogue reveals their relationship to each other—Hassan as son, and Ilia as father. In the prologue we see Hassan traveling from southern Nigeria along with many people—mostly Hausa men, Biroms, a few Yoruba traders who cluttered up the train with their wares, and one or two schoolboys who sit at the far corner of the carriage talking excitedly about their forthcoming holiday—to Jos in the northern part of Nigeria. Interest is not really in the journey but in the curiosity of the young boy. It is his curiosity that draws from one of the passengers, a dying old man, the tale of the feud between him and his adversary.

It is interesting to note that Hassan and his fellow travelers have been doing the train journey of some hundreds of miles for *two* days. This journey of some hundreds of miles was in the 1940s—a time when traveling by rail was not all that exciting. The construction of the railways in Nigeria and other parts of Africa during colonial days was motivated not by the need for human transportation but by the pursuit of economic gain: to transport raw materials like groundnut (peanut), cotton, cocoa, rubber, and other goods from northern Nigeria to the seaports in the South. These cash crops were shipped to British industries, where they were used to manufacture a variety of goods.

If there was any concern for human comfort in the coal-fueled trains, it was minimal. The sharp pain in the eyes that many travelers got from specks of coal dust was just one of the journey's many discomforts. Because the railroad builders sought to avoid such obstacles as high hills and solid rock, the routes were longer than they needed to be, which is partly why Hassan and the others have been traveling some hundreds of miles for two days. Even the train itself is exhausted. In the words of the young boy in the prologue, "My train was gasping and panting up the steep incline that leads on to the Bauchi plateau in northern Nigeria" (*Passport*, 5).

The boy's frustration and exhaustion reflects the experience of many who used the Nigerian railways in the 1940s and 1950s: "I had been travelling third class for two days and two sleepless nights with scarcely any room in which to stretch my legs; I felt bored to death, and anxious to get the journey over" (*Passport*, 5). Third-class coaches or cabins (or cars) were and are still for the masses. As popularly used in Africa, the masses are the numerous struggling people—those who are not privileged to afford second-class and first-class coaches fares. These are the people the youths fight for in *A Paradise for the Masses*.

During such a dull journey most travelers relieve their boredom by telling tales, singing, playing cards, and the like. Our young curious boy, Hassan, does his by reading, but it is almost futile: "There was nothing I could do to relieve the boredom. I had read the novel and magazines I had brought with me; the scenery was too familiar to excite me, and my temper was in no state to be improved by any undue mental exertion" (*Passport*, 5). It is in this state of boredom that he notices the old man who sits opposite him—very dirty and worn out. He sees this dirty old man bringing out a blue passport from his bag under his seat smiling at it and later putting it back in his bag. How such an old and physically unclean man can be in possession of a passport piques Hassan's curiosity: "In my boyish imagination, a man who owned such a valuable document could not look like this. Why, it did not seem to me that he could even read or write down his own name" (*Passport*, 7). His "boyish imagination" does not end by wondering. He probes further. His interest in the dirty old man and his passport causes him to ignore Kofi Usuman, a middle-aged man who, 10 years earlier, used to tell him and his age group "fantastic stories of the days when the first white man arrived in Nigeria." According to Hassan, "His imagination so illumined these stories that for us they became real. I had heard enough of these tales . . . and was in no mood now to recall them or to give an ear to fresh boasting" (*Passport*, 8). Apparently, Hassan has always loved to listen to stories—a speculation established as fact in the epilogue.

It is his interest in stories and of course his curiosity that propel him into a conversation with the strange old man. It is rare for a young African to initiate a conversation with an older stranger. As the old man later tells him, "My son, you are too curious. First you want to see the passport; and now you must know what I am talking about" (*Passport*, 10). In fact, Hassan's curiosity pays off for him because Mallam Ilia sees him as a worthy recipient of his rich tale of vengeance.

Like the traditional African folk tale, *The Passport of Mallam Ilia* has the physically present storyteller and the physically present listener. What sparks the tale's telling is Ilia's passport and Hassan's genuine deep interest in it (it is important to note that Hassan is Ilia's son, as later revealed in the epilogue):

> "That passport I saw just now. . . ."
>
> "Oh, that! I got that in 1927. It's twenty years old now, isn't it? Odd, how time flies."
>
> "Yes," I said.
>
> He nodded. "Twenty years. . . . But Allah be praised, those years were not wasted. I nearly missed him."
>
> "Missed him? Who?"
>
> He gave a guilty start, and glanced about him. "I beg for mercy, Mallam. I was really talking to myself. Would you like to see the passport?"
>
> I was still rather puzzled as I watched him bring it out and open it at the page containing the photograph. (*Passport*, 9–10)

Hassan knows there must be some story behind the passport, and the old man's statement, "I nearly missed him." The passport, issued in 1927 by the British colonial official, shows an Ilia 20 years younger, a man in his prime—very different from the old Ilia. When Hassan remarks about the difference, the old man's response piques Hassan's curiosity even more: "Twenty years is not a short time . . . but it was worth it. I did not give my life for nothing" (*Passport*, 10). "Give your life" puzzles Hassan. Very soon after the old man removes his robe and shows Hassan the "long deep flesh wound" under his heart. With this deadly wound that he sustained in the last fight with his adversary, Mallam Usuman, during this same train journey, he tells Hassan his story.

The Passport of Mallam Ilia, then, is the tale of a dying man recorded by an enthusiastic youth. The health of the old man and Hassan's problem in recording his words lend credence and plausibility to *The Passport of Mallam Ilia* as a tale:

> There were times when he appeared quite normal, but his pulse was very low, and his voice almost inaudible, so that often I had to guess and suggest and gesticulate before a nod of his grey head told me that I had got his meaning right. . . . The original was perhaps not quite as coherent as what follows, but the tale is, in essentials, what Mallam Ilia recounted to me, and I have as far as possible preserved his personal touch; for that grand old man was a great story teller, and a devout follower of the Prophet. (*Passport,* 12)

In the prologue and epilogue Hassan's first-person narrative lends immediacy and authenticity to what he puts down as an interested listener. It also draws children and young adults closer to his experience. Similarly, Mallam Ilia's first-person narrative gives his tale a factual dimension.

Like *An African Night's Entertainment*, *The Passport of Mallam Ilia* is an intriguing story of vengeance told with energy and precision. It is the story of a long feud between two men, Mallam Ilia and Mallam Usuman, from their youth through adulthood. When Ilia wins as his wife Zarah, the daughter of Kanemi, a Tuareg prince, in the deadly gladiatorial game of *shanci* by defeating 10 competitors, including Usuman, Usuman plots to steal her by all means from Ilia. One of his plots is to tell lies about Ilia that lead to his arrest and imprisonment. The false charge leveled against Ilia by Usuman and his henchmen is that Ilia's horse trampled a child to death. Without a fair hearing or trial, Ilia is thrown in jail only to come out during the British invasion and conquest of Kano. In Ilia's absence in jail, Usuman makes several advances to

Zarah. Usuman finds in the disturbances of the British invasion of Kano an opportunity to go into Zarah's room, obviously to seduce her.

Ilia, who has miraculously come out of jail as a result of the British invasion, rushes home to find Usuman with his wife, and he recklessly attacks him: "There behind lay my Zarah, petrified with fear and well-nigh fainting. The man was glowering at me, his sword drawn. One glance at those dark eyebrows and I recognized him—Usuman, the thief, cheat, highway robber, murderer—the man who had put me in prison out of envy. I was almost mad with rage. With scarcely a thought for my own safety, and forgetting that I was entirely unarmed, I sprang at him" (*Passport, 29*). In this fight with Usuman, Ilia defends Zarah but accidently kills her with his bow and arrow when Usuman uses her as a shield. Like Abu Bakir in *An African Night's Entertainment*, Ilia swears vengeance and a substantive part of this novella deals with their several bloody encounters. Ilia exacts full revenge in his old age but dies very soon after as a result of the fatal injury he received during his last fight with Usuman on the train journey. As in *An African Night's Entertainment*—a tale of adventure, love, and vengeance where everyone is a loser—both Ilia and Usuman also lose in *The Passport of Mallam Ilia*.

As in *An African Night's Entertainment,* Ekwensi provides a frame for the narrative by having the dying Ilia tell his life story on a train to a schoolboy who, by coincidence, turns out to be his own son. While the old storyteller in *An African Night's Entertainment* tells an ancient tale of his people to a group of listeners, the old storyteller in *The Passport of Mallam Ilia* tells his own story (because he is a participant) to his own son. Mallam Ilia is good personified, and the dichotomy between good and evil in the story is quite prominent. The good Mallam Ilia—who has the chance to kill Usuman during the game of *shanci* to decide who should marry Zarah—spares his adversary. He spares him primarily because of his youthful goodness. This good act to an opponent who had all the traits of a scoundrel proves Ilia's undoing in his old age (Emenyonu 1974). In fact, his killing of Usuman would have ensured his enjoying Zarah as his wife.

Ekwensi's two works are similar but with some slight difference in their common subject of vengeance. In *An African Night's Entertainment* Abu Bakir is obsessed with vengeance and cannot think of anything positive to do when his betrothed is stolen from him. In *Passport of Mallam Ilia,* however, Ilia's desire for revenge is not an obsession. He is a devout Muslim—proud and confident of his physical power and his love for Zarah. To lose this dear wife through the hands of a scoundrel like

Usuman is to Ilia an insult and a humiliation, and her death must be avenged. He does not forget Zarah after he marries Dije. The picture of the fatal scene of his dying wife remains permanently in his memory, and he can recall it—"there she was, lying amidst the debris, bleeding, her lips trembling as she breathed his name." His desire to avenge Zarah's death does not, however, destroy his humanity. He takes care of the deserted child of his enemy, Usuman, and even gives him an education. Ilia the good man is only compelled to partake of evil in his desire to revenge. But the villain, Usuman, is a twisted personality whose perverse fulfillment is to do harm to others.

Because Usuman fails to win the *shanci* game and Zarah as wife, he declares that no other man, even the *shanci* winner Ilia, shall have her. Like such envious characters with an unethical frame of mind, Usuman even attempts seducing Zarah. It is this evil character whom Ilia, who wants to live a morally clean life "according to the Prophet (Muhammed)," wants to kill in a fair fight. The fair fight eventually takes place on a train traveling to Jos, but both men die as a result of the fight. Ilia's death, however, is presented with compassion and some satisfaction. When he regrets that he will not be able to see his wife, Dije, and his child again, his young listener reveals himself as the young son of Ilia and Dije. He authenticates this fact by showing the family talisman, a square parchment, written over in Arabic. Ilia is satisfied that his son knows his story and would hand it down to the next generation.

The story of Mallam Ilia the good man and Mallam Usuman the villain is a good illustration of the statement that when one gets into a fight with a skunk, although he may win the fight, he will never smell the same again. The moral of the story is evil is not an antidote for evil.

Undoubtedly, the graphic illustration of feuding, vengeance, and blood in *The Passport of Mallam Ilia* as well as in *An African Night's Entertainment* is depressing. Such negative emotions should not be dominant in works for children, and there must be a way out. Ekwensi's 1991 children's book, *Gone to Mecca*, is intended to contrast with the unquenchable thirst for vengeance that dominates *An African Night's Entertainment* and *The Passport of Mallam Ilia*.

Gone to Mecca

In Usuman, Abdul, and Dan Kyauta in *Gone to Mecca* is seen a reflection of significant positive growth in conscience and moral standards that augurs well for humanity. Such a lofty ideal is what the author wants the young population to aspire toward. Despite its brevity, *Gone to Mecca* negates the dominant feud of *An African Night's Entertainment* and *The Passport of Ilia,* Ekwensi's works of the 1960s. Mecca is the holy city of Muslims where pilgrims go for cleansing and spiritual renewal, especially after the traditional 30 days of fasting (the Ramadan). But not all Muslims outside Mecca can really afford such a potentially expensive pilgrimage. While some rich men make the pilgrimage for spiritual regeneration, some go for other reasons—commercial and otherwise. Ilia's adversary, Usuman, in *The Passport of Mallam Ilia,* goes on a pilgrimage to Mecca not for spiritual or moral rejuvenation but to cheat and defraud, and he distracts Ilia from his zest to live a pious Muslim life. But unlike Usuman the villain in *Passport,* Mallam Abdul, who is sponsored by Dan Kyauta in *Gone to Mecca,* makes his pilgrimage for purely spiritual matters as demanded by Islam.

Mallam Abdul is a poor farmer who on his own would not have been able to sponsor himself on a pilgrimage to Mecca. His sponsor, Dan Kyauta, does not pose as a superphilanthropist, and he has no self-aggrandizement whatsoever. Instead, the spirit of calmness, of one with a pious mission, is what is evident in his speech to his fellow pilgrims from Zaria on board the Nigeria Airways plane to Mecca. Mallam Abdul hears the speech like a lecture going on close beside him, and he strains his ears to listen:

> You are going to Mecca for prayer and devotion. You will meet hundreds of thousands of other pilgrims from all over the world, believers like yourself. . . . They have come to atone for their past misdeeds. It was the Holy Prophet who decreed that the devout must make this journey at least once in their lifetime. . . . It must do your spirit good. . . . When you return, if you have been true to your Maker, you will notice a new lease of life. . . . It is there in Mecca that you discover that before Allah, all men are equal. . . . Allah be praised![8]

Dan Kyauta's speech or lecture is really intended to drive home to the pilgrims and to the reader the true meaning of *hajj* (Muslim pilgrimage)—a journey with a noble mission to go near in soul to God. That such a lecture is by a true Muslim like Dan Kyauta is significant. It has more meaning when it is delivered by a clean vessel of God who demonstrates his faith in word and in practice. If it is otherwise given by a phoney, it would sound hoarse.

Dan Kyauta's annual practice is to finance the *hajj* of Muslims less fortunate. Mallam Abdul who benefits from Dan Kyauta's generosity describes Dan Kyauta in a positive light and attributes the success of his pilgrimage to Dan Kyauta himself: "My going to Mecca is the work of a man who has the fear of Allah in him. A man who knows that all wealth is from Allah the Merciful, and that we are nothing in his sight" (*Mecca*, 42). Unlike Dan Kyauta, Mallam Shehu, the rich man of *An African Night's Entertainment*, uses his wealth for selfish and evil purposes. He steals poor Abu Bakir's betrothed, Zainobe, setting in motion a chain of events culminating the destruction of himself and his wife, the scattering of his family, the madness and eventual disgraceful end of Kyauta, and the sadness, loneliness, and death of Zainobe.

If Mallam Shehu was a true Muslim in faith and in spirit, he would not use his wealth the way he does. Despite Mallam Sambo's advice to him to leave Zainobe on the grounds that it is not Allah's wish for him to have a child, Shehu adamantly refuses. Through misdirection, Mallam Shehu's wealth becomes, in the long run, a curse instead of a blessing. On the other hand, Dan Kyauta's wealth is a blessing that Mallam Abdul shares or benefits from.

In *Gone to Mecca* Mallam Abdul owes Mallam Usuman some money on his grains, which he bought on credit but does not pay for before he goes on *hajj*. That Abdul goes on *hajj* without paying his debt makes Usuman very bitter. But the bitterness seems misplaced because Mallam Abdul does not flee from his debt. In fact, it bothers Abdul that he did not have time to tell Usuman before he left for the *hajj*. In Zaria, Usuman boils with anger that Abdul lacks integrity for not paying him his money with which he expects to buy a ram to celebrate his Muslim Salla holiday. To make sure that Abdul has really gone to Mecca, Usuman sends his son Gambo to Abdul's house to inquire if it is true. Young Gambo rides to Abdul's house and instead of executing his father's errand, he joins his friend Yusufu to play ram games. According to the author, "Yusufu and Gambo were about the same age, and cared little for any differences between their fathers" (*Mecca*, 4).

The ram game is a fight between two rams that are usually pushed into it by humans. Two boys hold a ram each, standing opposite each other as if in an "on your marks" position in track (running) and push the rams toward each other at the signal of a boy who stands in the middle as referee. Both rams then charge against each other, lowering and butting head against head, horns interlocking and twisting, bodies quivering to their hoofs. Sometimes the fight can take a long time, and young boys enjoy watching it. This is what Gambo is enjoying with his friend Yusufu. After this fight, however, one of the rams furiously charges at Gambo and strikes him hard, breaking his ribs—an injury which sends him into the hospital. Gambo has obviously forgotten his errand, but his father Usuman who prepares to go to the Muslim praying ground anxiously expects him. Usuman's ready friend in heady jobs, Musa, tells him, "The ways of children are beyond the understanding of grown-up. . . . All of us were children once, and we behave the same way" (*Mecca,* 11). But many adults like Usuman do not seem to realize this fact. This is intended for Usuman to reflect on. This is part of the knowledge Usuman is expected to have in *Gone to Mecca.*

As far as Usuman is concerned, it is unfair for one man to slaughter four or five rams while his brothers in Allah have nothing for themselves. In this angry mood he forcefully needs justice his own way and employs Musa in carrying it out: "Musa, you will fetch me one or two of Abdul's rams to this house. You will take them inside the yard and lock them up till I return. He who denies his fellow man rams for the Sallah shall have no rams for himself. . . . That is Usuman's law" (*Mecca,* 13). "Usuman's law" recalls the villain Usuman and all the negative spirit he personifies in *The Passport of Mallam Ilia.* Like Usuman of *Passport,* who covets Ilia's wife and his achievement, Usuman of *Gone to Mecca* covets, to a certain extent, Abdul's good luck in going on a *hajj* to Mecca. Unlike Usuman of *Passport,* whose villainy never wears off, Usuman of *Gone to Mecca* gradually comes out of his shell of covetousness and bitterness when he meets Mallam Abdul who has genuinely and dutifully performed his *hajj* and returned.

Abdul informs Usuman that his *hajj* was financed by Dan Kyauta and that he was not rich enough to sponsor himself. This information reduces Usuman's hostility and resentment against Abdul, and he is at ease. Usuman changes from the pilgrimage topic to his son Gambo, who was almost killed by Abdul's ram, and Abdul instantly responds with sympathy and readily wants to see young Gambo in the hospital. After the visit, Usuman and Abdul are deep in thought. The story of Gambo's near-fatal injury resulting from the attack from Abdul's ram recalls Usuman's fabricated story of Ilia's horse trampling a child to death in *The Passport of Mallam Ilia.* Unlike Usuman's true story of an actual attack by a ram in *Gone to Mecca,* Usuman's made-up story of Ilia's horse killing a child is primarily designed to incriminate Ilia. The ram story is real from a plain, blunt mind in *Gone to Mecca,* but the horse story is the evil product of a villainous mind in *The Passport of Mallam Ilia.*

After the story of the ram's attack on his son, Usuman asks Abdul about the money he owes him. Abdul minces no words and expresses no hurt feelings that Usuman has forcefully seized two of his rams as ransom for his debt. Instead, he accepts Usuman's arrangement—to take the ram that knocked down his son while Abdul takes the other one and settles his debt. Abdul does not think his pride is hurt when Usuman seizes his rams. He looks more refined and cherishes lofty ideals of love and harbors no evil against anybody after his pilgrimage to Mecca. He tells Usuman, "Going to Mecca has taught me a lot. . . . Yes, worldly things are nothing. . . . Before Allah, all men are equal. . . . No one is favored above the other. . . . We are in this world only for a short while, so why make enemies? . . . Let us do good to our fellowmen while we can. . . . These are the commands of the Prophet" (*Mecca*, 48). This positive spirit affects Usuman, who had been in a fighting mood before he went to meet Abdul but returns a changed man filled with peace and happiness: "In the new presence of Alhaji Abdul, Mallam Usuman suddenly found that he could feel no anger" (*Mecca*, 48).

Perhaps the older Cyprian Ekwensi's desire is to illustrate the true spirit of religion—one of love. In various cultures where religions still create sporadic crises, *Gone to Mecca* in its simplicity and brevity drives home what true Islam as well as other religions should have as their ultimate goal—love for one's neighbor and peace with him, and one's spiritual uplifting. Its tone of peace and reconciliation is a contrast to that of *An African Night's Entertainment* and *Passport*.

Unlike *An African Night's Entertainment* and *The Passport of Mallam Ilia, The Drummer Boy* (1960) and *Trouble in Form Six* (1966) are very simple works. *The Drummer Boy* stresses that children should live an exemplary life even if they are physically handicapped like the blind drummer boy. *Trouble in Form Six* is about events at Ilubi College, a traditional Nigerian high school where children live in dorms according to strict rules enforced by house masters, prefects, and principals. Although *Trouble in Form Six* is about Akin Tayo, the high school radical, one cannot categorically assert that it is a novel of character, because Akin Tayo is not a fully rounded character. Why is he a radical and what is his family or economic background? Such information would have been helpful in realizing the real essence of Tayo's radicalism. It does not have sufficient literary merit to justify analysis except to note that it mirrors some aspects of a traditional African high school. Similarly, Ekwensi's short story "Motherless Baby" (1980) is thin. As its title suggests, the story deals with unwed motherhood. It is the moving story of an adolescent schoolgirl who makes her own decisions. She falls in love with a popular bandleader and subsequently has a baby out of wedlock. Apart from delineating that misfortune follows irresponsible behavior "Motherless Baby" is not rich enough to merit discussion.

Like "Motherless Baby," Ekwensi's earlier work, *When Love Whispers* (1948), is also thin. Its theme is the prerogative of parents to choose husbands for their daughters and the consequences of stubbornly imposing such choices on unwilling daughters like Ashoka. Ashoka's marriage to an illiterate traditional village ruler is dry and unfulfilling. *When Love Whispers* essentially heralds the theme of young adult love and marriage, which is quite common in African prose fiction for youth.

Juju Rock

Like *Trouble in Form Six, Juju Rock* which was published in 1966 and revised in 1971, is one of the adventures of a high school student, 15-year-old Rikku. The primary purpose of Ekwensi's revision was to remove what some critics noted as "reverberations with echoes from *Treasure Island* and *King Solomon's Mines*."[9] It is primarily a book of entertainment rather than of moral value. Ekwensi strives for a thrilling wild, wild west. It is a story of some Europeans looking for a lost gold mine in Juju Rock in Africa, and they need a map to locate it. One of them, Rikku's benefactor, Captain Plowman, who was in an earlier trip to this gold mine in Juju Rock, had the secret to the treasure. But he did not return. To find old Captain Plowman and the treasure hunt is the main mission of the Europeans. It is the newspaper advertisement for a boy to lead them to Juju Rock that brings Rikku into the story. Perhaps Rikku also wants to locate his old benefactor.

The trip to Juju Rock in the northern grasslands of Nigeria is the central controlling theme of the novel. The rather mysterious appearance of George, the college's night watchman; the irrepressible taxi driver who takes Rikku in his cab to the European adventurers; and the orgies of the secret society people are tangential to the major action of the novel—the treasure hunt. The novel is essentially a suspenseful thriller. The reference to *King Solomon's Mines* and "wild west" stories in *Juju Rock* indicates that Ekwensi strives to make the reader associate his novel with "real-life adventure stories" or thrillers that pique high school students' interest.

Through Rikku's courage, the Europeans are able to locate the gold mine. Its hero certainly has commendable qualities of courage and loyalty, but the reader—and, indeed, the hero and author—have to be somewhat aware of the limitations of these virtues by the end of the book. The plot of *Juju Rock* is arresting but not morally serious and at times morally corrupt. We can accept the fact that the hero, Rikku, has gone with the English crooks because he wants to save his benefactor, but his ultimate inability to question the morality of his benefactor's actions— seeing him only as the good man of the piece—is surely disturbing. His benefactor certainly is a man of charm, feeling, and generosity, but at the same time one has to notice that he has led an expedition to "discover" a Nigerian gold mine for a British company and is prepared to take advantage of a chief's friendship and generosity in showing him the mine when it cannot be in the interests of the chief's people to have the mine exploited by foreigners. There is even gold on the surface. Why not let the chief's own people exploit the mine?

Even more disturbing perhaps is Rikku's attempt to save the white crooks whom he knows to have murdered Africans. Admittedly the latter are out to kill, but are they any worse than the white crooks? Very possibly they are better. Moreover, by attempting this deed of daring, Rikku almost loses the chance to ensure that his benefactor, whom he has just rescued, is conveyed to safety. One wonders whether Ekwensi has not taken over some of the white imperialist's moral bias along with the form of his adventure story here.

What instantly emerges in most of these works is Ekwensi's knack for didacticism. For him, books for children and youth must be strongly related to the age group for which they are intended. In addition, "They must be simple and direct, rather than circuitous and unnecessarily verbose. They must contain credible characters—boys, girls, men, women, pets, families, teachers, traders, workers—characters we can believe in, however eccentric. They must project high moral standards of honesty, courage, truth, honor and all those good things that lift man from the level of the savage and make him a finer being" (Ekwensi 1981, 4). His concern for nonlaborious communication with children and youth apparently explains the brevity of his works for juveniles and a deliberate choice to state his morals directly at the end of the novels. He states at the end of *The Drummer Boy*, "Akin, the Drummer Boy, was radiating, in a manner to make everyone think only of doing good, of being good, and of living a clean life."[10] And at the end of *An African Night's Entertainment*: "one must not take it upon oneself to inflict vengeance. But you can see the moral for yourselves" (*African Night*, 94).

It is clear that *The Passport of Mallam Ilia* preaches against feud and vengeance. Everyone loses at the end of the novel, and the moral is clearly stated. While *Juju Rock* does not bluntly set out to preach, it extols the qualities of courage and loyalty. In their didactic orientation, Ekwensi's children's books provide a cultural and intellectual service to the African community, whose adults feel it is their duty to teach the young. Ekwensi's writings for children and young adults are a watershed in the development of written African children's literature, which peaked in the 1970s. Quite a number of the recurrent themes in African young adult literature are contained in various degrees in Ekwensi's works.

In his literature for children as in his novel for adults like *People of the City,* Ekwensi's major focus is on Nigerian society. His conception of the children's literature genre is one of a major instrument for positive change:

> All teachers, [educators], local authorities, state governments, and the Federal Government owe it as a duty to our junior citizens to ensure that sterling qualities are inculcated in junior minds in their formative years. We will then hear less of the lament about irresponsible youth. . . . Nigerian literature in schools is one sure way of achieving this objective but it must not be left to chance. There must be concerted planning with authors, publishing houses, [educators], and parents. Herein lies the future of Junior Literature in our great country. (Ekwensi 1981, 7)

In Nigeria and other African countries that are literally plagued by various social malaise, the importance and the relevance of children's literature cannot be overemphasized.

Conclusion

Ekwensi's versatility in writing is his relative ease in switching from traditional folk tales to contemporary realistic fiction, and his ability to cast a contemporary life story in the mold of African folk tale. An old storyteller tells the story of *An African Night's Entertainment* to a group of interested listeners under a moonlit night—a traditional setting for African folk narratives. But old Mallam Ilia tells his story, *The Passport of Mallam Ilia,* to an interested youth on a train journey; the train is basically an image of contemporary life.

All told, Cyprian Ekwensi's impact on African literature is quite significant. His adult novels *People of the City* and *Jagua Nana* and his youth novel *When Love Whispers* deal with urban themes, especially the lure of the city, which *Director!*, *Naira Power,* and *For Mbatha and Rabeka* deal with in various degrees. In African children's literature one can use Ekwensi today as a central figure in tracing literary themes ranging from those couched in the mold of the folk tale in print through those in realistic fiction for young adults. And almost all his successful youth novels deal with the Muslims of the northern part of Nigeria.

Perhaps it is Ekwensi's childhood in the Muslim north of Nigeria that has tremendously shaped his literary imagination. *An African Night's Entertainment* is essentially a traditional tale of the Hausa people, and like it *The Passport of Mallam Ilia* deals mainly with the Hausas. In fact, it is in Kano, a modern Hausa-Fulani metropolis, that Mallam Ilia spends his childhood and young adult days. It is in Kano that he takes part in the deadly game of *shanci*. And Ekwensi's fastidiousness to details in depicting Hausa-Fulani Muslim culture indicates his strong knowledge of it. For example, relaxing in the evening at the front of one's house to spin and share yarns is quite operative in Hausa culture and in other African cultures as well. This is what young Ilia is doing with his friends when El Kanemi meets him and later invites him to compete in the *shanci* game. It is this same spirit of relaxing and sharing yarns that is contained in the introduction to *An African Night's Entertainment*. And in both works the influence of Islam, the predominant religion of the Hausa-Fulani, is quite pervasive. Similarly, Ekwensi's 1962 adult work, *Burning Grass*, is a tale of the Fulanis, and the flavor of Islam is quite strong in the novel. *Gone to Mecca* is also about Hausa Muslim folks, mainly of Zaria. In its spirit of reconciliation and goodwill to all, *Gone to Mecca* reflects a more sober and philosophical Ekwensi.

In 1987 Ernest Emenyonu, Ekwensi's foremost apologist, edited *The Essential Ekwensi: A Literary Celebration of Cyprian Ekwensi's Sixty-fifth Birthday,* a collection of essays specifically written for the literary celebration of his birthday. The collection reflects the special features of "Ekwensi the man" and "Ekwensi the artist." The essays provide an insight into Ekwensi's versatility as an artist and reveal his humble wisdom, his avid observation, and his sensitivity to his African environment. He is the oldest African writer discussed in this study. For more than 50 years his interest in youth and the dynamics of change in society has not diminished. He stated in 1988,

The "information explosion" has shattered the boundaries of the sharp distinction between adolescents and adults. Sex education, family planning, birth control, political assassination, political manipulation, curruption, rape, kidnapping—all these aspects of modern life which were rarities in our time, are today, commonplace. Coupled with this is the rapid physical growth of adolescence which makes a sixteen-year-old taller and heavier than both parents and therefore creates the illusion of having "arrived." The adolescent world of today is well ahead of that of previous generations. Parents and teachers no longer hold a monopoly on knowledge, though they may claim to have more wisdom. Even so, parents and teachers would be ill-advised not to listen to the adolescent point of view.[11]

Accustomed from as far back as the 1940s to writing for young people, Ekwensi believes that "solid chunks of description must give way to functional description. We are not in the age of Dickens when the author pauses to take an inventory of the furniture in the room" (1988, 96). Cyprian Ekwensi in theory and in practice has always advocated a realistic creation, visibility, and relevance of African children's literature. He strongly asserts that "the writer for adolescent and teenage readers must be inspired and motivated to educate, entertain and inform the young and in the process leave a message of lasting impact which is unconsciously and painlessly absorbed" (1988, 96). His works for children and young adults have accomplished that, and they continue to have enduring value for Africa's young population and its adult population as well.

Chapter Two

The Bride Price: A Masterpiece of African Youth Literature

Winner of the Jock Campbell Award for her novel, *The Slave Girl* (1977), Buchi Emecheta, who writes for both children and adults, has emerged in recent years as one of Africa's leading female writers. Her youth novels—*The Bride Price, Naira Power,* and *A Kind of Marriage*—have almost an equal appeal to both young and old. While she focuses on traditional African society and modern African society in these works, she sensitively goes into the stresses and strains of growing up; furthermore, she offers a profound insight into human relationships. Some of her works selected for discussion in this book are the most successful in the present body of African literature for children and young adults.

Perhaps only a few African writers can match Buchi Emecheta's compassion and sensitivity when dealing with African adolescent girls or African women. Katherine Frank (1982) makes an interesting observation about Buchi Emecheta's oeuvre, which I believe can be conveniently used as an inroad into a critique of her works: "Taken together, in fact, Emecheta's novels compose the most exhaustive and moving portrayal extant of the African woman, and unparalleled portrayal in African fiction and with few equals in other literatures as well. The entire realm of African female experience can be found in these books, from birth to death, with all the intermediate steps of childhood, adolescence, marriage, and motherhood" (Frank, 476). For the purpose of this study, I will concentrate mainly on her works that deal with childhood, adolescence, and marriage. The topics are quite fascinating from an African female writer who has experienced all. In discussing Emecheta's works for children and young adults I will of necessity make reference to some of her works for adults to throw more light on the topics under scrutiny.

At a very young age, Buchi Emecheta lost her father, who was a railway porter in Lagos. This event is echoed in her fiction, as we see in the death of Aku-nna's father, Ezekiel Odia, in *The Bride Price*. The impact of Ezekiel Odia's death on Aku-nna reflects that of Buchi Emecheta's father's death on her. At age 10 she won a scholarphip to a Christian mission school, the Methodist Girls High School Lagos, but by the time she was only 17 she had left school, married, and had a child. At age 22 she left her husband and earned an honors degree in sociology at the University of London while supporting her five children in England, where she still lives. These interesting episodes are reflected in her works.

Her first venture into writing, the manuscript of what later became *The Bride Price*, is, like her life, an interesting one. The manuscript that would have passed into oblivion inexorably surfaced as *The Bride Price*. The first manuscript of this novel was burnt by her husband, but she kept the vision of the book alive and revised it.

The Bride Price stands shoulder high among the novels in this study. Possessing the personality and craftsmanship of its author, *The Bride Price* deals with a variety of topics—traditions and customs, prejudice and discrimination, the distorted concept of dowry, polygamy and its attendant problems, and, above all, the fate of the teenage Aku-nna, who dares to assert herself as an individual in a conservative traditional African society, Ibuza. (Although in other works Ibuza is sometimes spelled *Ibussa* or *Ibusa*, it is the same town.) A major aspect of African marriage tradition that the novel deals with is the bride price.

The institution of the bride price, which is really called *dowry* in Africa, is meant to promote interaction between the families of a couple and not necessarily a commercial exercise. As contained in Ezekiel Mpahlele's *Father Come Home*, a South African youth novel to be discussed later, "The bride wealth . . . was not a selling price. It was a bond made holy by ancient custom and therefore valued by the ancestors. To scorn the idea was to rebuke the ancestors."[1] One cannot really quantify the amount of money spent on the upbringing of a daughter or a son. If one wants to make a monetary profit on his or her daughter, then the bride price will be a colossal amount that many men cannot pay.

The bride price is essentially a token of appreciation. To pay a bride price presupposes that the girl is valued and worthy of appreciation beyond the monetary price itself. It also indicates that the bridegroom's family appreciates and commends the bride's parents for successfully raising their daughter to marriageable age because it is strongly believed in Africa that it is more difficult to raise a daughter than to raise a son. To a certain extent, this is true. Like all women, African girls are especially attractive in their prime. Usually it is their appearance that initially draws male admirers to them. Love may develop later. Some lustful men set eyes on them and entice them mainly with money and material goods, primarily to sleep with them, and sometimes to have them as "kept women." The promising careers of many young African girls have been ruined by ignoble wealthy men. But the girls who are able to escape the various traps set by dubious men are valued, and their parents are always commended. As the givers of such a respectable young girl in marriage, her parents are entitled to a price from the man's family. The bride price, which was not meant as a commercial transaction, is sometimes turned into one by some greedy African parents, thereby losing its true meaning.

The tradition of bride price is so entrenched in the psyche of some African communities that the near commercial flavor of the institution is either glossed over or accepted as normal. For example, bride prices are comparatively very high in the Igbo ethnic group, and usually their adults use the fetched high price on other things—to buy or trade or take a chieftaincy title to enhance their social position in their community. It is this commercial side of the bride price that Buchi Emecheta condemns in *The Bride Price*. But it does not seem to be accepted by even some African female critics like Chikwenye Ogunyemi, who is also an Igbo. In fact, Ogunyemi's stance on Emecheta's handling of the bride price makes one sometimes very uneasy, especially because she is a female. She believes that in *The Bride Price* Emecheta writes about Africa with a Western sensibility, so much so that her attack on the tradition of bride price with its feminist thrust becomes suspect; she is no longer "one of us."[2] Ogunyemi's stance can only be taken with a grain of salt. Emecheta's attack on the bride price does not seem to have a rigidly feminist thrust really. The attack is a realistic exposure of the perverted meaning of the institution.

The Bride Price as a Youth Novel

The Bride Price has been highly praised by critics in England, America, and Africa. The Londond *Times* called it "totally fascinating vivid and exciting." The London *Observer* described it as "sympathetic and touching." *West Africa* appraised it as "skillful . . . the reader is caught up with the very real people who inhabit her pages," and *Library Journal* praised it as "a fast-moving story with characters the readers can care about." It is the apparent clarity of the content and the intriguing nature of the form of *The Bride Price* that makes it fascinating.

In brief, the novel is the poignant love story of Aku-nna, an Igbo girl whose mother has been inherited by her Uncle Okonkwo into his polygamous home very soon after her husband's death, and Chike, son of an educated, prosperous, former slave, Ofulue. They are drawn together despite all obstacles standing between them and their happiness; the most powerful one is the weight of tribal lore and custom. Fleeing an unwanted marriage to join Chike, and her uncle's refusal to accept the required bride price from Chike's family, contribute to Aku-nna's haunting fear that she will die in childbirth—the fate (according to tribal lore) awaiting every young girl whose bride price is not paid.

If Okonkwo can hastily inherit his brother's wife, Ma Blackie, and with lightning speed impregnate her, one would be tempted to dub him a doer and a no-nonsense person. But these enviable characteristics disappear in his attitude toward Aku-nna who he regards as a money-fetching commodity. As far as he is concerned, Aku-nna's schooling would make her fetch more money in her bride price. While he readily and selfishly habilitates Aku-nna's mother, Ma Blackie, in Ibuza, he virtually leaves Aku-nna to her own devices. But he knows deep down in his heart that Aku-nna is a potential asset only because of her bride price. In Emecheta's skilled hands, Okonkwo is artistically invested with lifelike attributes and emerges as a real, selfish, and reactionary African. It is not really the bride price institution that Emecheta condemns in *The Bride Price* but its commercial side—Okonkwo's conception of it as the be-all and end-all as far as Aku-nna is concerned—and the Ibuza community's general perception of it as a girl's supreme asset.

As a business matter it virtually reduces the girl to a mere commodity for "sale" for profit. The novel is quite rich and, to a certain extent, complex. It is perhaps because of the novel's richness and complexity that some find it difficult to call it a young adult novel even when the heroine is a teenager. The New York publishing house George Braziller does not include it in its list of Emecheta's novels for young adults.

When I contributed an essay on Emecheta for the third edition of *Twentieth Century Children's Writers* (1989), I discussed *The Bride Price* as a young adult novel. I do not recant this stance. The novel's heroine is presented in her late childhood and early adolescence. All the trappings of female puberty—menarche, loneliness, and first love—suggest the beginning development of Aku-nna's young adulthood. Her development is plagued early by two traumatic experiences—the death of her father, and her subsequent relocation from cosmopolitan Lagos into a conservative, traditional, and relatively rural community, Ibuza, where she really experiences the pain of loneliness. We the readers are made to experience Aku-nna's plight in Okonkwo's home, the antagonisms of

Okonkwo's wives and sons toward her, and the dreariness of the whole household. The girl's point of view is quite prominent in the novel, and it outweighs that of the adults. It is Aku-nna that really lingers in the reader's memory. Without the teenage Aku-nna, there is no novel.

Movement Out of Lagos and Relocation in Ibuza

Right from the time of her father's death, Aku-nna is subjected to a series of demands of tradition. While it is natural to be depressed at the passing of one's father, this emotional depression is not really expected to continue for too long and dominate one's thoughts. The two children of Ezekiel Odia, Aku-nna and Nna-nndo, weep bitterly when their father dies. While grown-up men restrain Nna-nndo from hurting himself while howling and throwing himself down, they spur Aku-nna on: "Nna-nndo soon finished crying, but Aku-nna was *encouraged* to continue; girls were supposed to exhibit more emotion" (my italics).[3] As a result of the much-encouraged wailing, Aku-nna temporarily loses her voice. After her father's burial, Aku-nna's mind is filled with numerous thoughts as they prepare to leave Lagos for Ibuza:

> Aku-nna remembered only scraps of stories about what life in Ibuza would be like. She knew she would have to marry, and that the bride price she would fetch would help to pay the school fees for her brother Nna-Nndo. She did not mind that; at least it would mean that she would be well fed. What she feared was the type of man who would be chosen for her. She would have liked to marry someone living in Lagos, so that she would not who have to work on a farm and carry cassava. She had heard stories of how strenuous farm life could be for a woman. She had heard that a farmer husband did not give housekeeping money, as her father had given her mother. There were so many questions she would have liked to ask, but that was regarded as bad manners to be too inquisitive. (*Bride Price*, 52–53)

In fact, the experience for Aku-nna and Nna-nndo is an uprooting from the warmth and security of Lagos to an Ibuza unknown. It is also an uprooting from cosmopolitanism to traditionalism. Being unused to the traditional ways of rural Ibuza is all the more reason that Aku-nna's mother should devote attention, especially to Aku-nna, to assist in lessening her pain of transition from Lagos life to Ibuza life. The final departure out of Lagos, which is couched in sadness and an image of mad frenzy, seems to deepen the pain and confusion of Aku-nna and Nna-nndo. It also foreshadows the life of pain that Aku-nna, Nna-nndo, and Ma Blackie are to live there: "The mammy-lorry groaned, shook from side-to-side like a huge earthquake, eased itself from its resting place, coughed out loud smoke, started to move jerkingly . . . then suddenly gathered speed . . . the mammy-lorry raced forward at a lunatic speed, out of Lagos" (*Bride Price*, 58). On arrival in Asaba, Aku-nna's keen observation of some of the men passengers and the driver going into town and her questions about them elicit an explanation from her mother. Her mother explains to her that most rich traders keep mistresses who they spend the rest of the night with in town. The revelation shocks Aku-nna, and she wonders if her father behaved that way, if all men behave like that. According to Emecheta, "The whole adult world was becoming too complicated, so Aku-nna stopped thinking about it, followed her mother's example and dropped off to sleep" (*Bride Price*, 61).

What is interesting is that Ma Blackie readily explains to Aku-nna that some men have extramarital relationships. This ready explanation and Aku-nna's falling asleep following her mother's example indicate the close relationship between Aku-nna and Ma Blackie. But this relationship collapses in Okonkwo's polygamous home in Ibuza. Soon Aku-nna's cousin, Ogugua, who is also her age, readily establishes a friendly relationship with her. In fact, she explains to her as far as she could, in their first happy meeting, after their arrival in Ibuza, the custom of inheriting wives:

> "My parents have been telling me so much about you—that you're very clever at school and all that. Now we're going to be friends. We shall be like sisters, especially if your mother chooses to be with my father."
>
> "Why should my mother choose your father? How come?" Aku-nna asked, puzzled. The two girls had lagged behind engrossed in their gossip.
>
> Ogugua burst out laughing. "You're almost fourteen years old now and you still don't know the customs of our Ibuza people? Your mother is inherited by my father, you see, just as he will inherit everything your father worked for."
>
> "Oh, dear!" exclaimed Aku-nna, as if in physical pain. "How can my mother fit into that type of life?" (*Bride Price*, 64)

The stark reality that her mother is going to be inherited is devastating to Aku-nna. Unlike young Aku-nna, her mother, Ma Blackie, knows this custom, and it is not strange to her. This partly explains her ready adjustment to it and her later involvement in the politics of Okonkwo's polygamous home. The difference between a country or rural Ibuza teenager, Ogugua, and a cosmopolitan Lagos teenager, Aku-nna, is there. When Ogugua shows her a woman who has been inherited by actually pointing at her, she adds that she is blessed—blessed especially because she has a son. Aku-nna regards it as just like "stories read in books." But Ogugua knows it is real. Emecheta uses Aku-nna's familiarity with books and Ogugua's familiarity with oral tales to depict the difference between them: "Her cousin did not know about stories in books, but she did know a great number of folk stories that were told by moonlight and handed down from generation-to-generation" (*Bride Price*, 65).

Obviously, if Aku-nna was going to be happy in Ibuza she had quite a good deal of adjustment to make. In fact, Emecheta's interest and empathy undoubtedly lies with Aku-nna, the girl who dares to assert herself as an independent mind.

Emecheta's Feminism in *The Bride Price*

Emecheta draws attention in this novel to some aspects of the injustice and humiliation that many African women have suffered for a long time. In Africa every woman is expected to marry and to be fertile in her reproductive years, and she is blamed for infertility or barrenness when in actuality the fault may lie with the man.

Only a brief picture of Ezekiel Odia and Ma Blackie's marriage is given—one of sadness. The root source of the sadness is the "great issue of childlessness." Although they have already had two children, Aku-nna and Nna-nndo, Ma Blackie's inability to get pregnant with a third child is blamed on her. The womenfolk in the same compound make songs about her "childlessness." Because of the lack of sophisticated gynecologists and of course poor technology at the time of the novel, no one really knows if the problem is with her husband, who has been sick with a swollen foot.

This speculation is significant, especially when one realizes that Ma Blackie gets pregnant in no time with Okonkwo after he inherits her as his wife. Therefore, Ma Blackie is blameless in her childlessness. This little episode is Emecheta's way of drawing Africans into a reassessment of who is responsible for barrenness, to know who has a problem instead of hastily blaming the woman who might not be the cause.

It is interesting to know where the blame is usually from. The family of the man and the larger society usually regard the woman as the problem. Quite a number of families have been known to arrange for other women for their sons especially when their wives do not get pregnant. For example, Charles's parents bring young Obioma to him when his wife, Maria, is unable to have more children in *A Kind of Marriage*. In modern times it is becoming the other way round. If a young woman does not get pregnant on time for her husband, she soon comes under serious pressure from her family and her friends to leave the man. Such pressure is not usually overt but subtle. Although she bears the brunt of accusation for the inability to become pregnant, the African woman has traditionally been marginalized in marriage. Emecheta essentially uses Ma Blackie's inability to get pregnant for Ezekiel Odia, and her swift pregnancy for Okonkwo, as a preliminary to comment on other myriad matters affecting the African woman.

Emecheta uses Aku-nna's fate to comment on various issues in traditional African adult world, and feminist consciousness is quite prominent in the novel. The author prepares the reader for this consciousness by hinting early in the novel the woman's marginalized position in Africa: "It is so even today in Nigeria, when you have lost your father you have lost your parents. Your mother is only a woman and women are supposed to be boneless. A fatherless family is a family without a head, a family without shelter, a family without parents, in fact a non-existing family. Such traditions do not change very much" (*Bride Price*, 28). The near nonexistence of a family after the death of the man of the house is borne out in some tribes by the practice of inheriting his widow like a material good. By such practice a family is dissolved, and custom sanctions it. Nancy Topping Bazin rightly observes that the belief in such dissolution of a family when a father dies enhances male privilege, for the mother is inherited by her husband's brother without any regard for how his wife, or wives, may feel about it.[4] While it enhances male privilege, it degrades and dehumanizes the widow and the children, especially the daughter. To the Ibuza Igbo community, Ma Blackie is now a property for inheritance, and Aku-nna is an "orphan," and her aunt calls her that. But the reader knows that she is not an orphan; after all, she still has a mother.

Unlike this insignificance of women in Ibuza Igbo society, in a matriarchy society like the Ashanti of Ghana, a woman enjoys definite inheritance and property rights, and elderly women are consulted in the making of community decisions.[5] Other matrilineal societies in Africa

are the Bemba of Zambia; the Yao of Malawi, Mozambique, and
Tanzania; the Wollof of Senegal; and the Baule of the Ivory Coast. As
noted by Mario Azevedo in *Africana Studies: A Survey of Africa and the
African Diaspora* (1993), although descent is reckoned through women in
matrilineal societies, it is men and not women who dominate the public
forums of power.[6] That a female writer discusses the issue of bride price
is gratifying because it is an "insider's" view of the whole issue. This is
why Rolf Solberg can assert that

> one of the ways of correcting one's faulty image of the African woman
> would be through the reading of creative literature. But even then one is
> in danger of acquiring biased information. . . . What one should really
> look for is the African woman seen from the "inside," in other words ren-
> dered by women. However, African women writers are few and far
> between. It is all the more exciting to come across Nigerian Buchi
> Emecheta, a writer with no less than five novels to her name . . . and
> what is more: they are all very readable books.[7]

Emecheta draws attention in her works to the age-old "insignificance"
of the female sex in ancient Africa and, to a certain extent, in some parts
of Africa today. The protagonist of her *Second Class Citizen* (1975), Adah,
"was a girl who arrived when everyone was expecting and predicting a
boy. Since she was such a disappointment to her parents, to her immediate family, to her tribe, nobody thought of recording her birth. She was
so insignificant." This insignificance is also glaring in *The Bride Price*.
Despite Aku-nna's age and inexperience in *The Bride Price*, she is aware
of her ephemerality simply because of her sex: "Aku-nna knew that she
was too insignificant to be regarded as a blessing to this unfortunate
marriage. Not only was she a girl but she was much too thin for the
approval of her parents, who would rather have a strong plump little girl
for a daughter" (*Bride Price*, 58). She suffers already a psychological feeling of inadequacy at home because she is a girl. This feeling of inadequacy is intensified after her father's death and her mother's neglecting
her as a result of immersing herself in the politics of Okonkwo's polygamous home in Ibuza.

Okonkwo's Polygamous Home

When Okonkwo neglects his first two wives and devotes all his time to
his new one, Ezebona, there is unhappiness and jealousy among them.
When Okonkwo increases the number of his wives to four after inherit-

ing Ma Blackie, he is so blinded by the novelty and excitement of his new addition that he does not realize his problem has increased. First, Okonkwo's wives envy Ma Blackie because she belongs to the "elite." They regard her as an elite simply because her children attend school. This envy is not limited to the adults. It spills over to the children and young adults in the household. Led by Iloba, Okonkwo's senior son, Okonkwo's children question why Aku-nna should be in school and accuse their father of it. In his defense, Okonkwo reveals his selfishness; his wife and children are satisfied to know that Aku-nna's education is mainly for commercial reason: "'Aku-nna and Ogugua will get married at about the same time. Their bride prices will come to me. You see the trend today, that the educated girls fetch more money.' Now his sons smiled. And so did his young wife who, on the pretext of clearing the goats' droppings was listening to everything. . . . His sons were pacified, and wondered to themselves at the cleverness and experience their father had just displayed" (*Bride Price,* 75).

The reaction of Okonkwo's wife and sons are a composite picture of envy and jealousy that are symptomatic of competition and rivalry in polygamous homes. Iloba, who Emecheta describes as a youth of 20, knows he cannot be anything more than a farmer. But he does not want anybody, even the newcomers already used to school in Lagos, to be more sophisticated than he, who has lived all his life in rural Ibuza. Beside Okonkwo's children, his senior wife, Ngbeke, is very inquisitive about the affairs of Aku-nna, primarily out of envy. She sarcastically calls her "the Big Miss in the family" in the presence of others in the house. In a fit of jealousy, she uncontrollably vents her disgust for Aku-nna and her mother, while subtly extolling the virtues of her own daughter, Ogugua:

> "I don't see any strength in that girl. Can you see her bearing children, that one? Her hips are so narrow, and she has not even started to men- struate yet; we are not even sure yet that she is a woman. Look at your sister—they are of the same age, and she started almost a year ago. . . . That Aku-nna will come to no good, I tell you. She and her mother are too proud," Ngbeke concluded, now puffing and swallowing harder than ever. (*Bride Price,* 77–78)

There is no indication that Aku-nna is proud. If she is proud, she would not have fallen in love with an *osu* (a slave) like Chike. Ngbeke resents Ma Blackie for stealing the show in the family she has helped Okonkwo to build. Out of spite and envy she dubs the beautiful Aku-nna an *ogban-*

je (children who, in African mythology, die young usually several times mainly to torment their mothers). To Aku-nna, her cousin Ogugua is friendly but gullible and cannot be trusted to keep secrets. Her brother Nna-nndo is too young and too spoiled to be any consolation to her. In her loneliness in this unhealthy polygamous home, Aku-nna dies a death of the spirit.

Aku-nna's Physical and Emotional Maturation in Ibuza

The Bride Price is a novel of character dealing with Aku-nna's problems, of hopes, fears, and death. Death removes Aku-nna's father early in the novel, and the primary concern of the novel—how Aku-nna lives her life without the protection of a father—is pathetically told. The novel reveals the mind and character of an African teenage girl who, because of her desperate need for love, goes against the age-old customs and practices of her community and meets a tragic end in the process. The action progresses chronologically, and no flashbacks are used. There are no subplots.

An African female critic has remarked about Emecheta's works:

> The spectrum of modern African writing is given wider dimension by the novels of Buchi Emecheta. This is a most welcome phenomenon primarily because it has filled the gaping gender gap between male and female characterization, and shown the other side of the coin. The rural, backhouse, timid subservient lack-lustre woman has been replaced by her modern counterpart, a full-rounded human being, rotational, individualistic and assertive, fitting for claiming and keeping her own.[8]

In the same vein, Cynthia Ward opines that "for literary critics seeking authentic representations of the African woman, the works of Anglo-Nigerian novelist Buchi Emecheta provide a veritable gold mine."[9] It is the apparent clarity of the content and the intriguing nature of the form of *The Bride Price* that make it fascinating.

The stance of the novel is clear—to depict the selfishness and hypocrisy of the African male adult world (especially the Ibuza Igbo society) and the dehumanization and stifling of African womanhood. The author says, "There were men who would go about raping virgins of thirteen and fourteen, and still expect the women they married to be as chaste as flower buds" (*Bride Price*, 84). Herein lies one aspect of selfishness that Emecheta is concerned with in the novel. If some African men have boundless freedom to violate the virginity of African young adult girls, there is no reason that they should expect to marry virgins. But it is often otherwise. The effect of such selfishness and rigid customs on the teenage girl is the story of *The Bride Price*.

Emecheta manifests a superb knowledge of the biological development of women. For example, her sensitivity to Aku-nna's menarche—her transition into womanhood—is fascinating:

> She swirled round quickly, looked and saw that there was blood smeared on a part of the hem of her dress. At first she was frightened, thinking that she had hurt herself. Then common sense took over, and she knew what was happening to her. She had heard about it from her friends so many times, she had seen it happen to many women, she had been told about it often by her mother and she knew the responsibility that went with it. She was now fully grown . . . all at once she was seized by a severe cramp; her feet felt like giving way, small pains like needles shot in her back and she could feel something warm running down her legs. What should she do now? (*Bride Price*, 92)

In this natural cycle of menstruation, however, Aku-nna is regarded as unclean by Ibuza community. She must not go to the stream, she must not enter her stepfather's house, nor the house of any *Eze* chief until it was all over (*Bride Price*, 115). But her physical maturation into young adulthood is not really the author's major interest; it is, rather, the psychological stresses she experiences in her bid to assert herself as a person in a reactionary environment. Many of the reflections in Emecheta's novels are of her own life and the lives of people close to and around her.[10] She herself asserts that the events that found her "in the ditch" and submerged her humiliatingly as a "second-class citizen" are 80 percent autobiographical.[11] There are autobiographical elements also in *The Bride Price*. She states,

> In *The Bride Price* I created a girl, Aku-nna, who had an almost identical upbringing to mine, and who deliberately chose her own husband because she was "modern" but was not quite strong enough to shake off all the tradition and taboos that had gone into making her the type of girl she was. Guilt for going against her mother and her uncle killed her when she was about to give birth to her first baby.
>
> Aku-nna died the death I ought to have died. In real life, due to malnutrition and anaemia, I had a very bad time with my first daughter. I was in labor for days, and became so exhausted that when she was actually born I knew I was losing consciousness.[12]

Ma Blackie, who gradually involves herself in the politics of Okonkwo's polygamous home, starts neglecting Aku-nna, and her uncle is interested mainly in the bride price she would fetch him. Like her uncle, her father's ambition in regard to his daughter was fixed: he had named her Aku-nna, meaning literally, "father's wealth," knowing that the only consolation he could count on from her would be her bride price. To him, this was something to look forward to (*Bride Price,* 10). Okonkwo only continues what her father missed.

The Nonconformist Teenage Heroine and the Conformist Teenage Girls

Of all the various marriages depicted in *The Bride Price*, only that of Aku-nna and Chike is given human dimension. Unlike theirs, the marriage of Aunt Uzo, "who is probably between the ages of sixteen and eighteen or nineteen," and Dogo is determined mainly by commerce. Dogo, a tall man who was an army driver during World War II, wants to marry with the army money he received. Despite his exposure to Lagos cosmopolitan life, Aku-nna's father, Ezekiel Odia, advises Dogo like a traditional Ibuza man: "My cousin's daughter is grown now. She comes from a very tall family too, so why don't you pay for her?" (*Bride Price,* 22). Ezekiel Odia does not think of the existence of mutual love as a prerequisite for a marriage between his cousin's daughter and Dogo. Dogo has the money and is able to pay, and in the end Uzo is brought to Lagos from Ibuza to be married to him. Emecheta sarcastically describes this dry marriage-by-purchase and its hungry product: "Dogo liked Uzo and Dogo paid for Uzo, and Nna helped them to get a room in Akinwunmi Street and now they had this fat, greedy baby who was eating Auntie Uzo up, making her look too old for her age, making her dry, giving her the appearance of a female giant" (*Bride Price,* 22).

Like Aunt Uzo, Rebecca is another young and inexperienced Ibuza girl, who Emecheta considers too young and too beautiful for Uncle Richard, who never stops beating her "for making eyes at other men" (*Bride Price,* 35). As a result of continued ill treatment of her, Richard eventually loses his wife. Like Uzo and Rebecca, Alice, at 14, is already a bride to a clerk. She shares a congested kitchen with the numerous occupants of the 16-room house on Akinwunmi Street in Yaba, Lagos, where Aku-nna and her parents lived before relocating to Ibuza. Their marriage is plagued by poverty mainly because the parties were not economically and emotionally ready for it.

By presenting the marriages of these young and inexperienced teenage girls as dull and unfulfilling, Emecheta seems to suggest that one must be emotionally and psychologically mature enough before he or she marries. Unlike Uzo, Rebecca, and Alice, who abide by the traditions of their society by accepting their husbands who paid their bride prices, Aku-nna wants a man who really loves her and who she of course loves. She wants love and happiness in her marriage.

The Bride Price, then, deals with the problem of the nonconformist teenager in a conservative and traditional African society. The main conflict is between Aku-nna's choice of waiting for her husband who would pay a bride price to her selfish, ambitious uncle, or choosing the *osu* Chike, whom she falls in love with at 15. Aku-nna's love knows no social taboos or barriers. She escapes forced marriage with Okoboshi and finally elopes with Chike to Ughelli. The strength of Aku-nna's love for Chike is demonstrated by her disregard for the tradition of waiting for the husband who would pay the bride price to her uncle or guardian. But she unfortunately dies after giving birth by caesarean section in Ughelli. Aku-nna's death soon after childbirth seems, on the surface, to vindicate the tradition of the land: if you are to be free of disaster and to live a peaceful life, accept the husband chosen for you. But Emecheta takes this traditional belief with a grain of salt as evidenced later in the story.

Aku-nna's hopes, fears, and dreams are treated seriously, reflecting her attitudes toward them. Her hopes of getting a higher education crumble with the death of her father. Without a father she comes under the guardianship of her selfish uncle. Lacking the love and care she desperately needs, she embraces a social outcast, Chike, who provides it. She exhibits many emotions, ranging from depression to steadfastness in love. Without her father she thinks she has no more shelter. She thinks her loneliness is complete because her mother does not have time for her. But her love for Chike cannot be snuffed out by custom and traditional values, and at her dying moment she expresses satisfaction over her rather brief but wonderful time with Chike: "I told you that I would not keep our love a secret. Now, with our little girl, everybody will know. They will all know how passionately we love each other. Our love will never die. . . . Let us call her Joy too, the same name we gave to the bed on which she was conceived" (*Bride Price*, 167).

Aku-nna is a developing character learning to make independent decisions rather than abiding by the conventions of society. Her task of learning to be independent amounts to a kind of rebellion, and in the process her life ends tragically. The adults who could have nurtured her to some degree of maturity and happiness are either too selfish or too busy to devote some attention to her. Okonkwo reveals the character of an adult who considers a young adult, especially a girl, only as financial asset. He knows the bride price will aid him in his ambition to become an *obi* (an Igbo chief) and receive the respected Eze title. But he makes no financial contribution to Aku-nna's schooling even after the death of her father. Only her mother pays.

Okonkwo is portrayed as a self-centered, conceited adult who uses traditions to further his selfish ends. After inheriting Aku-nna's mother, reason and moral precept demand that he is duty bound to take care of her and her children. But like a number of irresponsible men, he craftily steers clear of the burden of financing Aku-nna's schooling. Yet he wants her educated because educated girls fetch more bride price. Although Ma Blackie pays for Aku-nna's elementary schooling after her husband's death, she does not help Aku-nna to solve her emotional problems. Consequently, Aku-nna learns to make herself happy, especially with her sweetheart, Chike, and she learns to cope with the pain of her father's death by herself.

Emecheta's novel is better literature than a majority of the novels considered in this study. Compared with the welter of paper-thin characters who dominate many novels written for adolescents, Aku-nna emerges as a flesh-and-blood person. Like Patty in Bette Greene's *The Summer of My German Soldier,* who falls in love with an enemy prisoner, Aku-nna has equally been starved of love and care and falls deeply in love with Chike, an *osu* who, according to Ibuza society, is not free to mix with freeborns.

The *Osu* Tradition

The *osu* tradition is an old one in the Igbo community. Quite a number of captives during intertribal wars were dedicated by the victors to their various gods as *osus* (slaves). They were sold and bought. As outcasts who were not free to mix with others in the Igbo society, they and their descendants had their exclusive domain and were allowed to marry only within their group. Any love relationship between a freeborn and an osu was frowned on, and to a certain extent traditionalists still frown on it today. In Chinua Achebe's *No Longer at Ease* (1960), Obi Okonkwo's Igbo community disapproves of his love relationship with Clara in Lagos because she is an *osu*. Because of the age-old segregation from their own people, the *osus* readily embraced the Christian missionaries who regarded them as human beings when they came to West Africa in the nineteenth century. Their swift acceptance of the missionaries provided an opportunity for them to become some of the first groups of Africans to receive a Western education. In *The Bride Price* Chike's father is one of the most educated and one of the wealthiest in the Ibuza community, but the Igbo community still regards him as an *osu*. Neither the German soldier, Anton, in *The Summer of My German Soldier* nor Chike in *The Bride Price* are looked on favorably in Jenkinsville, Arkansas, or Ibuza, respectively. But Patty and Aku-nna find that these social outcasts provide the love and care that they need in their period of emotional depression.[13]

The man-made *osu* institution has the potential of wrecking love relationships. Although Ma Blackie likes Chike, she cannot accept him as "the man for her daughter" simply because he is an *osu*. Aku-nna finds the whole *osu* institution disturbing: "Oh, what kind of savage custom was it that could be so heartless and make so many people unhappy?" (*Bride Price*, 122). Aku-nna and Chike are compelled to elope from their community to Ughelli, only for Aku-nna to die soon after giving birth.

Unlike Chike, who humanely shows his love in a civilized manner to Aku-nna, the deformed Okoboshi crudely shows his by kidnapping and attempting to rape her—an action accepted by the old Ibuza Igbo community in the novel. As a matter of fact, it is to forestall any marriage with Chike that Okoboshi kidnaps her, not any feeling for her. She escapes, however, by telling a lie that her virginity has been lost to Chike. For "losing" her virginity she is brutally beaten by Okoboshi, ill treated by his relations, and shunned by Ibuza community. While the traditional Ibuza community endorses these crude actions, it does not endorse the civilized and humane one of Chike simply because he is an *osu*. The author uses Okoboshi's deformity to reflect his bestiality. His attempt at consummating his forced marriage to Aku-nna is offensive: "The very next minute he was upon her pulling her roughly by the arm, twisting the arm so much that she screamed out of pain. He forced her onto the bed, still holding on to her arm, which she felt going numb . . . then she kicked him in the chest, he slapped her very hard, and she could smell the gin on his breath. . . . His chest was heaving up and down like a disturbed sea" (*Bride Price*, 137–38).

Like the brute he is, Okoboshi caps his catalog of battering with this revolting act—the height of insult in various African cultures: "He filled his mouth with soapy saliva and spat, *plop*, in her face between her nose and her mouth. The spit revolted her and she almost vomited" (*Bride Price*, 139). Determined to fight Okoboshi and not yield to any forced sex with him, "a kind of strength came to her, from where she did not know. She knew only that, for once in her life, she intended to stand up for herself, to fight for herself for her honor" (*Bride Price*, 136).

Young Aku-nna cannot fully understand why Ibuza people are against her relationship with Chike, her only love in a barren Ibuza. She muses, *"How simple our lives would have been but for the interference of our parents" (Bride Price*, 139; italics in original). Caught in the web of Ibuza Igbo tradition, Aku-nna is in despair.

Aku-nna's Elopement and Death in Ughelli

Aku-nna's elopement with Chike from Ibuza to Ughelli is her final emancipatory act, reflecting her disgust with reactionary traditions and desire to satisfy a major need—that of self-worth. But Aku-nna's escape from Okoboshi and her elopement with Chike are offensive to Okonkwo, who considers the "rebellion" an outrageous discourtesy and an insult to his person. Besides, her action also denies him the bride price he expects. Parenthetically, he feels his prerogative by tradition to choose a husband for Aku-nna has been completely ignored, and he retaliates very viciously on Aku-nna and her mother. He divorces Ma Blackie in the traditional Ibuza way by publicly exposing his bare posterior toward her face. This is a rare act and, according to the author, "his relatives and friends who stood by covered their faces in shame, for this was not a step commonly taken by Ibuza men" (*Bride Price*, 155). This custom is not common to all African communities.

To kill Aku-nna for her disobedience and rebellion, Okonkwo makes a small doll in the exact image of her, pierces the heart of the doll with a needle and puts it in front of his *chi*—his personal god. With the act, he believes Aku-nna will die very slowly and painfully. According to the author, "It was evident that it worked, though nobody was sure how because those who knew the art would not submit it to scientific investigation" (*Bride Price*, 165). Okonkwo's disowning of Ma Blackie and his diabolical art to annihilate Aku-nna for letting him down—people whom he is expected to take care of—indicates his intense selfishness and villainy. Seen in this light, we the readers can conclude that Okonkwo has always regarded Aku-nna and Ma Blackie as inherited living property to enhance his masculine image and never as those he should take care of.

Although Aku-nna dies in childbirth, she is satisfied with her brief pleasant period of fulfillment with Chike, and the author brings the novel to a close:

> So it was that Chike and Aku-nna substantiated the traditional superstition they had unknowingly set out to eradicate. Every girl born in Ibuza after Aku-nna's death was told her story, to reinforce the old taboos of the land. If a girl wishes to live long and see her children's children, she must accept the husband chosen for her by her people, and the bride price must be paid. If the bride price was not paid she would never survive the birth of her first child. It was a psychological hold over every young girl that would continue to exist, even in the face of every modernization, until the present day. Why this is so, is as the saying goes, anybody's guess. (*Bride Price*, 168)

The relationship between content and form appears simple, but it is quite dense. Sometimes, however, critics seem to miss this point. A hasty or superficial reading of the novel may lead one to conclude that the novel is didactic and that the author's didactic concern is in seeming to stress the need for conformity to traditional cultural ways of life. Actually, to reach such a conclusion is a misjudgment of the importance of the plot and the role of the narrator.[14]

Read in this way, as quite a number of critics have done, one might come to a conclusion that Buchi Emecheta never really intends. One of the most perceptive critics of African literature, Ernest Emenyonu, falls into this trap. Recently he stated about the conclusion to the novel:

> This is an unsatisfactory ending for it confirms the traditional superstition that the author knowingly (unlike her fictional heroine) set out to eradicate. It removes the sense of commitment in Buchi Emecheta's fiction and makes her no more than a reporter who succeeds in narrating the woes of African womanhood, echoing its agonies, exhibiting its wounds, while firmly withholding a balm for its gaping sores. (Emenyonu 1988, 135)

To Chikwenye Ogunyemi, "Aku-nna's defiance of tradition brings about her end in a devastating way. It is incongruous that the feminist Emecheta should permit such failure considering the fact that she [Emecheta] came out unscathed after her own deviation from African norm" (1983, 70–71).

Another critic, Kirsten Holst Petersen, uneasily steers a middle course between medical reason and psychological reason as the cause of Aku-nna's death; her own conclusion is not really different from that of Emenyonu:

> Tradition takes its revenge. The bride price has not been paid, and according to tradition the bride must die in childbirth—which is exactly what Aku-nna does. The explanation given for her death hovers uneasily between the psychological and the medical. The book thus ends with the defeat of progressive forces. Such apparent defeatism is somewhat surprising from an author who so far has celebrated achievement.[15]

It is equally somewhat surprising that Petersen—who acknowledges Emecheta as one who "shows courage in challenging traditional male attitudes to gender roles; anger and iconoclastic contempt for unjust institutions, no matter how time honored or revered they are; and a willingness to seek new ways to subvert what she sees as the unjust subjugation of women in the name of tradition" (1991, 283)—can come to such a conclusion.

In almost the same vein, like the aforementioned critics, Helen Chukwuma states that "Aku-nna wins the battle but loses the war. Her death negates her entire struggle for freedom and she dies under the same yoke she seeks to overcome" (1989, 8). Similarly, the American critic Nancy Topping Bazin maintains that "*The Bride Price* could itself be used as a story that warns young people of what happens to disobedient girls" (1989, 8). Emenyonu's, Ogunyemi's, Peterson's, Chukwuma's, and Bazin's observations do not seem strong enough to stand on their own. Any literary critic who understands the mind behind *The Bride Price* will not completely share the conclusions of the aforementioned critics. Emecheta has an obligation to convince the reader that this literary work is worthwhile. She is not a reporter who succeeds in narrating the woes of African womanhood, echoing its agonies and exhibiting its wounds, but a talented artist in control of her craft. Emecheta uses the life of a young teenage girl to reflect on the rigid traditions of a conservative African community, Ibuza, and to examine the deficiencies of the bride price institution.

In her choice of an *osu* as a life partner in the world of rigid traditions, Aku-nna reveals the real search for independence and self-worth. *The Bride Price* is not a complete disaster story of Aku-nna. The author does not criticize her. Neither does she condemn her. If the author wants to make a severe judgment on Aku-nna, her matrimonial life would have been a miserable one. Instead, the author presents her matrimonial life as pleasant. Emecheta's narrative voice has a mediative weariness. She presents herself as an author disillusioned but not so deeply cynical as to think that traditions that seem inhuman and barbaric will last forever. However objective she tries to be, it is difficult to eliminate absolutely her personal style. It is this unique personal style that is essentially the medium and the substance out of which character, event, and plot are woven.[16]

The narrator does not say anything positive about the traditional ways of life discussed in the novel. All those aspects of tradition it considers—such as making someone an *osu*, a slave or outcast, inheriting wives, and the custom of "bride price"—show the destructive side of such practices. Despite the fact that Chike's father is one of the wealthiest and most educated people in Ibuza community, he and his family are regarded as slaves because one of his ancestors had been sold into slavery. For purposes of tradition and custom Chike cannot marry a freeborn like Aku-nna. Despite this social taboo, Chike and Aku-nna elope. One cannot categorically assert that this rebellion brings about the death of Aku-nna in childbirth. It might have been accidental. It was birth by caesarean section. According to the doctor, "She was in an extremely anaemic condition" (*Bride Price*, 156). At a time when medicine was not as sophisticated as it is today in Africa, such a tragedy was not unusual. But be this as it may, even on her deathbed, Aku-nna insists that her marriage has been a happy one and that the choice of the name Joy should reflect the happiness of the union. In some cultures of black Africa where the names of people have meaning to mark the circumstances surrounding their birth, the name Joy is formidable. Joy the daughter seems to represent the new free generation of African females, which Aku-nna seems to herald.

Certainly in this case one may say that Aku-nna's short-lived happiness did bring more joy than an arranged marriage by tradition might have brought. Such a marriage would have been determined by material (the bride price), not human gain. Such a price would have reduced Aku-nna to an expensive commodity rather than a human being with feelings and emotions. Not only does tradition in this novel never take a step in the right direction, but those who rebel against tradition—the girl, the young man Chike, and his father—are always seen in the best of light.

Aku-nna dies but not without experiencing fulfillment in her love and marriage. She is even happy at death—a death that her young brother, Nna-nndo, who steadily matures into a disciplined teenager, witnesses. Like his sister, he breaks out of traditional shackles and objectively looks at human beings as they are and not as stigmatized by their conservative and prejudiced society. Chike's compassion and care for his sister and for himself, Nna-nndo, makes a deep and lasting impression on the boy. Denied very early in life a male role model as a result of his father's death, Nna-nndo finds Chike, an *osu,* his ideal hero, "the type of man he hoped he would grow up to be" (*Bride Price,* 165). Nna-nndo's new frame of mind suggests that the next generation will not be ruled by retrogressive traditions. Chike gives love and fulfillment and subliminally radiates the positive spirit of a role model to Nna-nndo.

Surely, Nna-nndo's brief stay with Chike and Aku-nna in Ughelli is more fulfilling than his long stay in Okonkwo's household in Ibuza: "These past months Nna-nndo had lived with them had inspired him to do better for himself. He had forgotten the crude life of Ibuza, and was thankful to Chike and his sister for making this new existence possible for him" (*Bride Price,* 165). Emecheta here minces no words in describing Ibuza in unpalatable, stifling terms, and one wonders if she has not gone too far. As one of Ibuza parentage, Buchi Emecheta knows, presumably, the spirit of Ibuza traditions that she finds offensive. Like Lagos and Ughelli, Ibuza is a real place. It is not a town or location in the world of folklore or myth. It is apparent in the novel that Aku-nna and her brother had more joy in Lagos and in Ughelli than their hometown, Ibuza, primarily as a result of their association with Chike. Rooted in the world of realism, *The Bride Price* is a powerful depiction of what a strong-willed young woman encounters in a conservative society—one that does not even have regard for an achiever because he is a slave.

Chike's father is an achiever and has trained his children, who, in turn, are an asset to Ibuza. Through the positive and constructive presence of the *osus* in Ibuza, Emecheta points to the need to treat a person as an individual and not as a stereotype. Those who rebel against traditions—Aku-nna especially—are the ones who make the human moves even at the cost of material sacrifice, and their shortcomings, if they can be viewed as such, are forgivable. In other words, the plot seems to say, a short and sweet marriage is better than a drawn-out life of misery with the wrong partner. Even this, however, is not the point of the novel. The narrator's role here is quite significant.

The narrator's comment at the end of the novel—"If a girl wishes to live long and see her children's children, she must accept the husband chosen for her by her people, and the bride price must be paid"—does not mean that people ought to conform to tradition, as a hasty and superficial reading might lead one to conclude. Rather, given the plot, it means—and this does seem to be the point of the book—that nonconformism against inhuman customs seems to lead to disaster. Isn't such tragedy as a result of nonconformism chilling and shocking? Isn't this something we should protest and fight against (perhaps unto death)? The narrator is omniscient and leads us into the thoughts of those we should sympathize with—thus playing the classic role of an omniscient narrator. Still, it seems the author does not want her work to be obviously didactic, and therefore she makes the narrator hold back when it comes to direct criticism. She wants her readers to be active, wants them to put two and two together, for then their sense of revulsion will be strongly realized. In short, the book, for all its protest, seems a beautiful example of nondidactic art.

Chapter Three
Young Adult Love and Marriage

Young adult love and marriage are of overwhelming importance in contemporary African children's and youth literature and in many novels dealing with this subject. Its overwhelming importance is also traceable in the ancient traditionsal tales of the people. Let me illustrate with one example—Cyprian Ekwensi's *The Boa Suitor* (1966). All the young men in an African village court a pretty girl, and a boa who has borrowed a human body and a human voice defeats every other person in the courting competition and marries her. But when she finds out that she is married to a boa, she runs away to her parents. But she is sent back by her parents who respect the sanctity of marriage. In her third escape from the boa she manages to convince her parents that her husband is a boa and not a human being. Her parents take her back, and the boa is killed. As Eckhard Breitinger rightfully observes, "This story about marriage and divorce presented to children at a non-marriageable age seems to be meant to illustrate the functioning, the rules and the value rating of important social institutions. It illustrates society as an organism working along certain rules even in cases of violation of rules."[1] In a precognitive way of understanding, the children learn about African adult social world. The intent, of course, is to further and secure their integration into African marriage culture.

As cultural products, such literature mirrors contemporary African social order. In Africa the concept that a family is a very important unit of the society is still very strong. The family is regarded as a major institution that can ensure perpetuation of African society and instill traditional positive values and faith in the next generation. There is a strong belief that family or home training and education of the young is important for their future development. The beginning of a family is traceable to young adulthood when a young man and a young woman express their sincere feeling to each other during courtship. While the young adults may sometimes become infatuated with each other and become somewhat irrational in their love affair, African adults are always around to put them right.

Long ago marriages were almost completely arranged by the families of both parties, and the practice still exists in some African societies. Families of both parties may not openly come out to approve or disapprove the courtship of their young adults. But when such a love affair is developing into a marriage, which is strongly regarded as a lifetime commitment by the two parties, African adults—especially the parents of both parties—play a major role either to approve or disapprove it. Absolute freedom for African young adults in the final choice of their spouses does not generally exist. It is not my intention here to discuss all the numerous and varied aspects of young adult love and marriage in Africa but to look at how the theme is explored in African youth fiction.

The African novels that deal with young adult love and marriage look like romances to Jurgen Martini, Wendy Griswold, and Virginia Coulon.[2] It is important to note, however, that these novels go beyond the entertainment of romances to explore the African heritage in love, matrimonial affairs, and family life. They thereby offer solid instruction to young adults who will one day begin a family and perpetuate the unit of society. They counteract the tendency of young adults to be captivated by appearances, and they are not extensions of Western romances per se.

The number of novels that deal with young adult love and marriage in Africa is quite staggering, and it is impossible to cover all of them in a work like this. I have selected Buchi Emecheta's *A Kind of Marriage* as my primary focus in this chapter because it deals with monogamy, polygamy, the age-old interference of in-laws in marriage affairs, and two young adult products—one from a legal marriage and the other from a forced marriage. David Maillu's *For Mbatha and Rabeka* and Jide Oguntoye's *Too Cold for Comfort* I selected primarily to illuminate how one party's devotion of his or her attention elsewhere outside his or her marriage or love affair can negatively affect it.

For Mbatha and Rabeka

The Kenyan young adult novel *For Mbatha and Rabeka* realistically deals with what divided attention can do to a love relationship. An ideal love affair is between two—a male and a female—and not three. A tripartite love relationship as seen in that of Rabeka, Mbatha, and Mawa lacks a center. According to David Maillu, "The triangle could be turned three ways: one with Mawa hoisted and placed at the top angle; two, Rabeka sitting at the top angle with both men fighting each other from the two bottom angles; or three, with Josef Mbatha crucified with grief at the top angle by the two people, Rabeka and Mawa, at the bottom angles, smiling and kissing each other waiting for the moment when they could meet at the centre."[3] Without a discerning spirit, Rabeka fails to see beyond the mask of sophistication and friendliness that Mawa puts on, and she fails to discover his inner person. This is why she becomes a victim of deception. If Rabeka had had an indomitable spirit in her love relationship with Mbatha, Mawa would not have succeeded in conning her.

Like Rabeka, Mbatha is also innocent of the ways of young women or even of men. He lacks a grasp of the psychology of women, especially his ignorance of the cultural assumption among some Africans that "woman feels and man reasons out" (*Mbatha*, 88). He loves and trusts Rabeka without reservation. On receipt of Rabeka's farewell letter, "he felt wounded, mercilessly hit like an animal." For the *first* time in his life, he thinks seriously about the complexity of women:

> Of all the things he had never imagined could happen to him, this was one of them. But it happened. . . . He had become a victim of his own dreams. . . . The Rabeka he had cherished in a thousand and one ways and for many years, had taken the soup of his life and poured it on the ground.
> He sat down again and went through the letter, this time very carefully, trying to digest every word, every sense, every implication, the psychology of the writer and women as a whole. (*Mbatha*, 105)

Released after six weeks' hospitalization, he becomes a withdrawn character. His note through his junior niece to Rabeka on her wedding day is based not on love but as a token of good memories. Rabeka's response to it, and their flight later after Mawa fails to show up at the wedding, are described in animal terms, and only Mawa's absence from the wedding ceremony provides Mbatha and Rabeka the opportunity to patch up and restore their old relationship: "They leapt onto each other, and acting instinctively, both raced like frightened thieves down the slope, down into the forest of eucalyptus, into the bush and into the cliffs still holding hands" (*Mbatha*, 148). Very soon after, Mbatha's madness descends on him and he pounces violently on Rabeka, but a few moments later they are in a love embrace. It is only in the last paragraph of the novel that the reader knows that Mbatha and Rabeka finally come together. Although Mbatha and Rabeka come together again, all indications are that their love may not retain its old purity and intensity. As the title *For Mbatha and Rabeka* suggests, the novel's content is primarily for growing young adults who will one day find themselves in love. The novel's thrust, then, is to reflect various forces that can affect love affairs and even marriages.

Too Cold for Comfort

Like Rabeka, who removes her attention from her young sweetheart, Mbatha, and devotes it to a charming fraud, Mawa, Hannah Ologun removes hers from her husband and new marriage and devotes it to a so-called spiritual church, the Holy of Holies. In Hannah's case it is a devotion ignited by an excessive and irrational yearning for spiritual fulfillment. Whether prompted by secular or religious reasons, the result of devoting one's attention outside a love affair or marriage is the same—a weakening or breakup of the affair or marriage. In *Too Cold for Comfort* Hannah's obsession with distorted Christian ideals she has learned in a fake church ruins her sex life with her husband and almost breaks up her marriage. Under the influence of Holy of Holies, Hannah regards sex, which her young husband, Kolade Omola, like most people, enjoys, as evil. Kolade's complaint to his mother-in-law reveals a picture of a cold marriage:

> "She does not believe in caring for the sexual desires of a husband. If I try to love her ten times, she would have declared eight of the ten moves as sinful, shunning me like a leper. How do I reconcile this with the tenet of monogamy ma?"
>
> Lady Ologun nodded.
>
> "That's the crux of the matter," he continued. "I tried to educate her, she branded me an agent of Satan."[4]

Kolade's complaint captures the frustration in his checkered history of his new but turbulent marriage to Hannah. Hannah's misunderstanding of Christian morality as a result of her membership in a cult comes to the fore and ruins even their wedding night, when couples typically consummate their marriage. Her behavior on their wedding night is dramatic and shocking enough to warrant quoting this long passage:

> Kolade had kissed her passionately and dragged her down to bed. She noticed her *iro* [a wrapper] falling off and . . . "That is temptation," her voice rang out. She had some inner caution, a sort of voice akin to the "voice of God" which had cautioned her against falling for the lustful

advances of Dr. Kole Tokulo over the years. As she had reacted obediently to his voice so she would now.

"Stop that, Kolade," she said in a high, hard and resolute tone, pulling him off and gasping, her eyes flashing in bewilderment.

"What? Why?" perplexed, Kolade asked.

"Don't you know what you are doing?"

"What if I know? Is it anything wrong?"

"Wrong. Yes."

"Don't you know right things should be done at the right time? That otherwise they become wrong?"

"Wonderful. What time is better than now?"[5]

"You don't know. Man of small faith."

"Hannah . . . Hannah . . . you . . . you are beating me hollow." Kolade stammered and trembled, full of sudden doubt.

This was not the Hannah he had dreamt of a few days before his wedding but a fanatic of the sort he would least like to encounter.

"Are you loose sexually?" Hannah rebuked him. "I arrived only few minutes ago; now you come to pounce on me. . . . This is unlike the follower of Jesus Christ you claim to be. No Christian rushes into things. We should pray, consult God, seek his approval and blessings."

"Good sermon," Kolade snapped back, shaking his head pitifully. He could see Hannah's mind was enslaved to dogma. He kept his distance on the bed and gazed at her. "Have you forgotten that our marriage was blessed by God and man in a memorable wedding ceremony only today?" (*Too Cold*, 25–26)

This unusual atmosphere henceforth characterizes their lovemaking—or lack of it. Hannah's regular denial of Kolade's sexual gratification frustrates him. He consequently begins to regard his matrimonial home as a prison.

His purchase of a "Liberate Yourself" T-shirt indicates his desire to get out of his marriage with Hannah, whom he soon regards as "an incorrigible bigot" who sleeps like "a big log of wood in the night" (*Too Cold*, 57). To Kolade, "sex is an instinctive thing, despite the lessons or story of Adam and Eve: too natural for a timetable." On the other hand, to Hannah Ologun, prayers should be said and a divine sign must be received before lovemaking. The two cannot arrive at a compromise. This is too much for Kolade to bear, and he becomes unfaithful. As far as Kolade is concerned, "an unsexy wife is a sad disappointment" (*Too Cold*, 59). It is Hannah's deviant attitude toward sex that her mother wants to correct when she promises to tell her that "sex is the bolt to wedlock. When a lock has no bolt in it, it is no lock at all" (*Too Cold*, 146).

Hannah has the potential of becoming a good wife. She is quite faithful, but her flaw is that she allows the dogma of her so-called spiritual church to corrupt her and make her believe that prayers have to be said even before making love. With such distortion deeply lodged in her mind, she finds it difficult to have sex with her husband without a tinge of guilt. According to the author, "Hannah preferred to believe she had no sexual feeling for her husband. To be jealous was sinful while to have sexual feeling was to succumb to temptation" (*Too Cold*, 107). She essentially denies herself her human nature.

The young couple's incessant arguments and scuffles over religion and sex draw their neighbors' attention. In fact, it is the neighbors' intervention one day that saves them from killing or fatally injuring each other in one of their frequent disagreements. The author graphically paints the erosion of their privacy: "These neighbors made a series of such interventions thereafter. . . . Each time they quarreled, the neighbors found their excuses too flimsy. While some neighbors disbelieved their statements, some took the couple at their word and blamed their differences on immaturity" (*Too Cold*, 65). The respect accorded privacy in Africa is not as strong as that obtainable in Western culture. When there is commotion in a house, the neighbors go in to assist in any way they can. Today, however, such a gesture is not as strong as it used to be. That neighbors now know about their sex life—that Hannah is frigid and Kolade is not sexually satisfied—indicates the decrepit state of their marriage.

There does not seem to be anything to really bind Hannah and Kolade in marriage. Sex, which should draw them into a deep satisfying intimacy, seems to scatter them. Both Hannah and Kolade illustrate the offensive and unhealthy nature of conjugal sexual relationship. Kolade fantasizes sexual fulfillment with Hannah during courtship but degenerates into violence, recklessness, and infidelity after their marriage. Husband and wife come to see sex from different perspectives. Unlike some women, who use sex for commercial purposes, Hannah uses it as a means to draw Kolade into her brand of religious belief. This is why she wants Kolade to pray with her before lovemaking. In desperation, young Kolade sometimes acquiesces. But he does *not* believe in praying before sex. To a certain extent, however, Kolade uses sex to dominate and control Hannah. This is why he sometimes boxes and muffles her into submission. In some sections of the Western world, such action would be considered rape. In Africa, however, a husband raping his wife would sound ludicrous. For a wife to deny her husband sex is to encourage him to develop interest in other women, which does not augur well for the success of the marriage. Hannah also uses sex as an instrument of power. If she can pressure an irrepressible Kolade into doing what he does not believe—to pray before sex—Hannah is indeed powerful. Neither Kolade's perspective about sex nor Hannah's is completely right. Each is tinged with selfishness, and the spirit of sharing and giving that permeates a genuine sexual relationship is absent. In fact, sex has no pleasure for Hannah. She sees it as a price she must pay in marriage. Giving her body grudgingly and sparingly to Kolade takes out the joy and fulfillment in lovemaking. She seems to see the man in her life as an "intruder" into her chaste "religious" body. She would rather listen to the perverted sermons and doctrines of the Holy of Holies than to develop a deep intimacy with her husband. In her obsession with her church's deviant ideals of morality and in her immense satisfaction with its pastor, Hannah virtually substitutes her home life with her church. By frequently denying her husband sex or engaging in it sparingly and selfishly with him, Hannah is unable to grow spiritually; her action only stunts her spiritual development and dampens her marriage.

In Africa, any force, person, or group of people who attempt in any way to disrupt or break a marriage is condemned. Such a group is the Holy of Holies, whose deviant doctrines negatively affect the marriage of Kolade and Hannah. Claiming to be a deeply spiritual church, the Holy of Holies is a congregation of shams led by an untrained, self-appointed "minister" of God who is sly enough to recommend a holy bath with black soap to Hannah to cure her marital problem. One of the church's members, Kole Tokulo, a medical doctor, is an emotionally disturbed man whom Kolade still considers a rival for Hannah's love, even after Hannah turned down his marriage proposal. He is an irresponsible playboy: "Dr. Tokulo did not believe in the indispensability of women in a man's life although he would pay dearly for amorous pursuits. He was never impressed by talk of homebuilding and hated the idea of being tied down in matrimony" (*Too Cold,* 15). With such questionable characters making up the Holy of Holies church, Kolade is not at ease with Hannah's membership in it, even before his wedding: "Kokade could never see the logical basis of a religion or any church which did not insist on morality. . . . Kolade could not be made to believe that there was more honor in being a church member than not. He was perturbed about the safety of his fiancée in the hands of people like Dr. Tokulo, in such a church of hypocrites" (*Too Cold,* 15–16).

Children and young adults are all too often attracted to churches or other religious organizations or clubs that are deceptive. They are either too trusting or not old and experienced enough to detect this deception in the groups they join. To a certain extent, their male-dominated society and culture make African women especially susceptible to the influence of various religions and of practitioners of witchcraft. African women usually turn to them for guidance or protection against their so-called enemies and for magical influence in matters of love, and thus they sometimes come under the control of tricksters.

Although the leader of the Holy of Holies is a fraud, Hannah believes him to be a man of God. In *A Kind of Marriage* Bintu, who listens to Amina's tale of Ubakanma, expresses her fear of some of these leaders of certain religious groups: "I knew that if you allowed some of the Wolis [prophet in Yoruba language] to penetrate into your family they could actually control your private lives."[6] The alfa in Buchi Emecheta's *Naira Power* is a fake, and he swindles Lemonu out of his money and deadens his intelligence. Many of these self-proclaimed prophets care more about themselves than anyone else, yet their gullible followers believe they are "divine." Psychologically astute, they deceive and manipulate others, taking advantage of their weaknesses.

People who manipulate others actually exist in contemporary Africa and other parts of the world. Children's literature that addresses this sometimes complex and intricate world of deception affords vicarious experience reading for children and youth. A true presentation of deceptive churches, cults, or witchcraft practitioners and their modus operandi is invaluable. Michael D. Langone's stress that "practical curricula should be developed to teach young people how to maintain a critical autonomy in a world bent on influencing them to do things that are not always in their own best interest"[7] is apt. Young adults need a lot of guidance in a world that is increasingly becoming fraudulent even in religious matters, and African children's literature does provide edifying reading about them. Against this backdrop of the functional nature of literature for African children and young adults, the critical perspectives of some well-meaning Western critics sometimes miss the mark.

Criticism of both children's literature and African literature demands special considerations that go beyond the criticism of English literature in general (Schmidt 1981, 6). But some Western critics do not seem to be aware of any special considerations. Virginia Coulon, Misty Bastian, Wendy Griswold, and Jurgen Martini have written in quite intriguing ways about African children's literature. In 1987, with Misty Bastian, Wendy Griswold wrote an essay that she considered a preliminary study of the Nigerian romance novel. She followed two years later with an essay in which she asserts that "the question of cross-cultural transfers and transformation—what happens when cultural forms from one society are transported to and reconstructed in another—intrigues anyone who tries to understand how culture operates in the modern world" (1989, 75). Seen in this light, Griswold is one of the scholars whose broad-mindedness expresses itself in looking at the subtleties of multiculturalism. In concluding their 1987 essay, Griswold and Bastian observe that local context has influenced the narrative form of many Nigerian romances, while social changes shaped by Western models have influenced their content (351).

As I have earlier indicated, some of the novels have the semblance of romance, but the successful ones go beyond its parameters. They are not just extravagant tales for escapist tendencies: the situations they depict are real. They are not deliberate imitations of Western models. African children's literature that does not go beyond an elementary imitation of European and American children's literature will make no important contribution to world culture.[8]

Wendy Griswold is so caught up in her focus on literary transmission from one culture to another that she seems to forget the rationale behind Hannah's frigidity—her distorted understanding of Christian religion that spells the crisis in her marriage. In fact, it is Hannah's obsession with distorted ideals of Christianity that is the novel's crux. If Griswold has lived for a considerable length of time in Africa, perhaps she would have had some opportunity to see and appreciate firsthand what havoc sick religiosity has done and still does do to some people and some communities. Especially in contemporary times, when it is becoming increasingly difficult for many to differentiate between the genuine and the counterfeit or quack religious groups and their leaders, African children's fiction that addresses religious hypocrisy is relevant and topical.

One-third of those who died in the Jim Jones People's Temple massacre in Jonestown, Guyana, in 1978 were children. Children and youth were also consumed in the inferno that destroyed David Koresh's Branch Davidian sect in Waco, Texas, in 1993. They unfortunately trusted and believed Jim Jones and David Koresh were divine. Such absolute trust in someone who's regarded as a spiritual leader can be very dangerous. In David Halperin's words, the Jonestown tragedy stands as a menacing backdrop when considering the potentially destructive impact of a cult on its members.[9]

For some African and even non-African youths who believe that membership in eccentric fundamentalist groups or cults is the way to

salvation or heaven, *Too Cold for Comfort* is a demonstration of the consequences of such mistaken beliefs. *Too Cold for Comfort* has the capacity and
strength to engage and sustain our interest and vicarious experience of
life. It subtly stresses the need for a thorough understanding of Christian
morality rather than a superficial or perverted understanding of it, and
the need to rationally balance it with one's domestic life.

A Kind of Marriage

> Whenever I failed in anything I always remembered what I considered
> my greatest failure—the inability to make my marriage work. (*Head*,
> 165)

Buchi Emecheta continues her interesting reflection on love and marriage in *A Kind of Marriage*. The story is narrated by Amina to her listener, Auntie Bintu—not in a car under a tropical rainstorm as in *Naira
Power* but this time in a restaurant. When Auntie Bintu returns once
more from Britain to Nigeria she expects Amina, her sister-in-law, to
have plenty of stories for her—after all, last time she visited she heard
the sad tale of Ramonu (in *Naira Power*). She is not disappointed by
Amina's tale. It is full of unexpected twists as she unfolds the tortured
history of Afam, the son of Charles Ubakanma and the woman his parents pressure him to marry secretly when his first wife is unable to have
more than one child.

Set mainly in Lagos against a brief background of the Nigerian civil
war and on a few occasions in England, *A Kind of Marriage* deals essentially with marriage—a polygamous one riddled with discord. At the
end of the novel Amina asks Auntie Bintu, "What do we need men for
really?" Her response is somewhat sarcastic: "We need them to give us
babies, and after that I don't know." From the first page to the last, the
novel deals with the marriage of Charles and Maria, which is harmonious
initially but a disaster at the end. This disaster is a result of Charles's
inability to ward off traditional parental pressures that started the
unhappiness in his home.

While working in the Nigerian Office in London during the colonial
days when Nigeria was a British colony, Charles Ubakanma married
Maria, a nursing sister. Maria's inability to have another child after her
first and only one, Osita, does not detract from the happiness in the
marriage: "Life was very sweet for them because despite the cold weath-

er over there in England, they had a big house and servants" (*Marriage*, 26). Implied in this statement is that it is not really the number of children that necessarily brings happiness into the home: though Ubaks (Charles Ubakanma) wanted many more sons and daughters after Osita, none came. And Maria was beautiful and a good hostess and so Ubaks learned to live like a European, with just one baby son and a beautiful wife and hostess (*Marriage*, 26). In this harmonious state Charles does not realize that Maria has "failed" him by giving him only one son.

The family name—"Ubakanma"—means the large family is better. Perhaps fate dealt unfairly with Charles when he found himself saddled with such a name. It is a credit to Charles that he initially does not fuss about it and does not go after other women to have more children. On his arrival in Nigeria, however, things start taking a different turn. Charles begins mysterious tours in his government job, especially on the weekends. It is through these frequent weekend trips to his hometown, Ibuza, that he gets entangled with a young girl, Obioma, setting the stage for the beginning of his matrimonial problems.

Maria does not complacently accept her inability to have more children. As a nurse, she consults doctors who perform surgery on her, but still she in unable to conceive. She initially accepts her fate, but in desperation and despite all her education and sophistication, she joins the Celestial Apostolic Faith, hoping that her membership in it and the Faith's "spiritual powers" will bring her more children. But Maria ends her association with Celestial Apostolic Faith when the members invite her to make love with Charles in their church's altar—their "prerequisite" for pregnancy, especially for women desperately wanting babies.

Charles is a quite responsible husband but succumbs to the wishes of his parents to have more grandchildren. One cannot really condemn his parents. Their generation is interested in having a lot of children. This is why they bring an attractive young girl to him to sleep with at night. His reaction to his parents bringing Obioma to him in bed at night is one of shock, because he never expected it: "He could remember how very nervous he had been the first night with Obioma. . . . He had not paid any particular attention to what his father was saying until he felt Obioma in his bed at the dead of the night (*Marriage*, 67). He protests, but his protest is followed by his old father's use of psychology—to put a finger of doubt on his son's manhood by asking, "Is there something wrong with you, son? Are you impotent and are you not man enough to admit it? Will you allow people to blame it on your wife, Maria?"

(*Marriage,* 67–68). Charles's father knows the right questions to ask. To put any question of doubt on the sexual health of an African male or any man amounts to casting aspersion on his manhood.

Despite this, Charles initially insists on rejecting Obioma but finally yields under his father's pressure. His lovemaking to Obioma is devoid of real fulfillment: "He remembered the superior feeling he felt when he was making love to Obioma who was then little more than a child. His feeling of guilt had to be deadened and he heard himself promising to look after her" (*Marriage,* 68). At a somewhat unguarded moment he allows his parents to intrude into his matrimonial home to the point of ruining it. The intrusion, of course, is not malevolent; the aging parents' interest is for Charles to have another son beside Osita to fulfill the meaning of their family name.

Multiple wives obviously provide more children for a man. It was a practice accepted for a long time, and it is still accepted in many parts of Africa. But as it is, Charles is forced into this practice by his parents. In a polygamous setting the wives compete among each other, and their children do the same. It is this unhealthy rivalry and competition that Maria fears. Charles's affair with Obioma produces Afam, who becomes Osita's rival and later his killer.

Unlike Maria, who compliments Charles's life, Obioma could only flatter his ego as a man, because of her complete dependence on him. Flattering a man's ego is not what makes a marriage strong. Sharing life and experience together is absent in the Charles-Obioma relationship. Charles is not proud of Obioma because she is an illiterate, far below him socially. While he has an eye on working in the Foreign Service, he does not dream of ever presenting someone like Obioma as his wife, to people in foreign/diplomatic circles, even though she is wife number two. Social compatibility therefore is necessary for a successful marriage.

Unlike Obioma, Maria is Charles's pride. Quite unlike the practice of most African women, Maria operates a common bank account with her husband. Unlike many African women who believe that the man spend more in the up bringing of their children, she regard's herself as an equal partner in the upbringing of Osita. Unfortunately, this partnership is severely shaken after she learns of Charles's affair with Obioma. She minces no words in telling Charles her new mind: "Charles, I understand you could not help the pressure your family put you under . . . you must appreciate the fact that though my son Osita, God bless him, is your first son, he will be out-numbered. So if you don't mind, I will keep my income separate from now on so that my son can inherit my things. . . . Another thing, that woman is not coming to live with us in Lagos" (*Marriage*, 47).

Unlike most African women of past generations who appeared contented in sharing their husbands with other wives, modern-day African women do not tolerate it. An extramarital affair or an additional wife are grounds for strife in marriage or even outright divorce. Maria does not want Obioma in their house because, like most African men, Charles would dote on her as the new and fresh one. The result, of course, would be a neglect of the wife at home, and this is exactly what happens in Maria's case.

The beginning of separate accounts in Charles's home spells the beginning of the painful disunity in a marriage that has hitherto been a model. According to the narrator, "Maria watched helplessly as the marriage between her and Charles became completely invaded by his parents, then gradually by Afam's mother" (*Marriage*, 50). With her separate account, Maria alone courageously finances Osita's education in a posh private school in Lagos through medical school in Britain. Although Charles and Maria share the same bedroom, many a night Charles is not there, using Maria's refusal to contribute to the household budget as an excuse. While Charles concentrates on Obioma, Maria concentrates on Osita.

When Maria takes Osita to the United Kingdom, Afam, the product of Charles and Obioma's affair, comes to live with Charles at his home in Ikoyi, an elite, wealthy neighborhood in Lagos. Perhaps the invasion of Charles and Maria's marriage by young Afam proves to be the worst of all the invasions. Raised and pampered by his permissive grandmother in Ibuza, Afam becomes used to having his way in everything, and he carries this attitude into Charles's home. He displays his temper tantrum anytime he feels he is not having his way. Afam's tantrum is the talk of the Ikoyi neighborhood. Afam brings neighbors, including the unruly boys like himself, to invade Charles and Maria's home. (Ikoyi has been and still is a quite posh, exclusive neighborhood for upper- and middle-class people in Lagos.) The presence of an unruly boy like Afam and his noise are a nuisance. This is why he is the talk of the neighborhood. Afam's hot temper is strange to Maria because Osita has never displayed anything of the sort. When Maria gets up to go and help Charles to hush Afam in one of his unruly moments, Dr. Cooker, their neighbor, stops her:

Sit there, Maria, this is not your funeral, your husband's name is Ubakanma, the crowd is better. Well he's got one son too many for his crowd, let him deal with him. And you be careful with that boy, his mother's tongue is sharper than you realize.

"Is the mother here?" Maria asked aghast.

Mrs. Cooker looked at Maria with that sympathy which only women can feel for each other. She shook her head. "Thank goodness, she left just two weeks ago. But what a fight she put up when Charles told her to go back because you were returning. It was then we knew what was happening. We were wondering who she was. I thought she was a new maid but she soon left us in no doubt at all. It was devastating for Charles." (Marriage, 55; my italics)

I quote this passage at length to get the feel of Charles-Maria's home in the absence of Maria.

In the absence of Maria, in London with Osita, Obioma moves into Charles's home. Since there was no legal marriage between Charles and Obioma, the latter's stay with Charles in Maria's absence is a slight to Maria. Charles's inability to disclose the identity of Obioma to his neighbors reflects his consciousness of the fact that Obioma is absolutely inferior to Maria. It is this "inferiority" coupled with her comparatively tender age that makes the Cookers think she is a housemaid and not a wife. (Idayatu is thought of as a house girl for the same reason in *Naira Power*.) The Cookers' relating of what had been going on in Charles's house in Maria's absence indicates the extent to which young Afam and his mother exposed the house to the neighborhood. The once cherished privacy of the Ubakanmas is past.

The novel concentrates on the steady degeneration of Afam, the product of Charles and Obioma, into a failure as a youth. A truant, Afam goes to the lagoon to pick crabs when he should be in class in the private school that Osita himself attended. The school authority eventually expels him. Despite Afam's unruly behavior, Maria strives to establish love between him and Osita, but it is impossible.

At the height of envy and jealousy, Afam collects about six rough boys (the roughest in Ikoyi) who, after drinking most of the cans of beer in the refrigerator, collectively curse Osita's picture in a very malicious vein (it is this kind of jealousy and unhealthy rivalry that Maria fears). They do the cursing after forming a circle around it:

"May you roast in fire, forever and ever. May you never come home. . . ."

And Afam was urging them to put the greatest verbal damnation they could think of on the object [Osita's picture placed in the center of their circle]. But when the boys started to say things like, "May you never qualify as a doctor so that our friends here will inherit all Ubakanma's wealth" Afam burst out laughing. The laughter was hysterical, ringing eerily from one corner of the apartment to another. It was not the laughter of an innocent thirteen-year-old, but the laughter of a wild animal. (*Marriage*, 60)

This is a macabre scene of sorcery and black magic practice unexpected from an African youth of 13. Because Afam could not physically reach Osita, the target of his envy, he attempts reaching him spiritually but in a devilish way, pouring venom on his picture. What can produce a demonic 13-year-old? Afam's selfish desire to inherit all his father's wealth at his demise points to one of the most potentially explosive situations in African polygamous homes. Both youth and adult children by different mothers are sometimes painfully estranged from each other as a result of their frenzied desire to acquire much of their parents' estate. As it were, there is a certain degree of indwelling tension and rivalry between children by different mothers in a polygamous home, and between the mothers as well. Subsequently, cohesiveness in such polygamous homes, if any, is not strong.

There is no indication that Afam was initially capable of demonstrating warm feelings in Ibuza before he came to live with Charles in Lagos. According to Mrs. Cooker, "Afam's character is almost formed and he has been encouraged to have his way with his grandparents." Perhaps grandparents, out of excessive love, pamper and spoil their grandchildren. Afam is inevitably influenced and conditioned by his association with the neighborhood's young ruffians, and also through his contact with criminals in a remedial center he was sent to after his expulsion from the posh school in Lagos. To wish death to someone is malicious and evil. Afam and his group's cursing of Osita's picture and their subsequent shattering of the picture foreshadow the murder of Osita by Afam and his associates toward the end of the novel.

The cursing and shattering of Osita's picture accelerate the woes in Ubakanma's household: "Maria cried from shock and anger. She cried at what Allah had done to Charles and herself. She cried because of the unfairness of the whole thing" (*Marriage*, 62). As she cries, blood trickles from her forehead where Afam's boys had thrown cans of beer at her. For Charles, "his shock was beyond words": "He picked up the wife Allah had given him in the first place, the wife whose fate had been originally knotted up with his before he had allowed himself to be pushed into a situation he knew he really did not want and they both cried" (*Marriage,* 63). Charles and Maria are now superficially and uneasily united in sorrow through Afam and his activities but united in joy through Osita and his success.

Afam's rapid degeneration in behavior increasingly exposes Charles's private life to the neighborhood. To salvage some of his privacy, Charles decides to take him back to Ibuza. But on the eve of the trip, Afam runs away from home. The long tedious search for Afam exposes Charles's family more to the city of Lagos. The papers carry Maria's story. Insinuations arise: she is suspected of putting a curse on Afam because she could no longer have a child of her own. But we the readers know that Maria has put no curse on Afam.

Osita, who has been brought up to respect his father, returns from Britain on completion of his studies and marries. Osita has nothing against Afam. He wishes him well and wants him present at his wedding. At Osita's wedding, Afam looks respectable. When Osita and his wife go to Disneyland in California for their honeymoon, they leave their "new well-furnished flat to Afam to look after until their return!" (*Marriage,* 109). It is during this short period of Osita's absence that Afam sees firsthand his half-brother's affluence. Although Afam does not take anything away from Osita's apartment, the seeds of envy are already in his mind. According to the narrator, "But as soon as they returned then it dawned on Afam that the type of rich happiness that Osita was enjoying might never be his. He suppressed his fear and jealousy, but kept deluding himself that if only someone would lend him money to start his business, he would catch up with Osita" (*Marriage,* 111). What is prompting Afam to start a business is his envy of his brother and not his genuine desire to do so. He generates a competitive spirit within himself and an unhealthy game of rivalry with his brother. Although he suppresses his fear and jealousy about Osita's "rich happiness," these unhealthy emotions are already in him. It is also in Osita's absence that Afam suddenly realizes that "by shutting himself away in Ibusa, he was missing a great deal out of life" (*Marriage,* 110).

He needs money to open a bar in Ibuza but is afraid to ask his father. His application for a bank loan to start business has earlier on been turned down in Ibuza. It is at this point of frustration and bitterness that Charles invites all of them to a get-together dinner at his house, but the event turns out a disaster.

Osita finds the frustrated and bitter Afam talking back at their father at the table very shocking and vehemently insists on him apologizing to their father. Afam refuses. With disgust they all leave Afam at the table. Alone, Afam smashes all Maria's best china, which she had been collecting before Osita was born. He walks out of the house only to resurface again as a young robber in the midst of thieves to steal money from Osita. In the ensuing scuffle Osita is killed. Fearing the consequence of being caught, the other thieves kill Afam, who had got mad and attacked them for killing his brother. Since Osita is no more, life has no more meaning for Charles, and he commits suicide by taking sleeping tablets. Four weeks later, Charles's father dies. The name Ubakanma dies without fulfilling its meaning; Charles's father dies without a son or grandsons.

A Kind of Marriage highlights the difference between two young products of two different marriages—Osita, the blessed product of a legal one, and Afam, the unruly product of a forced marriage. Emecheta achieves her presentation through her use of symbols. She associates sunshine with Osita: "When Maria and Charles arrive in London for the graduation of their son Osita the *sun was shining.* It was not raining and it was not cold and all the parks, the front and back gardens of the houses in London were full of sweet smelling roses" (*Marriage,* 76). Osita's return from his honeymoon in Los Angeles is also permeated by sunshine. "It was shining all over Lagos and one look at the happy couple showed that it was shining in their faces and in their hearts as well" (*Marriage,* 111).

Whereas Osita radiates happiness into his family, Afam radiates the opposite. He takes robbers to Osita's house in "a pitch dark night." Emecheta describes him in bestial terms. Besides the spirit of destruction he carries about, he behaves like an animal. He laughs like a "wild animal" when he and his ruffians curse and shatter Osita's picture. Although he reacts against his friends' killing of his brother, he virtually participates in the killing because he brought them there. Even then his reaction is couched on bestial terms: "He got mad and started to attack them just like an enraged animal" (*Marriage,* 119). The contrast between the young adults, Osita and Afam, is didactic—meant to reflect that hard work and diligence are rewarding and idleness and daydreaming are not. It is also to illustrate that the product of one's real marriage is usually better than the product of a forced marriage.

Amina recalls her narration of *Naira Power,* which Auntie Bintu later puts in print, and tells Auntie Bintu, "You indirectly strengthened our marriage because from that story he knew my past which I had been carrying with me all the time . . . We can laugh about it sometimes and try to use the lesson we learned from the tragic death of Ramonu [in *Naira Power*] as a guide to the way we live now. That is why I am telling you Afam's story" (*Marriage*, 93). Besides offering a reflection of his parents' marital woes, Afam's story is meant to guide youths about how to live. It is diligence and hard work that propel Osita into the medical profession, while stubbornness and daydreaming push Afam into a life of crime. Through his waywardness and criminal tendencies, Afam quickens the death of his brother, his father, and his grandfather.

Emecheta's narrow view of the social institution of marriage is quite fascinating in *A Kind of Marriage*. At the beginning of the novel, Amina tells Auntie Bintu, "I am so glad our women are now doing something. They have been so silent and too obedient for far too long. They said we used to be like that in Old Africa. Those women then could keep families going when their men fold had gone. But now a family like that [Maria, Ruth, and her twin children] is not a family, and that kind of marriage is not a marriage. What, Auntie Bintu, is a marriage and what is a family?" (*Marriage*, 8). At the end of the novel Auntie Bintu answers the question: "I think Ruth, Maria and the twins have a kind of marriage and a family. The two women have now got into a kind of marriage and a family" (*Marriage*, 120).

Is marriage complete without a husband? Emecheta seems to say yes, but this is an extreme position. Hostility to marriage is quite visible in many of Emecheta's works, and *A Kind of Marriage*, published only in 1986, is no exception. Perhaps in this novel she advocates a marriage of women alone.When Amina asks Auntie Bintu what women really need men for, she replies that they need men mainly for procreation. It is Buchi Emecheta talking. Marriage is a good institution if it is one of true minds. To assert that the marriage of a man and a woman is unnecessary especially after children have been born into it, does not give *A Kind of Marriage* the desired ending young adults would love. Is Emecheta telling young girls to get married to men principally to have children? Emecheta had an unpleasant marriage and perhaps she uses her personal experience as a yardstick and makes universal statements based on her own experience. This idiosyncratic opinion mars the novel.

As in *Naira Power*, the technique of a storyteller narrating a story to an interesting listener is also used in *A Kind of Marriage*. In fact, it is the same narrator, Amina, and the same listener, Auntie Bintu. Unlike *Naira Power*, whose narrative takes place in a car forced to stop in a tropical rain storm, the story of *A Kind of Marriage* is told in a restaurant in a more relaxed atmosphere than the one in a car. It is quite possible to have such a long story over food and drinks in a restaurant—a situation reminiscent of Joseph Conrad's technique in *Lord Jim,* where Marlow tells the story of Lord Jim to a group of interested listeners in a hotel. This is more plausible than the narration in a car under a tropical storm. Quite a compact novel, *A Kind of Marriage* provides an illuminating discourse that individuals, couple inclusive, must create for themselves ways of living and codes of personal behavior to which they can freely commit themselves without allowing an invasion of their relationship or home. Its significance for young adults themselves is to have an idea of how their own marriage might be marred if they decide to live like Charles. In the present body of African children's and youth literature, *A Kind of Marriage* is an eccentric exposé of the weakness of some African men in marital affairs. Inferior to *Naira Power* and *The Bride Price*, this novel sacrifices artistic excellence for the sake of "a special kind of marriage—of women alone."

Chapter Four

Material Wealth, Greed, Corruption, and the African Young Adult

Authors who write literature for children want to cultivate raw sensibilities, to civilize unruly passions, and to reveal unsocial forces hostile to civilization.[1] Nowhere in African youth literature is this statement more correct and applicable than in Agbo Areo's *Director!* and in Buchi Emecheta's *Naira Power.* In both novels the destructive power of the love of money and material possession is central. With pathos the novels present young adults who are destroyed by the dishonorable pursuit of money and material possessions; they convincingly indict the adult population and, of course, the society that fails to provide positive direction for its youth. In the midst of abundant wealth and material goods in African cities, those who do not have enough, and even those who do, are sometimes tempted to steal—sometimes with weapons that include firearms.

There are various incidents of violent robbery in such large African cities as Accra, Ghana; Nairobi, Kenya; and Lagos, Nigeria. Violent robbery, especially armed robbery, is in fact primarily an urban phenomenon. This is why Agbo Areo's *Director!* and Buchi Emecheta's *Naira Power* are set mainly in African urban centers—Ibadan and Lagos, respectively. It was the menace of armed robbers that incited a BBC commentator in the 1980s to say that President Babangida of Nigeria was in control of 16 states and armed robbers were in control of three. (At the time Nigeria had 19 states.) Many of these armed robbers are youths from lower-class backgrounds. One cannot categorically assert that robbers are born and not made. While there might be a few pathological thieves, undoubtedly most of them are made especially by the prevalent socioeconomic conditions of their environment. David Aronson observes that "the powerful in Africa steal because they can; the poor steal to survive. Corruption in Africa, then, was born of the structural weaknesses of African political and civil society, and it is now a cause as well as a consequence of African poverty."[2]

While there are a few wealthy people, there are many poor ones:

> A society characterized by widening inequalities and looting of public treasury by those who have access to it; where ostentatious display of ill-gotten wealth is applauded; where criminals, men in positions of power and trust, and law enforcement agents tend to collude, and where the needs and aspirations of the majority are neglected is likely to breed armed robbers and other property-related offenses.[3]

Some adolescent girls and grown women who want a very quick way to money and material wealth find prostitution a ready avenue. Those who have no access to their country's treasury might out of frustration become violent robbers. Stephen Ekpenyong states that "armed robbery is the result of an overt emphasis on the accumulation of material wealth by any means, and the inability of the system to provide subsistence to many. Only if materialism is de-emphasized and a more humane and disciplined society created can the energies of the frustrated and trapped youth be channelled into areas productive to both themselves and society" (21).

The model of status that many adults display to society—acquisition of money and material goods, especially cars in *Director!*—is ignoble and petty. To imitate such a bent of the adults is in fact a miscalculation by the youths. It is the devastating effect of imitating these materialistic adult role models that *Director!* and *Naira Power* seriously address.

Director!

On the surface, *Director!* (1977) explores the theme of material wealth in modern Nigerian society and illustrates that stealing results in retribution. Its presentation, however, is quite complex and lifelike.[4] The motive behind the actions of the characters is not greed but rather fear of impotence.

The people of Kajola want to display their material achievement because they feel inferior to the people of Ibadan. The parents of the young adult hero, Akinduro Falana, want him educated to become someone important—a lawyer or a medical doctor. That a lawyer or a medical doctor may be better off financially is not stressed. Akinduro

Falana's parents leave him with his grandmother when they go to Benin Republic to trade. It is their stark ignorance about the psychological impact of parental absence on their son rather than their desire to trade that is felt in the novel.

Young Akinduro originally takes up armed robbery not so much on account of materialistic greed but because he has been dismissed from school for leading a riot and he needs to retrieve his self-image. Similarly, Akpan gets into the football-pools racket and armed robbery not so much on account of materialistic greed but because he has been dismissed from the police force for gross improper behavior—getting drunk in public. But one should realize that Akpan has never been a drunkard. His getting drunk in public is primarily as a result of excessive excitement after he gets a word of his promotion, which has eluded him for 11 years.

After his dismissal he survives on the football-pools racket that he became familiar with in the police force. Akinduro's contact with Akpan accelerates his plunge into the rat race for money and material goods. Backed by a common experience of expulsion or dismissal by their establishments, Akinduro and Akpan establish a formidable partnership. The partnership represents dogged determination to survive and get on in the society, which they believe has treated them unfairly. They go out to rob on the freeway at night when they have no money or when they run out of what they "sell"—for example, cement for building houses. But they run out of luck when they are finally arrested by the police.

Even Akinduro's failure at school is primarily the result of psychological stress rather than materialistic ambition. Neglected by his parents, overprotected and pampered by his grandmother, the boy does not go to school until the age of 10. Older than his peers and handicapped by a feeling of inferiority, he does not do well at school. Protecting himself with an "I don't care" attitude, he goes to Ibadan and throws himself into city life.

The author, Agbo Areo, succeeds in going into the particular psychological motive behind each move his young adult hero makes, giving the character a certain roundness. Readers feel some sympathy for him. He is not an evil we are taught to hate, however crudely he may chase money and girls. The novel primarily shows how the young adult hero's values are misguided. The novel's moral value lies in its ability to help the reader understand moral predicament as in its condemnation of materialism. This is the kind of moral value that lies in most literature cast in the mold of realistic fiction.

In the present body of African literature for children and youth, *Director!* provides to the reader a clear indictment of materialism. In its sister novel, *Naira Power*, we see the total ruin of a youth, Ramonu.

Naira Power

African culture has always loathed stealing, and various traditional stories and sayings are a testimony to this fact. For example, among the Edos the saying *"ekhue imun oyi vbe n'omun otienoren"* literally means that the feelings of shame that the relative of a thief has are not the same as the one the thief himself has. Its deep meaning really is that for someone to be known as the relative of a thief is enough ground to cast doubt seriously on his/her character even if he/she tries to live a morally upright life. Knowing that he or she is not highly regarded simply because of the shameful fact that his or her relation is a thief makes him/her very uneasy—more uneasy than the thief himself. People have been known to seclude themselves because of this. In *An African Night's Entertainment* Shehu and Zainobe pack out of their Galma community because of their son, Kyauta, who degenerates into a thief. The intensely depressed spirit of Mallam Shehu surfaces in his statement to his wife, Zainobe: "I am tired, I am sick of hiding myself in my own town. Better to go elsewhere—to a place where I'm not known—and make a fresh start, than to continue under this burden of shame" (*African Night,* 82).

Besides such shame, depriving someone of a possession he or she has judiciously worked to get can be very devastating emotionally to that person. This is why punishment for stealing has always been severe. In times past in some communities, the punishment for a thief was to have his toes and fingers cut off. This may sound draconian, but it shows the people's age-old loathing of robbery. Such treatment, however, is rare today.

As in Western countries, robbery has become sophisticated in Africa, with embezzlement and white-collar crime more common. Con artists also pose as pastors, alfas, *marabouts,* native doctors, or as any other spiritual leader and deceive gullible people, swindling them of their money. Unlike such subtle forms of theft, some robbers are violent, using guns and other weapons. Law-abiding citizens respond sometimes by forming civil-defense or vigilante groups to protect their neighborhoods from thieves. Armed with the knowledge that some robbers can go scot-free through connections, people at times administer instant justice by executing thieves when they are caught. This is Ramonu's fate in Buchi

Emecheta's *Naira Power.* In Ramonu's case, however, he is not the actual pickpocket. He is only mistaken for one in the dense mass of spectators at a soccer match in Lagos.

Stealing *naira*—government currency—from people is made easy because most people do their shopping with *naira* in their pockets. Paying by check is an almost nonexistent practice in some parts of Africa because technology has not yet developed to the point where every person can have personalized checks. The Nigerian National Security Minting Office, which itself prints bank checks, postage stamps, and *naira* notes, has a lot of work to do. An added responsibility of printing millions of personalized checks would be too much for this office. (The currency notes of some African countries are printed overseas.) More important, a larger proportion of the populace are not literate enough to use checks. In addition, many traders do not accept checks. To trace the owner of a check returned for insufficient funds or the like would be extremely difficult.

In Nigeria there is no credit bureau or sophisticated central computer system; there is no social security number system, and the telephone is not a very reliable means of communication. There are few telephones, and those available are sometimes faulty or do not work. Only a very few educated people or organizations use checks to pay during shopping, and even then such use is limited mainly to big department stores like those in the Western world. In the traditional African open market, checks are not used; all transactions are by cash. Some traders, especially the illiterates, can carry on themselves thousands of *naira* from one town to another by road to make their purchases. Such traders are the easy prey of highway robbers. People who ordinarily have petty cash on them wherever they go are also targets for pickpockets. It is this kind of pocketpicking that is depicted very early in *Naira Power.*

Like *Director!, Naira Power* explores the decadence that the excessive love of money can unleash on a society and its youth. The novel derives its title from the Nigerian currency, the *naira,* that the country adopted in the early 1970s. Before that the pounds, shillings, and pence of old British West Africa were used. In the 1970s the *naira* was one of the world's strongest currencies, but today it is weak. *Naira* power, then, is not permanent. It has proved a bubble whose deflation Nigerians and other Africans now live with.

The novel's major action begins with Bintu and Amina's witnessing the mob execution of Ramonu. This killing incites Amina to narrate the long story of Ramonu and his family background. The plot unfolds mainly through flashback, spanning from Ramonu's father, Lemonu's, coming from the Muslim north of Nigeria to Lagos in the colonial days, through his marriages and to his son's sudden jump into wealth and subsequent execution by an irate Lagos mob. In essence, Amina's story is a flashback that takes the reader back in time to see the family and society that raised Ramonu. This family and society were quite strong, and they cherished honesty, dedication, and hard work. But with time, these virtues—honesty, dedication, and hard work—gradually gave way to various societal ills that sensitive artists like Emecheta find offensive.

Buchi Emecheta expresses her disgust and indignation by exploiting the potential of a central symbol, money—the ignoble pursuit of it, its negative influence on a society, and its moral and spiritual destruction of a young adult male, Ramonu. Throughout the novel the reader is bombarded with the breakdown of law and order, the corruption of justice, murder to make more money, and sexual and mental seduction through *naira* power. The odor of corruption and social malaise assaults the reader's moral sensibility.

A novel with such a thematic thrust stands the risk of degenerating into a mere catalog of social vices. *Naira Power* does catalog a series of vices—stealing, deceit, murder—as well as the moral decadence associated with the pursuit of money. But this is not just mere documentation of depressing events. These events are filtered through the minds of Amina, the narrator, and Bintu, a willing and interested listener, who together form a central consciousness as well as a chorus. They comment on the social vices they see around them and how they affect the African young adult.

The willing listener is in all probability Buchi Emecheta herself. Though she lives in London with her children, she pays regular and long visits to Nigeria, which to her is still her home. She was a senior research fellow and writer-in-residence at the University of Calabar, Nigeria, in the 1980–81 academic year. The 1982 publication of *Naira Power* suggests that the novel is a record of what she saw firsthand in Nigeria. She writes in *Naira Power,*

> I am a woman who has stayed more than half her life in the United Kingdom pursuing one set of studies and then another. I am in my prime, thirty-five or so, but I still call Amina my wife. In our society, a wife marries the family, not just the husband. That is a custom that still cuts across religion and across time. It was like that when I was little, over twenty years ago, it was like that among the Kiriyos Christians, it

was still like that among Muslim families like ours. So, she even felt it an honor for me to refer to her as "Amina my wife." I could hear and feel the vibrant happiness when she called back, "Yes, Auntie."[5]

Emecheta was roughly 35 when she wrote *Naira Power*. Evidently Bintu, who is "thirty-five or so," is her persona. With such a warmth between her persona, Bintu, in the novel, and Amina, her sister-in-law, the reader expects an interesting yarn. This is why Amina confesses to Bintu alone that Ramonu, the smuggler and murderer, was the youth who deflowered her. It is in this same spirit of openness and trust that Amina narrates the tragic story of the youth, Ramonu, in a society where *naira* is supreme.

The manner in which the African society of *Naira Power* is presented is significant: it is shown in images of filth, congestion, and stagnation, as in this interchange between Amina and Bintu in the crowded marketplace:

Soon we neared the market and my sister-in-law brought out two pairs of gum boots. The mud around here had completely covered up the tarred roads. We put on the boots and waited, searching in vain for ways to escape from the traffic trap and park the car somewhere.

In desperation, Amina had to say, "Oh, it would have been quicker if we'd walked."

"If we had waded, you mean. How can one walk in a place like this? There are too many cars, motor-cycles, cycles, open gutters and wandering people. No, walking in this part of the country is out of the question. You'll get killed."

She sighed. "But only ten years ago, we could walk the streets of Lagos."

"Now you are beginning to sound like me. Ten fifteen years ago, were years before the oil boom, before Nigeria became rich. Now she is rich, we are all condemned to choke in our wealth." (*Naira,* 11)

These observations set the tone of the novel—one of disorder, depression, and frustration in the midst of abundance without real management and direction.

By concentrating on two families, the Lemonus and the Waabis, in Isalegangan, a depressed neighborhood in Lagos, Buchi Emecheta ensures that interest centers not only on horrid social issues associated with money and acquisition of material wealth, but on relationships as well. The shifting points of view in time from the present to the past and the delayed release of information essentially help the reader to be cautious and to revise his or her previous judgment. In essence, there should be no rush to condemn the murdered thief. It is through a comprehensive assemblage of all information and evidence that we can sift the author's intention.

The information that Ramonu was not the actual pickpocket at the soccer game is delayed until the end of the novel. That an innocent person has been killed in error is shocking. Nevertheless, Amina regards the whole grim incident as divine justice meted for Ramonu. According to her, "Today is the day of the owner who cannot be bought or bribed with naira. The Owner who sees and judges all things. Allah!" (*Naira,* 108).

Having watched the public killing of Ramonu, Amina goes back in time to narrate the story of Ramonu and Ramonu's father, Lemonu, and of the British colonial days in Nigeria and the moral values that were cherished then. In short, in Amina's story is glimpsed a panorama of Nigerian society from colonial days through the present. Although isolated cases of corruption arose, integrity, steadfastness, and dedication to duty were cherished. Although Oba Olekemeji's wife is arrested by Lemonu for storing dirty water, the oba still praises Lemonu for his courage, fearlessness, and, above all, dedication to duty. But such dedication has been weakened by the pursuit of money.

The Lure of *Naira*   In the 1970s a local popular musician recorded a series of songs that deal with the steady collapse of the morals of Edo women as a result of their love of *naira.* The artist sings in a melancholy tone that hunger impels the poor man to go to the farm, but what draws Edo women into prostitution is money. Although there is element of truth in this, some Edo women were infuriated, and they condemned the artist for making such a generalized slur against them. In *Director!* some of the female high school students are also drawn into prostitution for the money. In *Naira Power* money assumes the dimension of a demonic god.

Success as depicted in the novel is almost synonymous with possession of *naira.* Amina and Bintu conclude that *"the tragedy that was Ramonu was the fault of nobody, but that of a society that respects any fool who has naira. However intelligent or creative one is, if one has no naira, there is no place to rest. The language of naira is universal here"* (*Naira,* 102; my italics). Overtly, Emecheta's concern is not solely with Ramonu really but with the society that produced him.

The circumstances surrounding Ramonu's vigilante execution and such vigilante killings are significant. They epitomize what happens today in quite a number of contemporary African countries. Many people go to the National Stadium in Lagos to watch soccer matches. In the novel the game between Nigeria's team and an unidentified foreign team is to be played in the morning because of the humidity at noontime and toward evening. The many fans who want to have good seats go to the stadium the night before the game to secure them. They stay all night despite a heavy rainstorm, and to prevent getting wet they take shelter in the stadium; Ramonu is one of them.

During the game the next morning someone is attracted to a man who exposes a wad of *naira* in his wallet while buying his ticket. In such a thick crowd any pilfering can create confusion, especially when the pilferer cannot be readily identified. Ramonu is mistaken for the one who attempted picking the spectator's pocket. This spectator's shout of *ole!* (thief) stirs into action the crowd, which is already disappointed because their side was losing the game, and Amina narrates:

> Ramonu has provided a much more stimulating show. They were not going to miss this one. It was much more fun, because in this new show, they could all take part. Poor Ramonu was beaten, kicked and jostled about. He begged them to take him to the police, and of course you know what that would have meant, he would have bought his way out of trouble. They say the police do this to supplement their incomes, but I think it is part of the same illness the country suffers from. . . . *The organizers of the match at the stadium knew what would follow, and therefore advised the crowd to take him away somewhere else where his burnt body would be a warning to other thieves and at the same time would not offend our visiting players.* (*Naira*, 33; my italics)

Burning a human being to death is shocking and offensive, but it is a manifestation of indignation against stealing and a reflection of a lack of confidence in the police. The killing is also intended as a deterrent to anybody who wants to live like Ramonu.

The organizers of the match do not stop the restless crowd taking the law into their hands, and they do not want the foreign team to see it. Deep down in their hearts the organizers know such a barbaric act is outrageous, but it is the people's swiftest way to justice. This is a stark, harsh reality. In fact, traders and merchants in the Nigerian city of Onitsha took the laws into their hands and burnt alive thieves who menaced their business life in the 1970s. Onitsha has traditionally been a famous strong commercial center in West Africa, and the town's inhabitants are great traders and businessmen. Incessant stealing of their goods and merchandise is a threat to the fundamental source of their survival. Hence they took to the vigilante method in the 1970s to curb stealing. These traders' swift method without the police actually resulted in a significant drop in robbery incidents in Onitsha. It is this historical fact that Amina's husband, Nurudeen, refers to in his exhilaration and satisfaction over the killing of Ramonu.

As a matter of fact, at that time in Onitsha any shout of *ole!* was met with other people's response, "Wey tire wey tire?" This is because old and discarded tires were sometimes readily available to hang around the robber's neck. With gasoline and few matchsticks the robber was set ablaze. In *Naira Power* the mob's refusal to hand over Ramonu to the police and their actual murder of him is symptomatic of a breakdown of law and order. Such background information is necessary for an appreciation of this terrible scene of mob execution in *Naira Power*.

The Youth Ramonu and His Polygamous Home Background Ramonu pursues money to give him momentary power over people and justice. But when the power fails, he is burnt alive by an irate Lagos mob. His end is more swift, more abrupt, and more hopeless than the end of Akinduro Falana in *Director!* Like Akinduro Falana, he is a youth of his time. Unlike Akinduro Falana, who is taken to jail by the police and government officials, Ramonu is burnt alive by an irate mob who take the laws into their hands.

According to Amina,

> Ramonu was our friend. We all suspected what his business was. I have attended many of the parties he gave, yet I am reluctant to call him a thief. You know . . . everybody does it in Lagos. How can I explain it? It is considered clever here. For instance you know the government says no smuggling, and anybody who smuggles and brings in more foreign goods will be sent to jail. You remember that many of the senators returned in the same plane. You saw all the goods they brought in. You saw that all the airport officials were saying, "Yes sir, yes, sir," and nobody searched them. You saw one of them carrying a bale of lace openly, flouting the law they made for ordinary people like us. Well how then can we blame people like Amina if they refuse to work and clear the rubbish that is

choking the life out of the streets of Lagos? So if one can be out of work
and able to make it in "business," one is respected and dubbed clever.
(*Naira*, 30)

Evidently, physical and spiritual sordidness combine to make the society
a hideous one. In the absence of a sophisticated sewage system, quite a
number of people use the gutters as their refuse disposal heap. Their
rubbish choke the gutters, and the result is a stench that makes life
unpleasant in some neighborhoods. Furthermore, the rains can worsen
the situation by flooding out the debris from the gutters on to the roads.
Besides this physical squalor is hypocrisy.

If government officials can willfully violate the laws they have made
against smuggling, then they cannot expect their people to heed such
laws. It is this hypocritical and corrupt world that Ramonu is thrown
into by his father, Lemonu, a once upright and methodical man who
unfortunately allows himself to be manipulated by a fraudulent alfa
(Islamic spiritual leader) and later entangles himself in a matrimonial
web of four wives. The result is that his attention is always divided in
his home—one of the negative results of an African polygamous marriage.

Ramonu's parents' home, which is a morally dilapidated one, lacks
the necessary luster to spiritually nurture him about the ideals of life.
Children and youth need direction and, to a certain extent, control—
from their parents and their society as well. Without direction and control, youth is carried away by the society's prevailing tide of whatever
value it champions. In *Naira Power* this value is acquisition of money,
material wealth, and affluence. Without direction and control from his
parents, especially his father, who throws him out for sleeping with his
young wife, Idayatu, Ramonu immerses himself into his society—a society enslaved by money. He shamelessly, fraudulently, and inhumanly
acquires the money, acquires temporary power without control, and suffers a life devoid of positive direction. To understand Ramonu's waywardness, an understanding of Lemonu's polygamous home that
produced him is necessary.

Unsure of Lemonu's love, Kudi, his first wife and mother of Ramonu,
and Idayatu, his second wife, start patronizing a local soothsayer, Baba
Sule, who makes for them a love potion—love meat. Simbi, the third
wife, who lives outside Lemonu's house, goes regularly to her own soothsayer to make a different, more potent charm than love meat:

She wanted the Alhaji to desire her almost like food, she wanted the Alhaji to forget all the other children, the other wives had for him, so that he would spend all his money on her. Her Baba told her to get a photograph of the heir, Ramonu. And every evening she had to rain curses on this photo. That way, the curse would go on him and the other children. Also the Baba made her a medicine that would make the Alhaji impotent whenever he came to his other wives. [Alhaji, as used in Nigeria, is the title for a Muslim who has performed the holy pilgrimage to Mecca as demanded by Islam. In popular usage however, "Alhaji" is for those who are affluent.] (*Naira*, 64–65)

Evidently Simbi does not wish Ramonu and his brothers and sisters well; in fact, she wishes them evil. Through competition, Lemonu's wives reduce him to a mere instrument of manipulation by African medicine men. The result is that Lemonu desires Idayatu only after eating Idayatu's love meat, but when it comes to actual lovemaking he finds himself impotent and only howls in the night. When he goes to Simbi, however, he finds peace and potency.

The sexually starved young Idayatu becomes vulnerable to the 16-year-old Ramonu, who secretly eats the "love meat" meant only for his father. One night, probably under the influence of the love meat he eats secretly, Ramonu makes love to Idayatu, who lies seductively on her bed. Lemonu, who has just returned from Simbi's place, catches them in the act. Enraged, he chases his son with a cutlass and swears to kill him. Many Western readers and even some Africans may find it difficult to believe that the charm can work. Such charms are diabolical, and they work when people believe they can. The community that *Naira Power* deals with believes in the charms; consequently the charms work for them.

Idayatu's sex with Ramonu is reflective of actual situations in which African women have been caught having sex outside marriage, even with houseboys. Such clandestine affairs presumably result, in part, from the lack of satisfaction these women get from husbands they must share with other wives. The result is the beginning of discord in the home. Similarly, husbands have also been caught having sex with their housegirls.

Husbands and wives who condescend to having sex with housegirls and houseboys do not seem to take the feelings of their spouses seriously. For a man to submit to sex with a housegirl is an insult to his wife, who is supposed to be the housegirl's mistress. In extreme cases the housegirl may start claiming equality with the wife at home after sleeping with her husband. Pretty housegirls have been known to displace the legitimate wives. In Idayatu's case it is sex starvation that compels her to seduce Ramonu.

I have given this rather extensive background information to illustrate Ramonu's childhood home—polygamous, devoid of love, and politically divided. It is a place where there is no real communication between father and son or husband and wives, where secrecy seems to reign. But the secrecy is destroyed by the congestion in the house. Amina says, "They saw the danger [of Ramonmu eating the love meat] and, without saying anything to each other, they became more secretive. But how secretive could one be in a room swarming with children?" (*Naira*, 64).

This sense of congestion is conveyed in Amina's description of their residence: "There were six rooms in the main house facing each other. Each room was owned by one family. At the back of the house, there were three other rooms. Again each room was rented by one family. We lived at the back of the house, and we were considered lucky because there was a veranda running along those three rooms at the back. We were eleven in ours, but the Lemonu family were twenty-four, before I married and left" (*Naira*, 41). This seeming inability to control population growth incites Bintu to predict that "at the rate which we are going now, we shall soon be over one hundred and twenty million in about ten years" (*Naira*, 42). The prediction is not wrong. It is already a decade after this prediction and Nigeria's population is roughly around that figure. In Western countries a man may be the source of about 12 children, grandchildren, and great-grandchildren, but in Africa a man—especially one who practices polygamy or sleeps indiscriminately with women—may be the source of more than 100 children, grandchildren, and great-grandchildren.

Without privacy in Lemonu's house, Ramonu easily discovers the place of the hidden love meat and begins to eat it regularly. The result is disastrous for him. Ramonu's consumption of the love meat may be partly responsible for his having sex with his father's wife. But there is also rational explanation for his awful act. At 16, Ramonu's stirring of sexual desire expresses itself in his copulation with his father's young wife.

To a certain extent, Ramonu cannot absorb all the blame for his act. Ramonu would not have ventured near Idayatu if she was not so young. In African culture, where age is highly respected, a young man would not lust after a woman the age of, say, his mother. But if his father has a wife who is the young man's age mate, he might be "bold enough" to sleep with her, as Ramonu does with Idayatu. To bring a young wife into a house where there are sexually active boys provides a very tempting atmosphere. This is a mistake Lemonu does not seem to realize.

Despite this situation, Ramonu exhibits a depraved and unethical frame of mind in sleeping with his father's wife. His father is too outraged about his son's act to sit the young boy down and discipline and advise him. After Ramonu flees his father's home, Lemonu rains curses on his son's mother, Kudi, "for bringing ruin to his house" (*Naira*, 66). Such curses on Kudi are unfair because she did not bring the ruin. Instead, it is Lemonu's handiwork. He marries a very young woman whom he sexually starves as a result of the charm wrought on him by Simbi, the wife who lives outside his house. He stops caring for his senior wife, Kudi, and her five children, and refuses to send them to school. Kudi reacts to this lack of care by leaving his house, taking her two youngest children to Ajegunle, another densely populated ghettolike community in Lagos. This is a painful breakup of a family that was intact when only Kudi was the wife at home.

Buchi Emecheta's stance is clear. Lemonu's polygamous home renders him emotionally and mentally incapacitated, and he watches like a foolish weakling the steady disintegration of his family and cannot do anything to arrest it. The flight of his heir, Ramonu, from his house is a tragedy in African culture. The first son is traditionally expected to be very close, sooner or later, to his father because he takes over the affairs of his family on the father's demise or in his absence. But it is otherwise in Ramonu and his father's case. It is the cluttered, polygamous family—and the inherent problem in tackling the basic issues of keeping such a large family together—that Emecheta illustrates elaborately.

It does not seem to be Ramonu's steady degeneration into criminality that interests Emecheta but the family and society that produce him. This is why Ramonu's gradual and steady degeneration into a murderer and robber as well as a rich youth is not really illustrated. He simply, without explanation, returns with his ill-gotten wealth and begs his father for forgiveness. His father readily forgives him because of the money, not because of a change of heart.

Lemonu's Early Life in Lagos, the Frauds, and an Unhealthy Workplace   Lemonu is a Hausa by tribe and a Muslim by faith. Hausa is one of Nigeria's large ethnic groups that accepted Islam in the nineteenth century. They occupy the northern part of Nigeria and various parts of the western Sudan. It was the Fulani Jihad, led by Usman dan Fodio, that established Islam among the Hausas in Nigeria. There are a few Christians among them, but they are predominantly Muslims. The genuine Muslim does not take Islam only as a religion but as a way of life. Such is Lemonu before he messes up his life with many wives.

Marrying more than one woman in the Muslim culture is regarded as normal. The popular number of wives seems to be four. Marrying four wives is supported if the man can take care of them and if he is capable of handling the numerous attendant problems of a polygamous home. But even when it is obvious that for many of the men one wife is a handful, they still marry more. More wives seem to enhance the man's status in the community and provide some variety in the man's sexual life. Sometimes the wife may be very young—a tender teenager as reflected in Idayatu's case. It is because of this tender age that Kudi, Lemonu's senior wife, thought Idayatu to be a housegirl.

Before Lemonu gets entangled in the web of three wives, he lived an upright life. The death of his cows soon after his arrival in Lagos from the north bankrupts him financially. Knowing no one to help him in Lagos, he resorts to the quickest means to survive—begging for alms. He fakes blindness because many Africans would readily not give alms to physically healthy and able-bodied men whom they believe should be working. Begging for alms is the resourceful Lemonu's most expedient way to survive. It is during one of the begging sessions that he meets the alfa beggar. An alfa has a supernatural knowledge of the past, present, and future and the knowledge of charms to ward off evils and bad luck. In Gambia and some other African countries he is called a *marabout*. Through one of his customers, the alfa beggar helps Lemonu to secure a job as hygiene or sanitary inspector, whose principal duty is to search and kill mosquito larvae.

The alfa functions in this novel as a revealer of the deep fears and secrets in the minds of those who pretend to be friendly with each other in the workplace but are actually downright vicious. In reality envy and jealousy have a strong foothold in the deep recesses of their minds. In African culture it is common to find people who are older than their bosses or supervisors plotting to wreck their careers. Those younger can also do the same. Some even go as far as creating crises in the bosses' home, or the home of anyone else they want to disturb, by surreptitiously telling lies and poisoning the minds of spouses against each other. At unguarded moments and without a thorough probing of the source of conflicts, some marriages or homes have broken up through ignorance reflected in the parties' inability to correctly identify their crafty enemy.

Many of these vicious characters in the workplace resort to protecting themselves through various charms. They also protect themselves through strong prayers to God. It is this atmosphere of suspicion, envy, and jealousy that the alfa hints at in the following interchange between him and Lemonu:

> "I know some big men here. I always sew their charms for them, even though they are Kaferis [non-Muslims]."
>
> "You mean, Alfa, that the trouser-wearing Kaferis wear charms as well?"
>
> "Oh yes, they do. They always sit together there in their places of work, and they see too much of each other, so they become jealous of one another. So for protection and to give themselves confidence, they come to me in the evenings and I sew the leather charms for them." (*Naira,* 18–19)

There are also, however, some who have fraudulently risen by lying and do not want exposure. Some of these patronize native doctors as well as alfas to help them block all avenues of exposure, and some pose as holy men for people not to suspect them of fraudulent activities.

In such an unhealthy workplace a dedicated worker is soon disillusioned and either leaves, dies a death of the spirit, or becomes a sycophant. This illustrates the proverbial saying, "If you can't beat them, join them." This joining them is mirrored in the people's lackadaisical attitude to government or public work as observed by Bintu: "Our lack of enthusiasm for work that relates to the public is well-known. For example, a Nigerian businessman will work tirelessly night and day in his own private business, but, once that same person is employed in any kind of public work, he will go slack, and say 'Na government job, ino de finish' [It is government work and it is endless]" (*Naira,* 10). The result is mediocre productivity in the workplace. Emecheta uses the alfa's revelation about the workers consulting him to enhance the general tone of social malaise of *Naira Power.*

Lemonu's question, "You mean, Alfa, that the trouser-wearing Kaferis wear charms as well?," indicates a surprise. It also indicates Lemonu's innocence and lack of knowledge of the evil and dubious ways of many workers in Lagos, as well as his ignorance of human complexity. Being a very straightforward man, he readily believes every one is like him. He does not know that some of these workers can craftily disguise their vices as virtues and thus obscure the judgment of innocent, trusting people, putting them off their guards.

Despite the alfa's professed esoteric spiritual knowledge, he, too, is a pretender. He tells Lemonu, "If I were a young person like you, I wouldn't pretend to be blind. I know that there is nothing shameful in begging, but here in the South they have jobs which one can do and get paid. You will not be your own master, and most of them are not interesting jobs and you won't get the satisfaction of taking your own risks or of raising your own cattle by yourself, but it is a reliable way of life" (*Naira,* 18). If the alfa was a true spiritualist he would not be pretending to be blind and collecting money from goodwilled people. The alfa is a fraud who is also looking for money—for *naira* power. He wants to be his own master, and this he gets in his alfa or spiritual leadership position, which he confers on himself. There is no indication in the novel that he received any formal training in Islamic spiritual matters or theology. Interestingly enough, he strangely succeeds in swindling the Kaferis into believing him to be supernaturally wise. Undoubtedly, most of these Kaferis are literate and educated. But because of their weak minds and their numerous fears, they are easily susceptible to the wiles of a con man like the alfa.

Genuine Muslim spiritualists, alfas, and *marabouts* do exist, but the one in *Naira Power* is fake. As one who wants to be a master of himself, it is not surprising that he also desires power over others. The quickest way to such control is to boast about his "possession" of divine or supernatural knowledge without the necessary spiritual training. He easily extends this desire to have power over people to Lemonu. Gullible, too trusting, and naive, Lemonu readily and easily becomes manipulated by a fraud. Like Othello being deceived by the crafty Iago, Lemonu is conned by the fraudulent alfa.

The Fall of Lemonu   One should note that when Lemonu arrives in Lagos from the north of Nigeria he is completely outside the pale of organizational power. It is to forestall a complete ruin and survive in Lagos where he knows nobody that he fakes blindness and begs. His beggar associates, including the fake one, the alfa, are destitute. But Lemonu later rises from a very low to a high estate and esteem through honesty, straightforwardness, and his Islamic faith.

Although superficially dishonorable, pretending to be blind and begging are things Lemonu does to survive; he knows as a true Muslim that one can beg for alms as a poor and helpless person, which he actually is soon after the disastrous death of his cows. He also believes by his Islamic faith that benevolent people will help him, and he stops begging after securing a paying job.

In his job as sanitary inspector Lemonu's virtuous character surfaces. He is conscientious, and attempts to bribe him always fail. A fearless individual, he goes into people's homes to inspect drinking water. It is in one of these routine inspections that he arrests Oba Okelemeji's wives for poor sanitation. The British officials in the city council find the oba guilty and fine him heavily. When Nigeria was a British colony, its system of administration was indirect rule, with British government officials ruling the people through indigenous African obas (kings or emirs). Obas were politically powerful, as typified by Oba Olekemeji.

Although this powerful oba is found guilty, he appreciates a sense of duty. He commends Lemonu for his integrity and fearlessness: "He [the oba] told him that our part of the world needed men like him, men who were fearless, men who were brave and loyal" (*Naira,* 24). The oba demonstrates his appreciation by giving him a cow and bags of money for his courage and dedication to duty. There is no indication in the novel that Lemonu secretly looks for fame through his conscientiousness and dedication to duty: "As far as he was concerned, he was doing his duty" (*Naira,* 24). For such dedication Lemonu gets a promotion and the honorific appellations "the fearless" and "the blameless." These appellations are used in Africa for the few human beings of enviable integrity and proven honesty. Lemonu gets an additional title, "Alhaji," after his pilgrimage to Mecca.

With one wife, Kudi, at home, he has the peace of mind necessary to be dedicated, proud, and conscientious. But being unprepared really for marriage, he fails to realize its sacredness as a commitment between two people. For Lemonu, the result is disaster.

Overwhelmed by the oba's gifts—a cow, bags of money, and trays of *obis* (kola nuts)—he goes to the alfa for direction: "Alfa, what can I do now? Is it the will of Allah that I should accept gifts from Kaferis?" The oba only shows appreciation for courage and honesty as a person and not as Kaferi. The fraudulent alfa knows that Lemonu already has some high regard for him because he helped him to get his sanitary inspection job, and he cashes in on it by claiming more knowledge of the Koran and God's mind to himself:

> The alfa intoned a long passage of the Koran and chewed several kola nuts. Both of them sat in complete silence for a very long time, com-

municating with their minds, praying in their silent, simple way to Allah to give them guidance. Allah eventually made himself heard. For the alfa said, "My son, you are now a son to me." Lemonu nodded. "A worker is worthy of his rewards. You know Allah took your cows away, now he is returning them to you. Not in the form you expected, but in this form. Use the cow the Oba has given you to celebrate the coming Ramadan. Then take the money and go on a hajj to Mecca. On your way back, get yourself a nice girl from a good Muslim family and come and breed sons and daughters for Allah. I have said my own, and as Mohammed the servant of Allah is my witness, I spoke the truth to you." (*Naira*, 24–25)

That Lemonu is a steadfast Muslim is beyond doubt: he prays and lives a morally clean life. But he overextends this steadfastness and puts his mind without realizing it under the control of a fraud who claims to be a spiritual leader. In his gullibility he fails to recollect that the alfa once faked blindness to deceive people into giving him money, and he saw him doing it. If he realizes the wisdom in the saying that a leopard does not leave its black spots, he would have known that the alfa is a sham. In a moment of exhilaration he invites the alfa to come and stay with him, and the alfa readily accepts. With this invitation Lemonu completes the mortgaging of his conscience and the independence of his mind.

The autonomy and responsibility that his sanitary inspection job conferred on him is soon craftily eroded by the fraudulent alfa. The result is that Lemonu takes no decision without consulting the alfa. In short, his mind is now under the complete control of the alfa and he responds to his dictates. He performs his *hajj* to Mecca not out of his conviction that he is morally and spiritually prepared for it but as a response to the alfa's directive. Similarly he marries as a response to the alfa's directive. According to Emecheta, "As the alfa had *commanded*, he brought Kudi, Ramonu's mother, down to the South with him as his new wife" (*Naira*, 25; my italics). Overtly, besides his *hajj*, Lemonu's marriage to Kudi is an act of obedience to the alfa, not his own decision.

The alfa is not a blood relation of Lemonu and yet he gives the name Ramonu to Lemonu's first son just before he dies. The giving of names to babies is usually a prerogative of the baby's grandfather, father, or other respectable relative. In naming Lemonu's son, the alfa's mind virtually replaces Lemonu's.

What is intriguing in Lemonu's contact with the alfa is the reflection that charlatans have penetrated the once sacred realm of spiritual matters. Genuine spiritual leaders do not pretend and do not want to have undue influence over people to the point of smothering the independence of their minds. But the alfa crushes Lemonu's ability to reason. After the alfa's death Lemonu seems to grope in the dark: unable to make worthwhile reasonable decisions for himself, he ends up cluttering his life with many wives.

When he adds Idayatu, the second wife, and another mistress outside as his third wife, Lemonu's fortune starts taking a different turn. For beating Idayatu, whom Kudi has earlier thought was a housemaid because of her youth, Kudi is almost beaten to death by Lemonu. The truth of the matter dawns on her when Lemonu invites young Idayatu to sleep with him. Later, however, in the face of competition from Simbi, a strong rival outside, Kudi and Idayatu close ranks to ward her off from their husband. Their putting love meat into Lemonu's food indicates that their trust in him as husband and sex partner was severely shaken. They fear that Lemonu will neglect them and devote all his attention to Simbi. A once peaceful home turns into one of no trust or confidence and one of too many people.

Lemonu finds it difficult to support his children financially in school, and the shady Ramonu takes over running family affairs after his return as a rich youth five years after fleeing his father's rage. Only those Ramonu decides to pay for get to go to school. That the once upright Lemonu does not inquire about the source of his son's riches is an indication of the degree of his moral decadence. He takes Ramonu's help in paying fees as a relief, and therefore finds it difficult to probe the source of his wealth. With numerous children, financial assistance from any quarter—even a thief—is welcomed.

Toward the end of his life Lemonu finds his family completely cluttered and congested. Ramonu's attempt to rebuild his father's family is a failure:

> Ramonu brought his mother back, because he felt that he was rich enough to set them up comfortably. Kudi had left anyway simply because the Alhaji was poor and was taking it out on her. Now they were both old, there was no need for her to go to Baba Sule to help her prepare love meat. Idayatu never left, but the third wife did not live with them. . . . Sala, the youngest wife is now the troublesome one. She wants the kind of fun that the Alhaji can no longer give, so only Ramonu's money is holding her down. She's having children regularly though [and not by Lemonu]. (*Naira*, 96–97)

Ramonu's belief in the power of money infects his father's family, which is already in a shambles. By "buying" a fourth wife, Sala, for his father in his old age, he only compounds his problems.

His father watches helplessly as his fourth wife sleeps around with other men and brings their babies into his house. Lemonu's life ends in total disaster, as reflected in Amina and Bintu's discussion: "'How many children has he in all?' I asked. 'I don't know, Auntie, and *I don't think he knows either.*' 'It's shocking! Such socially irresponsible men should be sterilised'" (*Naira,* 97). In fact, for a paterfamilias not to know the exact number of his children is almost the height of irresponsibility, and this is crystallized in his total ignorance of the shameful death of Ramonu. Only Amina knows about the killing, and she does not disclose it to either Lemonu or Meriamo, Ramonu's young wife. Against this backdrop of a cluttered, congested, and irresponsible family, Ramonu's wayward and criminal personality is not a shock.

Ramonu and His Negative Spirit   Ramonu's death is sordid and offensive to the reader, but his crowd of executors take it as a pastime. Bintu graphically describes the horrid scene of mob rule or swift rough justice:

> I could not believe what I was seeing. The tyres were flung round his neck and his hands were tied to one of the concrete pillars under the flyover. Somebody poured some kerosene over him. He was now pleading that he would give them all the money he had. It was no use; the excited audience screamed as another man set fire to the kerosene. The man bleated in tortured pain, then the smoke choked the sound into unrecognizable grunting. As the tyres caught on fire, the young man's body became a blazing torch lighting up the greying day. Eventually the now subdued crowd started to file away in search of another pastime. The terrible stink of burning flesh and rubber filled the air. (*Naira,* 13–14)

Ramonu becomes a part of an evil group after his expulsion from his father's house. He makes money through his association with it and uses it to "help" his father, to put himself in fraudulent business, and to marry. How he joined the group is not illustrated. In fact, Ramonu is a hazy character throughout the novel. Perhaps his haziness is deliberate. The product of a family without its bearing is likely to be one without form and without direction. Having been chased out of the house by his father, Ramonu dives into a complex society where it takes even the cautious and experienced person a lot to survive.

Although Ramonu's sleeping with his father's young wife is an immoral act that most African men could not tolerate, Lemonu's chasing him out with a cutlass is a negation of a strong traditional African principle that one cannot drive out a bad child for the lion to feast on. The deep meaning of this principle is that the parents should be alive to their responsibility and should make their home a cozy haven for all children, irrespective of character bent—good or evil. If the children are good it is the parent's duty to nurture them into the best they can be. On the other hand, if some children show signs of waywardness or rebellion, it is the parents' duty to begin immediately to put them straight. Even if they seriously degenerate like Ramonu, their fathers are still duty-bound to correct them. They are not expected to be thrown into the streets. Unfortunately, however, many African men just cannot entertain the idea of their sons sleeping with their wives. Permanent rifts or estrangements have been known to come between father and son as a result of such sordid acts.

It is the same rift that comes between Ramonu and his father, but this rift swiftly and miraculously disappears primarily because of Ramonu's ill-gotten wealth, but it is a superficial disappearance. When Ramonu runs out of money and is unable to help his father, his father resumes cursing Ramonu and Ramonu's mother. It is not only the possession of money that matters but Ramonu's general attitude toward it: "Ramonu had so great a belief in the power of his ill-gotten money that he did not see any reason why he could not get what he wanted" (*Naira*, 79). With money as demonic god, unhealthy workplaces, and frauds all over the place, the society of *Naira Power* is like Matthew Arnold's "darkling plain where ignorant armies clash by night."

Without love at home, the morally sick society easily swallows up its young population like Ramonu. Withdrawal is almost impossible from a network of evil associates. Ramonu is delegated by this evil network to kill a whole family, parents and three children who decide to quit their group after making their fortune. After murdering them, Ramonu, under the alias Kinte Constantino, cuts off their heads to sell to unscrupulous people who use severed human heads to make a magic potion that is believed to bring wealth. But he is caught by policemen on the border between the Republic of Benin and Nigeria. Because Ramonu's nationality cannot be readily identified, the border policemen refer his matter to their Cotonou headquarters.

The newspaper calls him the "Mystery Man." During the trial the international nature of this smuggling and murder network surfaces. A white man shows up from Lagos to claim that "Kinte Constantino" was coming for him. A Ghanaian who lives at the border between Benin Republic and Nigeria claims that "Kinte Constantino's" taxi was rented from him and that he had left the cab where the five heads of a father, mother, and three children were found, in front of his house for many days. Although the jury sentences him to life in prison, he stays in jail for only about four years. The network of smugglers and murderers facilitates his escape from Cotonou Prison by bribing a guard to pretend to be asleep while Ramonu makes his escape. Money power renders the prison useless for keeping criminals. And Amina cynically mentions the people's contemporary weakness before money and subtly contrasts it with Lemonu's former integrity and uprightness: "What does the prison officer want but money? He will probably never earn five thousand naira in all his dying days, and if someone can offer him ten thousand naira, will he not pretend to be asleep when the prisoner escapes? Not everybody is like Alhaji who would rather arrest the Oba than accept his bribe" (*Naira,* 92).

Ramonu's long absence as a result of this ordeal is mysterious, and Lemonu does not inquire about his son's whereabouts. A few months after Ramonu's return, he lavishly celebrates the naming of his first daughter by lining the whole street with *naira.* After this display of wealth, a drug syndicate involving Ramonu is blown up in Nigeria, but he miraculously escapes conviction. He begins to sell all his possessions, however, including his house, perhaps to buy his way out of the serious drug-trafficking charge. With the auctioning of Ramonu's house, his young wife goes to live in Lemonu's house for a while. Ramonu's final journey is when he is mistaken for a pickpocket. The mob—accustomed to smugglers escaping conviction because of their money—take the laws into their own hands and kill Ramonu instantly. With nobody to claim the charred remains of his body, they bury it in a mass grave.

Before his killing, Ramonu's presence is almost like poison in the Isalegangan neighborhood, especially on the family of Waabi, Amina's father. Like a poisonous negative spirit in the community, he corrodes various people's minds with negative emotions. Although Amina's father knows Ramonu is a reprobate and has always advised Amina and her brother, Latifu, not to have any dealings with him, he himself is too weak before Ramonu's *naira* power, accepting money from him and praying for him. It is this weakness that Amina cashes in on when he advises her against any amorous relationship with him. It is also this weakness that Latifu cashes in on when their father tells him that he does not need Ramonu to introduce him to any line of business. In retrospect, Amina thinks of Ramonu as a bad influence: "Perhaps Ramonu's presence and his open show of wealth, despite a father's curse, contributed to our open disregard of our father's warnings. With Ramonu as a symbol of success, the warnings sounded like the ravings of a senile old man" (*Naira,* 74).

For Ramonu to be a symbol of success before Latifu spells a certain disaster for him and Amina. Their mother has already left her father's house, and Amina gets no genuine maternal advice from anybody in her family. She plunges into an illicit relationship with Ramonu because of his ill-gotten money. Furthermore, Ramonu uses his money to buy or influence every person connected to Amina, especially her aunt and her mother. It is during this period of courtship that almost develops into marriage that Ramonu seduces her. The aura of hypnosis is obvious here, with Ramonu as the seducer (the hypnotist) and Amina as the subject. Amina recalls,

> That night, Ramonu did not give me much time to wonder. . . . I simply followed him out to the car like a zombie, and not even when I saw him opening the door to one of those apartments could I say a word. [Zombie in Nigerian English is used for a person devoid of any ability to reason.]
> "Ours!" he said simply. It was a beautiful flat. . . . I felt his hand pulling me back inside the flat. He made such a beautiful and desperate love to me then. That type of "only love" a woman likes to remember to her dying days. (*Naira,* 82)

While Ramonu seduces Amina sexually, he seduces her brother mentally. Under Ramonu's influence, young Latifu storms out on his father with his few things because his father questions Ramonu's integrity and the source of his money. Amina recalls an unpleasant scene between her brother and father:

> Latifu was telling my father that he did not need his help to finish his commercial education if father did not want to pay. He could work for Ramonu on Saturdays, and that money would see him through college. . . . I was shocked. Such a thing was never allowed in our culture.
> My father was hurt, and I hated to see him brought so low by his own son. (*Naira,* 78–79)

In various ethnic groups in Africa, it is the height of insubordination for children to talk back to their parents, guardians, or elders, or behave in any unruly manner before them. Even when the parents are wrong, and regardless of their achievement, the children are still not expected to talk back but remain calm as much as possible. Even before Africans' contact with the Bible, the injunction of the Fifth Commandment had been very strong. It is part of the culture. In the workplace a young person by virtue of his position may be senior to people who are older than him or her in age. But at home it is different. This is why a number of young people have problems in the workplace with diehard traditionalists who strongly believe in age. In *Things Fall Apart* Achebe says that among these people "age is respected but achievement is revered." Even then such reverence is given to an achiever mainly by people who are not his relations or kinfolk.

When a son or daughter openly talks back at his or her parents, he or she is deemed insane or untrained, or a disgrace to the family or community. By such acts children reduce their parents' self-esteem and incapacitate them emotionally. The result is that the African parent feels he is a failure in his inability to discipline his children effectively. African culture does not expect parents to condone any insubordination from their children. There are instances of parents physically beating up their adult children when they openly talk back at them. But these instances are quite rare because each party knows what the culture expects of him or her. Amina and her brother never disrespected their father until a negative spirit, Ramonu, rubs some of his negative influence on them.

Emecheta's moral earnestness in *Naira Power* can hardly be faulted. The physical squalor and decay that reflect the moral and spiritual decadence of the people is captured in Bintu's observation:

> I looked further down, only to see a big open drain, static, its sides coated a sickly green. The water was not moving at all. . . .
> But when I was little, there used to be some men who came weekly to collect rubbish. "Are they all dead now, and if so, why can't we employ more people to collect rubbish?" I asked. (*Naira*, 9)

The good old days of rubbish collection and general sanitary inspection are gone. Today the static messy drain seems to reflect the abnormally dense population partially produced by some irresponsible polygamous men as a result of their endless sleeping around with many women.

To reduce traffic congestion, Lagos implemented a civil law declaring that cars with even-numbered plates can be driven on some days and cars with odd-numbered plates on others. But the law has proved useless. In fact, the law only aggravates the problem. Without a good and efficient public transportation system, quite a number of Lagos people possess two cars—one with even-numbered plates and the other with odd-numbered plates. Taking in the whole depressing atmosphere of congestion and squalor, Bintu describes their slow movement in this grim picture of traffic:

> I could not get out of the car or wade down to the market; I simply had to simmer down.
>   At last we started to inch our way forward amidst the tangled web of traffic and the unruly danfoes. These yellow mini-buses, breakers of all the traffic rules in the book, could go the wrong way whenever the mood took them; they could cut in front of you, oh, they could do anything. They were the terrors of the roads, next to the taxi drivers. (*Naira*, 11)

The whole story is narrated in a car in a rainstorm. The pouring rain echoes Amina's pouring out her story of Ramonu; the rain subsides with the story's tailing to its end. But here lies a seeming fault in the novel. Under such a strong tropical storm, which forces every vehicle to a standstill, it is almost implausible and unconvincing for Bintu to hear every word of Amina's story. Despite this incredibility, the pervading tone of the novel is one of disgust but not an absolutely hopeless one. Emecheta uses the steady disappearance of the cloud and the slow emergence of sunshine to reflect her hope in a better future: "A big cloud, that for a long time had shrouded all of us in semi-darkness was fast disappearing to give way to the determined brilliance of the sun" (*Naira*, 103).

The image of the cloud shrouding them in darkness suggests the death of all the positive spirit in humans, and the determined brilliance of the sun suggests a hope in the future that would be characterized by light and justice that would wipe out the darkness of corruption and moral decadence. In the present corpus of African young adult literature, *Naira Power* is the most thorough exposé of corruption and moral and spiritual decay in a society whose values seem limited to the acquisition of the money and material goods. A vicious and twisted young adult seducer, smuggler, and robber like Ramonu is the product of such a society. And by extension she indicates that there is in African storytelling and African fiction writing a continuum in aesthetics between the African past, present, and future.

Conclusion

Certainly the manner in which Buchi Emecheta tells the stories of *Naira Power* and *A Kind of Marriage* instantly suggests her desire to entertain and instruct. There are realistic historical facts in both novels. Both Amina's and Bintu's voices recall history of an emerging nation and focus on human relationships. The evolution of an African country from its colonial days through the present—a picture of the African family, of love and marriage, and of Africa's young population—is undeniably depicted in both novels. Narrated by a fine storyteller to a willing and interested listener, both novels are a fusion of storytelling and writing. They are strongly embellished and ornamented and given vitality with the intimate voices of the narrator and the listener. Brought to life in oral narrative art by two women, these novels tend to have more immediacy and impact on African young adults, for whom they were primarily written. Despite these narratives taking place in modern settings, the spirit of the folk tale is quite resonant in them. This is why Nancy Topping Bazin concludes that "Buchi Emecheta's later novels deal with serious themes within the controlled structure of tales someone might tell around a fire in an African village."[6]

Chapter Five

A Quest for Utopia: *A Paradise for the Masses* and African Youth Activism

Every African is interested in having a disciplined youth population. Nigeria's new national anthem points to its ideal image of an African youth:

> Help our youth the truth to know,
> in love and honesty to grow,
> And living just and true
> great lofty heights attain,
> To build a nation where
> peace and justice reign.

But there is a gap between this lofty desire and reality. To appeal to "love" and "honesty" in a country where corruption reigns, where exploitation, oppression, and violence are clearly more representative than "peace" or "justice," is farcical and cynical (Martini 1989, 45).

Besides greed for money and material possessions that rock the society, as we saw in the last chapter, political and civil disorganization is also a social malaise Africans must contend with. A picture of the disorganized world created by adults is visible in such African literature as Ayi Kwei Armah's *The Beautyful Ones Are Not Yet Born* (1968) and Ngugi wa Thiong'O's *Petals of Blood* (1977) and *Devil on the Cross* (1982). One of the powerful adults in *Devil on the Cross* implores his colleagues, "Let's join hands to do three things: to grab, to extort money, and to confiscate. . . . [I]f you find anything belonging to the masses, don't leave it behind, for if you don't look after yourself, who'll look after you?"[1] This is the philosophy he lives by—one of reckless selfishness. This philosophy ingrained in him and his fellow rulers results in the unhappiness and impoverishment of the people they are supposed to rule. Unlike this adult, the youths care for the masses, and their desire is to create a paradise for them.

Although some African young adults like Akinduro in *Director!* and Ramonu in *Naira Power* are swallowed up by an ethically and morally corrupt world, quite a number of others are not. In their high self-esteem, they believe they can transform their decadent society almost overnight into a utopia. Because of their age, inexperience, and lack of power and resources, however, they find it difficult to make any real changes. Furthermore, traditional authorities and the powers that be can use all tactics to sway them from their goal as evidenced in Agbo Areo's *A Paradise for the Masses*.

A Paradise for the Masses

A Paradise for the Masses is a flawed and topical yet realistic young adult novel. It is the story of a youth movement and its attempt to reform the corrupt mythical country of Gerinia. As glamorous and praiseworthy as this reform attempt is, the effort collapses as a result of internal and external pressures. "Gerinia" is an anagram of "Nigeria," and the virility and exuberance exhibited by the youth in the novel are a true reflection of youth activism in Nigeria and in other countries of the developing world.

The novel's plot revolves around the rise and fall of Diti Oba and the Gerinia Youth Movement (GYM). When Diti Oba accuses his employers, Hawk Gerinia Limited, of economic exploitation and sabotage of his country and resigns his appointment, he is immediately proclaimed a national hero by the country's youth. The sudden emergence of a popular youth leader scares the political rulers, who resolve to prevent Diti Oba from leading a strong rival political party of the masses. They offer a government post to him, a scholarship to his relative, and a sinecure post to his uncle, all of which he rejects. Police detention and death threats fail to win Diti over to the rulers. The beautiful, sophisticated television anchorwoman Agnes Ade is used to seduce him, and Diti's idealism crumbles while the popular youth movement fizzles out.

The Young Adult Characters

The young adult characters essentially dictate the action of the novel: Diti Oba, the main character; Ife Okeke, the young university lecturer; and Dogo Yawuri, Miss Banke Iroko, Augustine Etuk, Yaya, Osa Osifo, and Miss Pat Ogun, the illegitimate daughter of the finance minister. Diti Oba resigns his appointment as top management officer with the multinational merchandise company, Hawk Gerinia Limited, because of the company's "economic sabotage" of his country. Such a reason is not convincing, however. By writing a scathing letter of resignation to the editor of the *Gerinian Echo*, the country's most popular newspaper, he draws attention and publicity to himself. In a society where a top management officer in a multinational company is expected to be living reasonably comfortably, he is also expected to sing the praises of his company, not expose its ills or resign from it. For doing these things otherwise, Diti Oba carves a different picture of himself as one who loves his country and identifies with its suffering and not-so-well-off people. It is such a person that the youths, especially the students, admire.

It is not surprising that the National Union of Gerinian Students (NUGU) readily proclaims him a national hero. In fact, it is this kind of status that Diti Oba seeks. He believes such a position will launch him into higher realms in politics, especially because of this massive support from students. The press release by the Gerinian students is given wide publicity by radio and television stations, and Diti Oba suddenly becomes the celebrity, which he has secretly wanted to be: "Opportunity knocks only once, Diti thought, as the whole world seemed to have named him a hero. If he failed to grab it to really install and perpetuate his name before the euphoria died down, the opportunity might not come again. He therefore decided to form a youth movement."[2]

The *Gerinian Echo* issues its headline, "DITI OBA LEADS GERINIAN YOUTH." Another popular national newspaper, the *Gerinian Statesman*, welcomes the birth of the new youth force in a moving editorial, ending with a passionate appeal to the elders and the ruling class to give the youths a chance to contribute to the country's economic development, stability, and unity. According to the paper, "The youths were *crusaders* rather than revolutionaries" (my italics).

In contrast, the *Gerinian Crusader*, another national newspaper owned by one of the country's political parties, maintains a studied silence. The radio and television stations join in giving the movement adequate publicity. Feeling that the government could not be effectively influenced with daily academic analyses of events and moral sermons, the members of the executive committee devise a master action plan—to do a physical cleaning of their country, collecting litter and cleaning stinking gutters and rubbish heaps from various parts of the community. In communities where sewage systems are very poor, refuse pyramids are not uncommon. Unlike clearing of debris, which is comparatively easy, a deeper cleaning of the mind, of corruption and evil, is not. An external cleaning of the country's landscape does not necessarily mean a cleaning of characters who really make up the country. If the characters are not clean, the country will not be morally upright.

That most of the members have not the faintest idea about the ultimate purpose of this master action indicates that communication is poor and information is deliberately withheld by the executive in their selfish bid to attract attention. Instead of briefing the members, the movement's national secretariat prefers to issue press statements to draw nationwide attention to themselves, and they succeed in this effort. An excerpt of an interview illustrates that the youths' clean-up campaign as presented by Diti Oba is meant to draw national attention to the movement as a force to be reckoned with:

> "How often does your Movement hope to do this type of nationwide communal work, Mr. Oba?"
> "Only once—we hope."
> "Only once! Why . . . ?"
> "Yes, once," Diti cut in, "because we don't expect the filthy situation to remain with us all the time. We hope our symbolic action will influence government and the people to find a permanent solution to the problem." (*Paradise*, 16)

For Diti to cut in while the interviewer has something to ask smacks of a desire to stop the interviewer from probing into a logical question. And of course the logical question is not unexpected by Diti Oba. A one-time physical cleaning cannot offer a permanent solution to sanitation problems. It would involve a sustained physical cleaning as well as a spiritual cleaning of the country's people—a spiritual cleaning that manifests itself in sanitation consciousness.

Unfortunately, the humanitarian gesture of cleaning up the city steadily degenerates into confrontation with the government. Under the direction of special Action Squads, truckloads of stinking debris are emptied at the entrance gate of the minister of health's official residence, to block the way, and at the Ministry of Health. The youths also send a sarcastic note to the minister of health—"With love from the masses. We brought this from our markets. The Minister of Health is very efficient!" The invitation of the police to stop the students' unruly behavior worsens the situation. In a tough scuffle with the police, the students display their aggression by burning two vehicles given to them by patriotic citizens for their clean-up jobs.

What begins as a praiseworthy endeavor—cleaning the city's three markets of stinking rubbish heaps—ends up in confusion. The minister of health's residence and office, the City Council offices, the police headquarters, the fire station, and the streets all over the Government Residential Area (GRA) become stinking refuse heaps. Soiling clean places like the GRA, the police premises, and the like are a composite act of rebellion by the students. Perhaps one might excuse them for venting their pent-up anger against the minister of health for his insensitivity to sanitation in public places. But emptying debris on an official residence leads to confrontation with the ruling class. Only a portion of the youths—Diti Oba and a few others—actually know what the "action" is all about. The mass is only caught in the euphoria of hooliganism: "Even though less than twenty of them had foreknowledge of the 'action' plan, every one of the hundreds of them who had taken part in the action was glad and satisfied with the ultimate turn the action had taken, at least for the fun of it" (*Paradise,* 21).

While the dedication to the clean-up campaign is superficially patriotic, it is couched in selfishness. While the GYM claims to seek a paradise for the general public, the ruling Gerinian Democratic party's major concern is to prevent at all costs Diti Oba from leading the youths as a rival political party of the masses.

The Ruling Class and Its Tactics

The ruling party devises various methods to undermine Diti Oba, but, as I have noted, he rejects their job offers. Police detention and death threats also fail to win him over. The only solution comes when the anchorwoman Agnes Ade seduces him and puts the politicians' minds at rest. With this seduction, followed by a sudden marriage, the glamorous fight of the youths for a paradise for the masses dramatically and swiftly comes to a close.

In various African societies where affluence is not common, a government scholarship is always, to parents or guardians, a welcome relief from the financial burden of sponsoring their children through school or college. But to Diti Oba, the scholarship to his cousin is obviously intended by the ruling class to cause confusion among the youth movement and supporters in the university. Truly it does cause some confusion because the students believe Oba directly or indirectly influenced the award's being granted to his cousin. Besides suspicion from students, Diti Oba's extended family seriously chastises him for stating to the press that his cousin does not need a scholarship. Subtly torn by students and his family, Diti Oba's idealism is weakened.

The scholarship is followed closely by the government's appointment of his semi-literate uncle to the position of deputy governor of the Bank of Gerinia. As a member of the family, Diti Oba is expected to participate in the celebration of his appointment. The idea of such participation makes him ill at ease vis-à-vis his role as leader of a revolutionary movement:

> "How can I appear in the *aso ebi* [special dress for the occasion], join them in the thanksgiving service and still retain the full credibility of my followers! These smart chaps in the government are real devilish planners. I hope my colleagues will understand the whole devilish strategy against us." Diti finally decided that it was necessary to brief available members of his GYM executive on what his extended family was planning to do and the necessity for him to compromise and participate in the planned programme. (*Paradise*, 92–93)

According to the author, "The government's strategy in appointing a key member of Diti Oba's extended family—in the traditional acceptance, his father—to such a prestigious sinecure had the desired effect of exposing him to the criticism of several members of the GYM."

The rulers complete their ploy to stop Diti Oba and his movement through Agnes Ade, who for many years had been a prostitute in London. The trade minister says,

> I know a top-class girl he once visited. She is my girlfriend. I will talk to her; appeal to her to help us tame him, love him, and if necessary lure him to bed with her. We can then eventually negotiate a big post for him through her. That will break up their Movement if we get him to take a post. But if all that fails, we can then go ahead to get him poisoned or ultimately assassinated. (*Paradise*, 155)

That the trade minister offers to use his mistress as bait to stop Diti Oba and his movement from becoming a rival political party indicates the extent to which these rulers will go to destroy any opposition.

The rulers succeed in using Agnes Ade to seduce Diti because they know his weakness for women. In school Diti Oba and Agnes Ade had

had crushes on each other. Ade returns to Nigeria and becomes a news-caster after her years of prostitution in Britain. Through Pat Ogun, Agnes sends her regards to Diti Oba while he is in detention for his activities with the GYM. According to the author, "Thinking about Agnes eventually became the only recreation which gave Diti some intermittent periods of peace of mind" (*Paradise,* 72).

When Diti, upon release from his detention, visits Agnes Ade in her luxurious apartment in an elitist suburb in Lagos, his idealism is shaken. He enjoys her imported German beers, which are on the list of banned commodities, and compromises his fiery idealism and revolutionary bent:

> "I'm sorry. What would you like to drink? Beer? I have Becks and Heinekenes, or?"
> "I have never seen those two beers for the last eight years—since the government banned beer importation."
> "Have a Becks then!" She went to the refrigerator and brought out a cold bottle of beer and a Coca-Cola. "I get my supply through some staff of the Government House," referring to the beer.
> Diti controlled his revolutionary instinct, not to speak against government for stocking a beer it had banned and not to appear critical of, and discourteous to, his hostess. (*Paradise,* 83)

Diti Oba enjoys the banned beer and slowly realizes that he cannot go all out to fight the good fight. He compromises his ideals essentially to keep his growing relationship with Agnes Ade cordial. His instinctual self slowly begins to crush his idealism:

> The photographic beauty of Agnes which he had seen on television screen several nights was, after all, not exaggerated. It was real and fascinating. He was prepared to overlook her seeming arrogance. He wanted to be close to her. Indeed, he wanted to love her! A revolutionist is a human being, after all; and human beings want to love and be loved! Diti did not consider himself an exceptional human being who might not need a woman's love, and Agnes was the woman whose love he wanted. (*Paradise,* 84)

It is Diti Oba's weakness in his growing infatuation again for Agnes Ade that the rulers readily and craftily exploit to crush him and his youth movement.

Sociopolitical Consciousness in Gerinia

A major thematic thrust of this novel is that a people's level of sociopo-
litical consciousness needs to reach a certain degree of sophistication;
otherwise, they can be easily manipulated by political opportunists.
Although there is no clear indication of the level of sophistication of the
student body, it is clear that they regard anyone who behaves in line
with their expectations as their hero. When Diti Oba resigns his
appointment on the grounds that Hawk Nigeria Limited was "exploiting" his country, no one takes it upon himself or herself to probe deeply
into his rationale for resignation. Without a thorough knowledge of Diti
Oba and his motive for resigning, the students pledge to join his crusade
to wrest their country from the clutches of collaborators.

But the question of economic liberation of the country from predators
does not appear to be part of their agitation. Throughout their period of
agitation for a paradise for the masses, no well-constructed or well-
worded manifesto against foreign exploiters is issued. The intensity and
immediacy of their action seems directed toward Gerinia's corrupt ruling
class, and for a while their energy is directed toward a swift physical
cleaning of Gerinian cities. It is therefore not surprising that the same
Hawk Gerinia Limited from which Diti Oba resigns because of
"exploitation" later invites his wife to serve as the first and only woman
director of the company. This is the company's wedding present to the
Obas. But Diti Oba does not reject this invitation. By accepting it he
virtually aligns himself with his country's exploiters, which he had earlier discredited and rejected. Thus, there is no strong or decisive move
from Oba toward any revolution to create a paradise for the masses.
Instead, what is created is, according to Ife Okeke, "a paradise for a
phoney leader."

Besides Diti Oba's virtual alignment with his exploiters, Ife Okeke is
interested in external financial assistance for their movement from a
nameless government, little realizing that such assistance is capable of
seriously eroding their economic and political independence. When
invited to an international youth conference by a government whose
country is regarded as "the Mecca for revolutionary and subversive
youths," Ife Okeke is very excited. Unknown to Diti Oba, Ife Okeke has
been in touch with some officials of this government. A clandestine link
between Ife Okeke and the Gerinia Intelligence Service Diti Oba finds
unbelievable. Why Diti Oba and Ife Okeke were invited for briefing and
training in subversive activity is not clear, but it is quite apparent that

they do not know exactly the purpose of their invitation. Ife Okeke's involvement with the secret agents of this government, primarily for change in Gerinia, without the knowledge of Diti Oba, who is supposed to be the leader of the GYM, smacks of deceit. Despite Ife Okeke's erudition and his international exposure, he does not know that he is being used by secret agents of the nameless government to control or destabilize his country.

Diti Oba's quest for independence for his country and his concern for a paradise for the masses may be genuine, but his later behavior in accepting a political appointment as a commissioner from the same ruling party he earlier pitched himself against reveals him as a sham. The student body's general inability to probe deeply into the motives of those it holds in high esteem paves the way for their swindling by Diti Oba and Ife Okeke.

Although Ife Okeke resigns his university lectureship to devote his energy to the cause of the youth movement, the students are absolutely unaware of his secret contact with the agents of the nameless government. Perhaps he expected some special favor from this secret contact. With this in mind, his regular advocacy of confrontation with the ruling Democratic party instead of dialogue or diplomacy is a farce. It is this confrontational attitude of Ife Okeke that prevents him from being included on the deputation to the minister of education to discuss scholarship matters: Diti's fear was that "Ife could flare the minister, and the conversation might eventually turn to confrontation right in the minister's office" (*Paradise*, 70). The inability of the movement's executive members to understand one another and the inability of the general student body to identify their interest and educate the ruling party about their actual intentions essentially spell their failure.

The composition of the GYM's executive body aims at being broadly representational of the nation—Diti Oba is from the Yoruba tribe, Mallam Dogo Yawuri and Malam Yaya Yola are from the Hausa tribe, Ife Okeke is from the Igbo tribe, Augustine Etuk is from the Efik tribe, and Osa Osifo is from the Edo tribe. Although their ethnic groups are not identified really in the novel, it is ordinarily easy for an African to identify someone's tribe simply from his or her name. The GYM's executive body aspires to be truly national. In a country with numerous ethnic groups a representation of all the groups makes it acceptable to every Nigerian or African. Among the executive members, it is Diti Oba and Ife Okeke who are given prominence. But neither possesses the courage and resolution necessary to redeem his own life, let alone those of others.

Like the coals that glow darkly in Milton's hell, Diti Oba's partial and
sudden phenomenal rise to the status of a national hero serves to outline
the general quagmire. In a morally decadent society, any spark of decency is championed even when the spark is questionable. Diti Oba's resignation from Hawk Gerinia Limited because of the company's
exploitation of the country's resources is his private action to draw
national attention to himself.

Resignation of an appointment is usually not enough to make one a
national hero. But the students who seem to be looking for a figure they
can rally round make him one. They make him one because he virtually
aligns with them—in his resignation of his lucrative position with a rich
company. Toward the end of the novel Ife Okeke's confusion reflects the
general confusion of Gerinian students in their search for a worthy
leader:

> I'm here today to arouse the conscience and hope of the youths on this
> campus; those who still have both. . . . I have tried to analyze why it has
> been possible for a cheat to take the generality of the youths of this coun-
> try for a ride. . . . I have regretfully discovered the bastard initially
> became a hero through impulse; impulse is one thing which rules his life.
> He resigned his former job on impulse; the impulse infected us, and we
> made him a national hero, also through impulse. He has become a minis-
> ter through *impulse* and treachery. Now he is married by impulse! [In
> Africa a "real" marriage is an alliance between two families, not an
> alliance as a result of seduction.] This is the crux of our national prob-
> lems. (*Paradise*, 209)

If Diti Oba is seriously interested in transforming his country into a paradise for the masses, he should have lived an exemplary life. An astute
demonstration of leadership by example rather than precepts would have
really made him a hero. Lack of firmness of character makes him vulnerable to government control via a seductive woman. In fact, it is out of fright
and panic that the government takes the action of penetrating the youth
leadership to kill the movement and any rival political party. Ironically, it
is when Diti Oba should have been vigilant that he collapses.

Like Diti Oba, Ife Okeke resigns his lectureship in the university to
join forces with the youths. He does not, however, seem to be down to
earth in his communication with the youths or students. Because of his
profession he tends to do things too academically to the point of losing
touch with reality. He talks above the students' level of understanding.
On the issue of financial assistance for transforming the youths move-

ment into a political party, he launches into a lecture on Ralph Waldo Emerson's theory of politics, which has possessed the mind of men. But his listeners and quite a number of the Gerinian people are familiar with neither Emerson nor academic political science. Although toward the end of the novel he is able to recognize the impulsive nature of Diti Oba, he himself is equally impulsive but fails to recognize this. According to the author,

> Ife Okeke was one of the very young lecturers at the National University of Gerinia. He had his university education in England and the United States of America and so had been abroad for eight years . . . even though the white civilization of Britain and the USA had afforded him the opportunity of university education, he approximated the face of a white man to a black leprous person and so detested and shunned any white man. He held the firm conviction that every political and economic ill that afflicted a black nation was engineered and fuelled by the white man. (*Paradise,* 6–7)

Probably because of youth and inexperience, Ife Okeke is very emotional. Undoubtedly, his long period of studying in the West exposed him to the white man's culture. While he might have had some unpleasant experience there (the author mentions none), one wonders if he had no pleasant experience as well. His constant reminding himself of the dark, unpleasant side of his period overseas reveals some of his inadequacies. A conjecture might be that Okeke experienced loneliness and various aspects of culture shock and was probably homesick at times, in both Britain and the United States. His open antagonism toward whites is perhaps his own way to get even with them for some of his unpleasant experiences in their countries. But if he really hates whites, why did he study in their countries?

His hatred of the white man expresses itself in his ready teaming with Diti Oba—in one who could "expose the white predators of our wealth," as he puts it. He feels that the time has come for him "to avenge his country's ills on the Whites" (*Paradise,* 7). Vengeance on the whites is Ife Okeke's secret motive for joining the youth movement. It is this vengeance that he carries along and translates into confrontation when dealing with government officials—an attitude that makes some of his colleagues wince with fear and prevents them from including him in some delegations to government. His resignation of his lectureship with the National University is thoughtless—a decision taken at the spur of the moment in a euphoric atmosphere:

"I call on you again: up Gerinian youths!"

"Ye-e-s! Power to the youths!" . . .

"Finally before I step down from this rostrum," Ife Okeke announced, "on the strength of your pledge I resign my appointment as lecturer in this university and devote my full time to the cause of the Gerinian Youth Movement." (*Paradise,* 5, 6)

One does not have to resign his or her appointment to join a cause. Besides, there is no indication that the university has mistreated him in any manner. Since he gets his monthly pay from the university, one would have expected him to be very cautious before taking a sensitive decision to resign an appointment. But he lacks caution. In his irrationality he invests the opportunist Diti Oba with the honors of a messiah: "Diti is our man!" But he realizes too late the type of character Diti Oba is, and condemns him as an "apostate," "traitor," and "a phoney leader."

Ife Okeke's firsthand experience in the course of the youth movement and Diti Oba's betrayal of the youths jolt him to reflect on the complexity of the human character. He matures and begins to have some rudimentary grasp of human psychology. Instead of appealing to human emotions as he used to do, he now appeals to human conscience. He addressees a few students of the National University of Gerinia in their Student Union Center after Oba's betrayal: "I'm here today to arouse the conscience and hope of the youths. . . . I have known some treacherous elders; but I never imagined that treachery could hatch so rapidly in some youths as well! I never realized that we were working for a paradise for a phoney leader" (*Paradise,* 209). The relationship of Diti Oba and Ife Okeke seems based on deceit. Neither is really out to help the youth or the masses. Oba has some grasp of youth psychology and mass psychology and exploits it—an opportunist, indeed.

Like Diti Oba, who has an ulterior motive in the youth movement, Ife Okeke has his—vengeance on the whites. He keeps clandestine communication with officials of the nameless government secret from Diti Oba. This absence of mutual trust, especially among the two most vocal of the youths, is one of the major causes of the fall of the youth movement. This is why, at the apogee of the movement, when it is about to be transformed into a political party, the whole things collapses. It is not based on a solid foundation of trust.

Miss Pat Ogun, the rebellious illegitimate daughter of the finance minister and the youth movement sympathizer, has her selfish reason for aligning with the youths. Her identification with them *only* during their times of confrontation with government affords her the opportunity to dramatize her frustration about her parentage and society's hypocrisy. According to her, "There is nowhere in this country to which I cannot gain access. . . . I feel *amoral* about a number of things where many people have double moral standards, or are hypocritical about. I'm a free girl. I don't give myself some hypocritical restraints. . . . Take sex, for instance; I take it like, say, you want a meal, a drink or a cigarette. Have a good one and forget it till you need it again!" (*Paradise,* 144). Such a wayward girl finds nothing wrong or outrageous in having as her lover a minister in the same cabinet with her father. She functions as a revealer of the sordid private lives of top adult professionals and men in the ruling party. From her we learn some men's ability to keep their extramarital affairs secret from their trusting wives.

What is pathetic about it all is that some wives live in self-delusion that their husbands are faithful to them and have no other wives. Some of these men have wives and children outside wedlock. Such affairs may not be known until the death of the man, when the wives and children outside wedlock appear on the scene for the burial ceremony, or to share in the man's property. Pat Ogun, the product of an extramarital affair, gives a good description of the watchful eyes of a wife and the secrecy of her husband's affair: "Because his wife is possessive and is always craftily watching her man's movements, he cannot visit his mistress as regularly as both he and the mistress want. It's usually like sneaking out to meet her. But when the wife travels out to their home town for some wedding or funeral or when she goes on her annual summer shopping abroad, the man and his mistress have an age of bliss together" (*Paradise,* 56).

This affair does not give this mistress, the friend of Pat Ogun's mother's, regular fulfillment. Without seeing her lawyer lover for two weeks and with the attendant sexual starvation, she lures her driver into having sex with her. This starts a new relationship. In his reckless affair, the lawyer's cousin dies of *magun.* Although Diti Oba does not strongly believe in it, he gives an idea of what *magun* is according to the Yoruba tribe: "They assert it is a traditional spell cast on an adulterous woman by her husband; it catapults the illicit male lover to his death at the climax of their love making. The assertion is debatable. I don't believe" (*Paradise,* 59). Whether Diti Oba believes the potency of *magun* or not, a countless number of stories about deaths of unethical men through *magun* abound in the Yoruba tribe. The term is derived from two Yoruba words: *ma* (do not) and *gun* (climb). Thus *magun* means "do not climb," and as a spell it really means do not climb the woman in question and have sex with her. To do otherwise is to die.

The *magun* spell is not put frivolously on a wife. It is only done when husbands have enough grounds to suspect their wives of infidelity. These grounds include sudden change of a wife from modest outfit to gorgeous outfit, extra attention to her physical appearance, and a perceived neglect of her home. The spell can also be done on a wife by a very jealous husband who does not want any man to even smile at her.

What is intriguing about *magun* is that the wives do not usually know that the spell has been put on them by their suspicious and jealous husbands. They usually know after their healthy secret lover suddenly behaves strangely during the actual lovemaking. The male lover does not, in his own volition, get off the woman. He is thrown off her by forces that are invisible to the objective eye. Some of the victims make funny sounds after they are thrown off and die very soon after. Some can be rescued or saved from death, however, if a traditional African medicine man or doctor is readily available to help neutralize the power of the *magun* spell. But because lovemaking is usually private and a secret, help from a medicine man is rare. This is why more men are believed to die of it than are rescued. The cousin of the aforementioned adulterous lawyer is among the unfortunate ones. His life insurance company refuses to honor his wife's claim because, according to the company, their policy does not cover *magun*. It is this insurance that the lawyer struggles to get for his cousin's widow.

Like his dead cousin, the lawyer is also very unfaithful to his wife. He almost wrecks his home through maintaining another home outside wedlock. The belated discovery of this affair by his trusting wife is pathetically told by Pat Ogun to her interested listeners:

> The last time [her husband] was away to further persuade the Insurance Company, his wife went to their bookshelf to check for some law books. As she picked the book she wanted and opened it, an envelope fell out. . . . The letter was from the young boy he had by "the other woman," his mistress. The boy was writing from the boarding house reminding his "father" of his forthcoming eighth birthday anniversary asking him to send enough money to enable him mark the birthday by entertaining his friends in the boarding house. He also urged his "father" to please visit "mummy" regularly. (*Paradise*, 59, 60)

That her husband could keep an affair secret from her for such a long time is too much for her to bear, and she breaks down only to recover after 10 days in the hospital. What is interesting to note is the impact such clandestine affairs have on their innocent young adult products like Pat Ogun. They more often than not come to reject hypocrisy in its entirety and fight it recklessly.

While Pat Ogun's sympathy rests strongly with the youths, she has not an ounce of feeling for her father. In fact, she is instrumental in ruining him. When she gives to Diti Oba and his group the budget documents she has stolen from her father, it embarrasses him and sets off a chain of events culminating in his removal from his ministerial position. She had sworn never to forgive her father when he asserted in a magazine interview that illegitimate children had no right to inherit their father's property. Her deliberate embarrassing of her father is her way of getting even with him. Her relationship with her father is quite pathetic.

All in all, the operation of the youths is intriguing. Despite the fact that they have no sophisticated means of disseminating their ideas and opinions, they succeed regularly with their Committee for the Fabrication and Propagation of Rumors (CFPR). The youths use this ad hoc committee to intimidate the government to recapitulate some of its decisions. For example, the CFPR is instrumental in the release of Diti Oba and Ife Okeke from detention. Although the use of the CFPR is always successful, it is an evil propaganda machine. Through its use, the youths do not make themselves better than the elders or ruling class whom they accuse of lying and deceit. Their disseminating false reports to damage the credibility of others is evil and does not promise any hope for the masses in Gerinia. It only solidifies corrupt and dubious journalism, which distorts and suppresses information when editors and writers are paid exorbitant sums of money.

In their revolution the youths do not seem to have any answer as depicted in *A Paradise for the Masses.* G. G. Dara has observed that

> Areo's exploration of this subject [revolution] contains serious epistemological and theoretical contradictions. The drift of his argument or presentation follows the stereotyped liberal bourgeois one which sees youths as a one-dimensional bunch of self-seeking opportunists who are no better than the elders they rail against. . . . [A] fictive account of the dream of revolutionary engagement demands more dialectical handling than Areo displays in this novel.[3]

This observation must be taken with a grain of salt, however. The youths are not a "one-dimensional bunch"; they possess energy for constructive work, and Areo strives to present the Nigerian or African youth in quite a realistic manner. They are idealistic and recklessly courageous in their youthful exuberance, but because of inexperience they accept their idols without probing into these people's characters.

Diti Oba possesses a drive to stimulate work as demonstrated in the fantastic mobilization of the students into a thorough clean-up of the Gerinian cities. Deep down, however, he has an inkling for the good life reflected in enviable positions and material comfort. The impasse between Oba and the ruling party officials clearly illustrates this: "'The Prime Minister is giving you two ministerial posts, including that of the health ministry as well as the chairmanship of some government boards and corporations.' . . . Diti was silent. . . . A ministerial post suddenly became attractive to Diti; but was he not going to be renounced by the youths? He found himself in a dilemma" (*Paradise*, 29, 30). This sudden interest in a ministerial position foreshadows Diti Oba's later behavior and his acceptance of the position of minister of youth and sports in a regime he has always discredited, and in his wife's ready acceptance of an invitation to serve as the only woman director of Hawk Gerinia Limited, the company her husband had resigned from. It is because Agnes and Diti Oba are in the same frame of mind that Agnes could form the mental reply, "My husband and I are pleased to confirm acceptance" (*Paradise*, 208).

When Diti Oba says that he heard the news of the ministerial appointment for "the first time" on the radio he is lying. His reply to the GYM secretary's letter of inquiry about his position with the GYM after his ministerial appointment does not portray him as a fighter for a paradise for the masses: "As founder of GYM . . . I cannot imagine myself doing anything that can destroy its existence and solidarity. . . . [I]n the meantime, I am negotiating appropriate board membership, directorship and foreign ambassadorial posts for us all and our supporters throughout the country" (*Paradise*, 203). According to the author, "The letter worked wonders. Everyone was pacified. Ife Okeke had been ignored both by Diti and eventually by the other colleagues of the GYM executive." The GYM, which began as an enviable, promising, dynamic force, fizzles out in hypocrisy and shame.

Diti Oba destroys the existence and solidarity of the GYM by joining completely the regime he discredited. The other members of the executive except Ife Okeke destroy this same existence and solidarity by not condemning Diti Oba for his treacherous and traitorous behavior, and by being pacified by Oba's promise of various positions in the government. The dejected Ife Okeke, who speaks to a few students of the National

University of Gerinia inside the Student Union Center, is not very different from other members of the GYM executive. His secret connection with the officials of the nameless foreign government is unpatriotic.

Conclusion

This novel is quite pessimistic. Perhaps the only ray of hope is in Ife Okeke's "From its ashes a new force, named Gerinia Popular front is being born! . . . The new child is not going to be one of impulse" (*Paradise*, 210). Perhaps a popular movement promises more hope than an exclusive youth movement. All told, the GYM executive members are essentially weak. None of the youth characters comes out as a full, well-rounded character. No rich view or background of each character is provided for the reader to have some insight into each's psychological makeup. To a major extent, Areo's interest is in presenting some strength and the hypocrisy, fraudulence, and other weaknesses of youth.

Like the characterization of the youths, there is no seriousness in delineating the characters of the adults. Only their selfishness, greed, corruption, and Machiavellianism are highlighted. If any character had come to life the the novel would have been artistically stronger. As one critic wrote, "In the tradition of realistic fiction which the novel belongs, neither paleness of characters nor moral neutrality is an artistic merit" (Dara 1988).

Unlike many novels directed at African youths, *A Paradise for the Masses* deals with revolution—an attempt by African young adults to change an exploitative system into a better one for the masses. Against the background of contemporary world events, *A Paradise for the Masses* is a topical novel. In 1989 Chinese students demonstrated en masse for better conditions of living. And in Nigeria and other Third World countries, student unrest based on demands for better living conditions is relatively frequent. Despite its topicality and the weightiness of this revolutionary theme, there is no readily recognizable authorial intrusion. It is quite a credit to the author for being able to distance himself from his material. *A Paradise for the Masses* is valid not merely for the African youth reader but for any community at odds with itself and sorely in need of direction and light.

Chapter Six

African Children's and Youth Fiction about War

The recent bloody war in Rwanda and the distressing faces of both young and old in the war in Somalia are not new. Captured vividly on television and radio and in newspapers, they reflect starvation and hopelessness—usually the by-products of war. Before the Rwanda and Somali crises there had been wars and civil strife in Uganda, Sudan, Nigeria, Angola, Mozambique, and South Africa, in which quite a number of people suffered untold hardship. Zimbabwe fought a bloody war for independence. Even in countries like Kenya, Zambia, Malawi, and Sierra Leone, which have been relatively peaceful, there is discontent and dissatisfaction with their rulers. In Kenya there have been student unrest and aborted coup attempts, and that country's best-known writer, Ngugi wa Thiong'O, for political reasons, lives in exile in London. Why these wars, disturbances, and unrest exist is not difficult to explain.

As a result of the "artificial" creation of various African countries from different ethnic groups, they have latent in them numerous forces for civil strife. Put together by the colonial powers whose territorial ambitions had no regard for tribal domains or kingdoms, African countries are still really developing the spirit of nationhood. The colonial political boundary divides the Ewes between Ghana, a former British colony, and Togo, a former French colony. The Ewes in Ghana once agitated to join Togo. The Wollofs are found in Gambia and in Senegal. Nigeria is also a country of various ethnic groups. The secession of Biafra and the three years' civil war in Nigeria are a manifestation of the jellylike stability of one African country: it wobbles but does not break.

Youth formed a major proportion of the army during the three years' civil war in Nigeria. The fact that the federal army increased its troop strength from 9,000 to 40,000 within a matter of weeks soon after the proclamation of the state of Biafra on 26 May 1967, and that Biafra itself almost overnight raised an army of 25,000, is good evidence of the heavy involvement of the youth in the war (UNESCO 1987, 36).

The Cyclist is one youth novel set against a background of this civil war. It is important to note that the youth did not really have any voice in the various developments leading to the war, or in the end of it. They attended none of the peace conferences in Aburi, Ghana, or Kampala, Uganda, or within Nigeria itself. Because the youths were not overtly politically involved in the war, and also for political reasons, the author, Philip Phil-Ebosie, does not go into detail about the beginning and course of the war. As a matter of fact, the novel opens with the end of the war and the amnesty and reconciliation that were in progress. But politics is not really the focus of *The Cyclist;* it is, rather, the human emotions of love and jealousy.

During the war many marriages dissolved primarily because many men were absent from their homes. Some wives who thought their husbands dead in the war engaged in extramarital affairs; some were seduced by their husbands' friends. In *The Cyclist* John does not seduce Odigo's wife, Celina, because he paid the bride price and married her when she was not divorced and when the fate of Odigo—alive or dead—was unknown. And in Africa, until and unless the bride price is returned, a marriage is still de jure in place. In extreme cases, when a wife or her parents or her people have not returned the bride price to her husband and his people, any child or children she has for other men legally belong to her husband. It is the return of the bride price that spells the final dissolution of a marriage. But Odigo does not die in the war, and Celina's people have not returned the bride price to him or his people. Very much alive, Odigo returns to Luawa, his village, at the end of the war. Thus the author sets up a potentially explosive situation.

The Cyclist

The Cyclist is the story of young Odigo, who leaves his newly married wife, Celina, behind in rural Luawa for three years to fight for Biafra during the Nigerian civil war of the late 1960s and early 1970s. Because he is seriously wounded and captured by Nigerian soldiers for three years, there is no communication between him and Celina, his family, or his Luawa community. It is mainly the thought of Celina that sustains him during this trying period of loneliness. When he returns after three years at the end of the war, he finds out that Celina is already remarried to John, the cycle repairer. He resolves to get Celina back by any means, and making love to her is uppermost in his mind. Odigo's successful secret lovemaking to Celina at the beach is made known to John by his friend Akagha, the fisherman. With this knowledge, John resolves to kill Celina, whom he regards as unfaithful. She runs away from John to Odigo for protection, but it is useless. Armed with a cutlass, and in rage, John fatally wounds Odigo, who attempts to protect Celina by holding her in his arms. Before Odigo dies, however, he summons his last strength to fire two deadly shots at John, who is already standing over Celina to finish her off with his cutlass. John dies, falling over Celina and his cycle. This debilitating and traumatic experience of witnessing two young men bloodily wiping each other out is too much for Celina, and she goes mad.

Love and Jealousy   A major concern of this novel is love and jealousy: "Love grows when it is watered and allowed to grow."[1] Obviously it needs time. This novel contends that the love between Odigo and Celina looked promising in the light of the story of their early relationship and final events of the story. But this promising matrimonial bliss is cut short for two major reasons: the youthful exuberance and stubbornness of Odigo in rushing to join the Biafran army, and his grandmother's dislike of Celina, leading eventually to her expulsion from her matrimonial home.

Although Odigo is just tasting married life, which in most cases is glamorous initially, he joins the Biafran army on the spur of the moment, only to be absent from Celina for three years—too long a period for a newlywed girl or her relations or even some of her in-laws to wait for a man. It is this time span and the uncertainty of Odigo's survival that his grandmother uses to drive Celina out of her matrimonial home. Although three years is a long time to wait for Odigo, Celina does not think of leaving his home. She is pushed out. In their next to the last meeting before their tragic end, she tells Odigo, "I never left you. Grandma asked me to leave. Everybody thought you had died and you know she never liked me from the start" (*Cyclist,* 118). Celina is blameless. Theirs would have been a happy marriage, at least happier than Celina's marriage to John. There are enough indications about this in the novel.

Celina really loves Odigo, and Odigo's paramount thought while in the prisoner-of-war camp for three years is about her. Such thoughts, however, border on infatuation or obsession. But Celina does not love John the cycle repairer. Celina's lovemaking with John is mechanical and barren, while her lovemaking with Odigo is one of fulfillment. The marriage of John and Celina is an unhappy one.

Plaiting hair is one of the few jobs she ever knows in John's house. Plaiting hair is a skill common to many African girls, who learn it from more experienced African women. Plaiting hair is the traditional form of today's women's perming or fixing of their hair in salons. But unlike modern hair styling, much black thread is used in plaiting. Because of the texture of the African woman's hair, it is very easy to fix it with black thread. Being able to plait is not much of an achievement. In fact, although some women do hair plaiting as their means of livelihood, it is more or less a pastime and a time for gossip. Because of the recreational nature of hair plaiting, some Africans do not have a high regard for the modern occupation of hairdresser, even if it proves a lucrative one. Seen in this light, the hair plaiting Celina learns in John's house is very insignificant.

The atmosphere that prevails during John's lovemaking to Celina after learning of Odigo's return characterizes their whole relationship—one of militant command and servile obedience:

> "Go to the room," he commanded. Celina knew the meaning of that command. She went to the bedroom without replying. She was already undressed when John walked in. She lay down on the bed. As John lay on top of her, she turned her head; she had wished he would not want to do it today. If he had looked at her face he might have seen her fighting back the tears. She thought of Odigo, then decided there was no point in doing that. So she concentrated on keeping her mind blank. John had his reasons for making love now. He wanted to show that he owned her completely. He made love mechanically. They did not speak to each other throughout. They never normally did. (*Cyclist*, 55–56)

Unlike the foregoing emptiness, fullness and warmth characterize Odigo and Celina's lovemaking toward the end of the novel:

> A playful fight started between the two of them, each one trying to gain the upper hand against the other. But really it was an excuse for their bodies to touch and this they allowed to happen as much as possible, until Odigo overpowered Celina and pressed her fully against him. Celina succumbed with a soft cry.
> "Odigo."
> It was the signal that she was ready. . . . He started to undress her, she him. . . .

> They made love. . . . The rhythm of the waves provided the music
> to their movements, the wind gave them the song. (*Cyclist,* 119)

Evidently, even nature—the waves and the wind—joins to celebrate the lovemaking of Odigo and Celina. It is a truly harmonious relationship.

Odigo considers his payment of bride price as conferring ownership or possession of Celina on him. With such ownership, he believes he has every right to have sex with her anytime he wants it; but the presence of John, her new husband, makes him unsure of, and quite uneasy about, this right. This uneasiness explains the clandestine nature of Odigo's sex with Celina after his return from the war.

If lovemaking is a physical and subliminal expression of deep, sincere feelings between a man and a woman, that of Celina and John is absolutely not. Theirs is like that of a man who pays to have sex with a prostitute primarily to satisfy only his sexual urge. But payment of a bride price and length of stay together do not really guarantee a harmonious relationship between a couple. John's physical presence, even in lovemaking, is immaterial to Celina. She thinks always of Odigo instead. When John learns of Odigo's affair with Celina from his friend Akagha, he realizes the folly of believing his "complete ownership" of Celina. To him, Celina is a deceiver, and he resolves to kill her.

Another theme tucked into the novel is that possession of money may not necessarily guarantee happiness. Before the cyclist Zoro performs, he strikes a deal with John, the cycle repairer, to pay for the repair or tune-up after his performance. Zoro is an entertainer who goes to various places to do acrobatic rides with his cycle. Although John is aware of the scarcity of money in the village and knows that a quarter of the cyclist's earnings at the show "would quadruple what he could charge for the repairs," he wants half of what Zoro would realize from his cycle acrobatic performance. Obviously as interested in possessing money as he is in possessing Celina, he also wants to test Zoro's bargaining power and generosity.

After his show Zoro comes in happily to fulfill his promise of giving John half of his earnings from the show. But it is a different John that he meets. John has just heard Akagha's story of Odigo and Celina's secret affair, and he is already outraged emotionally: "Had he not just heard the story from Akagha he would have been happier to see Zoro. John's movement now did not coordinate with his thoughts" (*Cyclist,* 122–23). To the amazement of Zoro, John only counts out absentmindedly what he would have charged for his cycle repair under normal circumstances.

John's knowledge of Odigo's secret sex with his wife, Celina, is the root of his boundless jealousy.

Perhaps John has learned right there and then the predicament of someone who is painfully cheated. He senses Odigo has cheated him in making love to Celina, and he does not want to cheat Zoro of his earning by taking half of it. Although Zoro shares his earning equally with John, John does not seem interested anymore. What surfaces really is that the emotional stability that arises out of a strong and happy relationship, and personal well-being as well, is more important and desirable than possession of a lot of money. Closely related to this theme of love and happiness is a husband's and a wife's duty to each other.

Spousal Duty in Wartime and in Peacetime Of the three young men—Odigo, John, and Zoro the cyclist—only Zoro seems to have a solid and perfect idea of responsibility toward a "spouse." Odigo leaves the security of his home and the companionship of his new wife for the uncertainty of fighting in a war. If this is patriotism, it is a misplaced one, particularly early in marriage. He has just sworn to take care of his wife until death do them part. Ironically, he leaves her at a period when most couples are still in their honeymoon. It is clear that Odigo toys with the survival of his new marriage, especially at a time of war, when everyone needs protection. In the absence of Odigo, John pays the bride price and becomes Celina's husband.

Regardless of how John performs his duty as a husband, it is to his credit that he keeps and feeds Celina; hence in a moment of intense frustration, these are his major points of regret: "You will vomit every penny I paid for you and all the food you have eaten in this house" (*Cyclist,* 126). He physically beats her primarily because he feels cheated: "He had been living with a woman all these years, a woman that never gave him all of herself. . . . He felt cheated. He felt used" (*Cyclist,* 125–26). Their predicament is traceable to Odigo's three years' absence—their marriage is predicated on a weak presumption that Odigo would not return from the war.

Odigo has the chance of not joining the army because many young men (like him) had found a reason not to be in Luawa and thus escape conscription. But Odigo goes to join the army out of his own volition—out of youthful exuberance in the euphoric days of the Biafran secession. Therefore Odigo has quite a big share of blame in his decision to leave Celina. On the other hand, Zoro is not likely to behave the way Odigo does by leaving his wife to join the army to fight. This is evidenced in the discussion between him and John shortly before the former's acrobatic performance:

> "Are you married?" John asked. "I am married to my bike." They both laughed. "I take my bike everywhere I go. I sleep with it, I ride it and when I ride it it's like making love to it. . . . I was given a girl at Idumagbo, a virgin. They said she was mine to take with me and marry."
> "Did you?" John asked.
> "The temptation was there; fifteen-year-old girl, very attractive, succulent even, but I could not take her. *How would I look after her?* My life is like that of a gypsy. Always on the move." (*Cyclist*, 99–100; my italics)

Zoro continuously draws back from marriage even at peacetime, primarily because he believes his job as a roving entertainer cyclist would interfere with the performance of his role as a true and devoted husband. He would not want to abandon a wife for any length of time.

Against the background of war, the novel's action revolves around Odigo's sustained obsession with Celina. Soon after his illicit lovemaking to Celina, a painful chain of events is set in motion culminating in the violent deaths of Odigo and John and the resultant insanity of Celina. The novel's main action ends precisely at this juncture. In essence, with the death of the principal actors and the madness of Celina, Phil-Ebosie does not deem it important to go any further with the narrative. The madness of Celina is not elaborated upon. What is important is that she lives out her last days as a demented woman. Nevertheless, the author brings the novel to a close by inviting the reader to sympathize often with an insane woman who may not really be directly responsible for her madness: "Please always take pity on a mad woman, it may just be Celina. A woman who loved and lost" (*Cyclist*, 131).

In various African countries emotionally disturbed people are usually regarded as living in a world of their own, and the source of the madness is always a mystery. They are usually left undisturbed, but young children sometimes make fun of them. During major festive occasions like the World Black Festival of Arts and Culture in 1977 in Nigeria, the people with mental illnesses were collected from the streets of Lagos and isolated. After the festival, however, they came back. They are on the streets again today, although psychiatric hospitals and a few people adept at dealing with mental illness are now doing a lot to help these emotionally troubled people. With Celina's madness, Phil-Ebosie points out that the mentally ill are victims of circumstances beyond their control.

The novel successfully presents what might happen to relationships and homes when husbands are often separated from their wives, especially in times of war. At such times a wife is usually taken care of by her in-laws, her parents, and her friends. Unfortunately, however, it is during such times that she is susceptible to seduction—primarily by morally depraved acquaintances of her husband. Also, where the wife lives may be rendered uncomfortable. While the wife at home may choose to remain faithful before the possible return of her husband, pressure from relations or society may compel her to leave her matrimonial home or to seek male companionship. In the case of Celina, it is Odigo's grandmother who successfully pushes her out.

Celina's people do not seem to care about her during Odigo's absence—a duty they should have taken over when the grandmother was making life intolerable for Celina. In the words of Odigo's uncle, Kadiri, "The girl's relations said they had no hand in the matter any more and that she could live with whoever she wished" (*Cyclist,* 75). Such a statement severs any relationship with Celina at a time when she needs it most. Absolute callousness on the part of Celina's people is not, however, the reason for their inhuman behavior: part of it is poverty. Removing Celina from Odigo's house could have required Celina's family to repay to Odigo's family the bride price—money they did not have. Instead they decide to accept a dowry on Celina from John, with the idea that should Odigo's people demand the dowry, they could return it, but if not, they themselves would make some money. Celina is useful, it seems, only as long as she can bring in money.

Throughout her painful time with John, her relations do not bother to check on her. She needs some powerful advice from mature relations during her emotional trauma after Odigo's return, but, sadly enough, she gets none. With Celina's predicament, Phil-Ebosie subtly indicts this commercial side of the institution of the bride price. In addition, he subtly points out that there must be unanimous consent between both families of intending husband and wife or there will be problems, especially during the hard times of war or famine.

Odigo's grandmother had never supported Odigo's marriage to Celina, and when she finds an excuse to send her away, she does so without any regret. After Odigo's return she minces no words in restating her old negative position on the marriage: "'You know I never agreed to that marriage,' said Grandma. . . . 'She was doing nothing in the house. I didn't always know where she was, she never told me and there was a war on. She had no issue for my son, he had been gone for a good year so why should I continue to feed her?'" (*Cyclist*, 75). The grandmother has made Celina a victim of the age-old disease of in-laws interfering in a couple's marital affairs. Odigo is also a victim as well. He never intends to dismiss Celina from his life. Certainly it is Odigo's absence for three years during the war that gave his grandmother the liberty to "break" his marriage.

Two Different Young Adults   According to the author, "That he [Odigo] had joined the army at all was by chance and out of ignorance" (*Cyclist*, 1). Precisely, "he had enlisted because there were a lot of men his age there in uniform" (*Cyclist*, 47). Overtly, what propels Odigo to join the army is the need to feel united with his peers in a common cause. But he forgets that each of his peers has joined the army for a different reason. Unlike those who have joined out of joblessness, Odigo is employed as a palm-wine tapper and has steady work.

Palm-wine tapping is a popular African occupation, especially in the rural tropical areas where palm trees grow freely. Palm-wine tappers are experts who climb to the top of the palm trees and collect the juice into a calabash container through a siphon from the succulent top of the palm tree. The collected palm wine is taken down from the tree after a few days and left to ferment for later treatment. From the time of climbing through the final brewing of his palm wine, the palm-wine tapper is quite occupied. According to the author, "They [Kadiri and John] were both in the same boat, and Odigo definitely had the better prospects" (*Cyclist*, 38). Ironically, however, it is Odigo who goes to join the Biafran army. Individual palm-wine tapping does not have the dimension of a sophisticated brewery. Although the individual tapper does not really make a lot of money out of palm-wine business, he gets some measure of financial independence and personal well-being from it. In such a situation, he does not go borrowing. Modern brewing technology has almost overshadowed the palm-wine tappers today, and palm wine is now bottled and sold like the numerous African beers.

Unlike Kadiri, who does not leave his wife after four years of marriage, Odigo leaves his barely six months after his marriage. Celina's physical attraction may have lost its novelty for him. This speculation is given substance when one analyzes how Odigo first fell in love with Celina and his later behavior to 15-year-old Ekaete, whom his grandparents were arranging for him as a wife after his return from the war. Earlier on, it was Celina's dancing prowess that strongly attracted him, and "he never forgot her after that day, for he had fallen in love with her" (*Cyclist,* 83). Back in Luawa after the war, he is more interested in Ekaete's figure instead of trying to know and understand the young girl. His sudden grab at and subsequent squeezing of Ekaete's breast at their first meeting reveal him as merely a physical lover. According to the author, "What he needed was a woman—a woman like Celina; a woman to hold him in her arms and listen to his problems, listen to his story of the war; a woman whose body would respond to his in an adult way. Odigo thought of Celina again" (*Cyclist,* 106).

When he sees Celina at Zoro's show, he thinks not of having of a heart-to-heart discussion with her but of making love with her. He runs after her, and a little while later he succeeds in making love to her on the beach. To Odigo, only successful lovemaking brings him back to real life: "Odigo felt good. This was *the first time he had really felt good and happy since he came back*" (*Cyclist,* 120; my italics). He feels "high" and apparently ecstatic.

Odigo's idea of marriage does not seem to go beyond pleasure of the flesh. Such is not enough for a successful marriage. Odigo's love for Celina is infatuation; it is temporary, shallow, and empty: "Celina was the only woman who made him feel this way [nervous]" (*Cyclist,* 115). But true love is also one of responsibility that someone like Zoro is not ready for because of the nature of his job. For John, it is a different matter entirely: "John was not the kind of man who believed in love. He needed a woman in the house and that was that. He had one now, love might grow later but it wasn't important" (*Cyclist,* 52).

John and Celina have the potential to love each other, but both of them have a fault. John is the frigid type who needs encouragement from his partner to love: "She [Celina] had not allowed theirs [their love] to grow. He was not the type to show much emotion but he could have shown it if she had encouraged him. She did not. She frustrated his love. There was only a thin line between love and hate. He really could have loved her but now he hated her; hated her for cheating on him; hated her for being deceitful" (*Cyclist,* 126). Because Celina cannot encourage John because of her emotional tie to Odigo, communication between them is warped. John often commands Celina verbally and expects Celina to understand his commands and signals. With such a commanding and intimidating tendency, John frequently degenerates into a brute. In his bitterness over Odigo's return, the tilting of the basin of water held by his seven-year-old niece, Beaty, for him to wash his hands, infuriates him, and he uncontrollably gives her "a hard wet slap that made even Celina wince" (*Cyclist*, 55). Phil-Ebosie describes John's beating of his wife after her illicit lovemaking with Odigo in bestial terms: "John paced her like a stalking animal" (*Cyclist*, 128). Without regard to decency, John fiercely continues beating Celina even when she is almost naked. He resolves to kill her and Odigo with his cutlass.

Celina's major fault is her inability to completely forget Odigo in lovemaking, thereby committing adultery, at least mentally. Although Odigo and Celina are not divorced, Celina has been expelled from Odigo's family and now lives with John. It is impossible to be married to more than one man at the same time in Africa. But since John legitimately paid a bride price on her, he is her legitimate husband. This relationship is culturally sanctioned. John constantly refers to his payment of a bride price on her because he knows deep down that Odigo also has a legitimate claim on Celina—and an older and stronger one. For a wife to use "Sir" for her husband, as Celina does for John, indicates fear and distant relationship. On the other hand, she calls Odigo by his first name, which is an indication of closeness and intimacy.

It is Zoro who seems to understand what love really is in his attachment to his cycle:

> He caressed the cycle, like a lover, he held it like a baby. He spanked it, he loved it, rider and bicycle became one. . . . Zoro lifted the front wheel of the cycle. . . . Each move expressed love: love of life, love of pleasing and entertaining, love of understanding of the man for his bike and love from one to another. He spoke for Odigo, he spoke for Celina, he spoke for the whole village. (*Cyclist*, 113–14)

All the ingredients of love are distilled in Zoro, although such passionate love for an inanimate object could be considered abnormal. Phil-Ebosie could have given the reader a comprehensive background of Zoro to show why he behaves as he does. He even turns down marrying a beautiful young woman, whom many young African men would want.

Whereas Zoro caresses, holds, spanks, loves, and rides his bicycle to celebrate life, Odigo borrows and mechanically rides Mathias's bicycle for only one mission—to make love to Celina: "This was the chance he had waited for. This was the moment he had hoped for. He had stayed alive for this and although it wasn't exactly what he dreamt about, he knew that he had to make use of this moment" (*Cyclist,* 115). Odigo's love is natural but an essentially carnal one. Zoro's relationship with his cycle is the author's illustration of what a perfect relationship is. A transfer of Zoro's relationship with an inanimate object to one with a woman would depict the true kind of love the author endorses.

The Manifestation of True Love   The novel's action moves from Odigo's regular dreaming of Celina while in the POW camp to an actual physical union between them even though Celina is legitimately married to John. Physical union with Celina is what Odigo longs for, and after this the novel's major action ends. Despite Odigo's obsession with Celina, the novel's action is depicted mainly on a physical plane. Odigo's state of mind as well as that of other characters is not deeply emphasized.

The novel illustrates what real love is through Odigo, John, and Zoro. The author does this by putting these three characters in significant situations where they manifest their natural inclinations, and also in their respective relationships with a bicycle.

By leaving Celina to go to war, Odigo plunges her into an emotional problem: "Food was short and Celina had needed a man to lean on, to reassure her and to explain why they were at war. Some families had even left the village to go to somewhere where they thought they would be safer. Her parents had been amongst those who left, only to come back a year later more wretched than when they left. They were only too happy to receive the money from John the bicycle repairer for her" (*Cyclist,* 29). But John the cycle repairer "takes care" of Celina in Odigo's absence during the war and gives her some degree of reassurance, thereby alleviating some of her problem.

As a palm-wine tapper, Odigo knows it is taboo to climb a palm tree and steal someone's keg (calabash) of wine and drink it. But after returning from the war he climbs a tree, steals one, and drinks it, feeling only "a little uncomfortable" about it. He knows full well that tappers believe that before the third theft the thief would be caught. His stealing of someone else's palm wine to drink when he himself is a palm-wine tapper who is aware of the wrongness of such an act foreshadows his "stealing" of someone else's wife. To Odigo, Celina is almost synonymous with sex. Hence his idea of love does not have definite ideals or aims beyond lovemaking; love or marriage holds no deep meaning to him. He is only momentarily stimulated sexually, and the effect wears off rapidly.

Zoro the cyclist is the complete opposite of Odigo. In a relationship one should retain his or her unique personality instead of surrendering it completely to the relationship. Zoro does his in his relationship with his cycle: their respective uniqueness is almost lost in the image of the cyclist.

The Bicycle Symbol, the Gun, and the Hollow Tree   A close reading of this novel reveals Phil-Ebosie's attempt at developing the bicycle as a private or personal symbol to illustrate what love really is, and the gun and hollow tree as symbols of destruction. Through the respective relationships of three young men to a bicycle, the author probes into the inner natures of the characters themselves. The cycle is basically a neutral element in the novel—inanimate and man-made. The perceptive reader gets hidden information about the characters as they interact with the cycle.

Both John and Zoro "had a natural interest in bicycles" (*Cyclist,* 98); the cycle provides them a source of livelihood. While John repairs it, Zoro entertains with it. For John, the cycle symbolizes his attempt to repair himself and his home. He is a frigid lover without tender emotion, as revealed in his relationship with Celina. His tender act of repairing cycles is, however, a release of his emotion to repair, or to bring order out of chaos. Psychologically he is affected by his constructive attitude toward the cycle. Like Zoro, who is already one with his cycle, John aspires to be in complete harmony with it. By virtue of the fact that he provides a home for Celina in Odigo's absence, one can definitively maintain that he provides some repair and direction for Celina's life. But Odigo intrudes on this life and wrecks it.

Unlike Zoro and John, Odigo does not do anything constructive or positive to any bicycle. Instead he takes care of a deadly weapon—the gun he has kept in the hollow of a tree by the beach. Taking care of a gun that has been used in a civil war is ominous. It is this ominous and destructive inclination that engages Odigo. He borrows a bicycle from his friend Mathias for only one reason: to ride to the beach with Celina and there seduce her. As he rides the bicycle with Celina he realizes that joining the Biafran army to fight was an empty endeavor and that he has missed his wife. True to his sensuous character, the physical touch between his body and Celina's is enough to arouse him: "The touch discharged static electricity between the two of them. Odigo knew then

that he had to have her back at all costs" (*Cyclist,* 117). It is this excitement that brings his selfishness to its worst manifestation—he does not
care who gets hurt in his now unquenchable resolve to have Celina "at
all costs." He does make love with Celina on the beach. Against the
backdrop of this lovemaking with Celina, Odigo's taking care of his gun
conveys a sense of foreboding.

John, who repairs bicycles, has the potential to love Celina if only
Celina could encourage him. But Celina's heart is far away from him.
When she submits to making love with Odigo, John's previously constructive mind sadly degenerates into one intent on destruction. Unlike
Zoro, who rides to celebrate life, John, who had earlier repaired cycles,
now rides one with a mission to kill Celina and Odigo. After wounding
Odigo fatally with his cutlass, he goes after Celina. While standing over
her to deal her the death blow with his cutlass, he is shot dead by the
dying Odigo. John dies, falling half on top of her, half on his cycle. This
picture of a bloody tragic wreckage reflects the demise of John and his
effort to repair himself. Celina, whom he had once taken care of, has a
permanent breakdown.

Unlike John and Odigo, Zoro seems to have a mystical bent:

> He had slept on the beach the previous night. This was something he had
> done before and quite enjoyed. It gave him a certain amount of freedom:
> to think; freedom to be alone and to be one with the internal spirit with-
> in his body. It was this spirit that gave him the inner strength which
> helped him to perform. It gave him the strength to concentrate and a
> belief in his own invincibility. Zoro had lain on the beach the night before
> looking at the stars and watching the kerosene lights from the village go
> out one by one. In the early morning he had swum in the sea and had
> treated himself to a breakfast of fruits which he had plucked from the
> surrounding bushes. Later, he had taken a walk to the village square to
> study the layout and width and to create for himself a built-in atmos-
> phere for the performance. (*Cyclist,* 98)

A careful young man, he does not rush into anything. He goes not by
riding his cycle but by walking, to study and get acquainted with where
he will perform. He knows such study can minimize stage fright and
blunders. Mystically inclined, Zoro wants to be close to nature and is
interested in maximizing his spiritual potential in his love of meditation.
This bent of mind is reflected in his attention to the natural light of the
stars and the man-made kerosene lamp lights of the village beneath, and

in his conception of his bicycle. For him, his bicycle is more than a mere tool of entertainment. The spiritual significance of the bicycle explains the reverential awe with which he takes care of it.

The cycle is the link between him and success. In other words, without the cycle Zoro cannot be successful as an acrobatic entertainer. Similarly, without Zoro the bicycle is lifeless. The blending of Zoro and his bicycle produces the live cyclist. This cyclist has the attributes of Zoro and the attributes of the cycle. Indeed, Zoro and the bicycle symbolize a true marriage of mind and spirit. This bicycle symbol may pose quite a problem in interpretation because it is not a traditional symbol. The author invents this interesting cycle symbol in his novel. Even the experienced reader has to be alert to distill the intricacies of this cycle symbol.

The symbolism of the hollow tree is self-evident. The hollow tree on the beach houses Odigo's gun, a deadly weapon whose "protection" is questionable. The hollow tree section of the beach is where Odigo spends his last moments before John's arrival. His attempt at protecting Celina is hollow. He only succeeds in getting his gun out of the hollow tree to shoot John—a bloody act that contributes to Celina's madness. In essence, then, both the hollow tree section of the beach that has once been a nice spot for Odigo and Celina and the hollow tree itself provide nothing for them but emptiness.

All said, Phil-Ebosie projects Zoro's conception of love as the ideal, which may account for the novel's title. While Zoro goes on celebrating life with his cycle and obviously waits for a time when he can settle down and take care of a wife, Odigo, Celina, and John behave like animals. John shouts on Celina, "Come back here, you animal!" (*Cyclist,* 127). Running out of their home, John paces her "like a stalking animal" to meet Odigo by the hollow tree. Here their savagery comes to the surface, and they really behave like animals by wiping out each other.

Unlike this bestial behavior rooted in hatred and jealousy, genuine love promotes peace. Unlike Odigo, John is not completely of a sensuous frame of mind. He only needs some encouragement to become romantic. John's frigidity could be altered by favorable circumstances. Zoro the cyclist is the near perfect lover. In fact, the novel has an epigraph with a somewhat cosmic significance of love: "We are all born for love, it is the principle of existence and its only end . . . " (Disraeli). But such a global phenomenon of love must begin with the individual. When jealousy dominates one's mind, love is almost impossible. Through an interesting manipulation of the bicycle as a symbol of womanhood, the author depicts ideal love or marriage as a true blending of two souls—Zoro and the bicycle in the image of the cyclist. It is the intriguing symbol of the cycle and the realistic probing of the universal human emotion of love and jealousy against a background of war that makes *The Cyclist* richer than *Vicious Circle* and *A Child of War*.

Two Human Elements of War: Possession and Power   *The Cyclist* also deals realistically with two human elements that cause war—possession and power. In fact, the tone of tension, strife, and war permeates the novel. The author seems to use the "war" between Odigo and John as a microcosm of the larger reality—the Nigeria-Biafra war that has just ended at the novel's opening.

That he paid a dowry for Celina is unshakable in John's mind. He clings to this fact and guards it more jealously after learning of Odigo's return, because he knows full well that Odigo, whom he presumed dead, has not received back the bride price on Celina from her family. According to the author, "He was certian that he had done everything correctly and now he was determined not to let anybody usurp his rights. He felt almost ready to kill anybody who tried to unsettle his life now" (*Cyclist,* 52). While thinking seriously of his possession, Celina, and of course his power over her as her husband, he eats absentmindedly in his house, and the whole situation is tense, as seen in this charged interaction between him and Celina:

"They say Odigo is back," he said in an indifferent tone.
     "I don't know. I haven't seen him," answered Celina, trying to restrict the conversation.
     "Bring me some salt." Celina obeyed and brought some salt on a serving spoon.
     "Well that's their business. I paid your bride price to your people," continued John as he swallowed some yam. "We have stayed together for over a year now. Bring me some pepper." Celina walked out again and came back with some pepper. "I don't make trouble for anybody, so let nobody make trouble for me," he said looking up at Celina.
     Celina did not dare look at him. John continued to eat.
     "Let nobody come near my house," he said suddenly, indicating that he wanted to wash his hands. The meaning of what he was saying and who he was referring to was quite clear to Celina. (*Cyclist,* 54–55)

In his intense bitterness over Odigo's sudden return, he is virtually sitting on a keg of powder.

In various African cultures food is associated with abundance, happiness, and peace; hence the popular saying that the quickest way to a man's heart is through his stomach. Conversely, incessant preparation of a bland and tasteless diet by a wife is enough ground for strife. Because there is no indication that Celina is a bad cook, John's venting his anger on seven-year-old Beaty is totally inappropriate. Such African foods as pounded yam are traditionally eaten with the hands and not cutlery. If children or young adults are around, they are expected to hold a bowl or basin of water for the father, mother, or any adult to wash his or her hands before and after eating. This is the kind of chore Beaty does for John. A seven-year-old might easily tilt the bowl of water when handling it; there is nothing strange in this and there is no reason to fiercely slap the child for doing so.

Like animals that show a possessive sense of certain areas when feeding, and a possessive sense of some of the female of their species, John, the "paragon of animals," exhibits the same over Celina. Like animals that fiercely defend their territory or possessions against any intrusion, John defends his. His commanding Celina to go the room—his signal for sex—and his actual "lovemaking" soon after eating are mainly to psychologically and physically reassure himself that he possesses Celina. On the other hand, Odigo's clandestine lovemaking to Celina gives him a feeling of one who still possesses Celina, and as one who still has power over her. He thinks of killing John because he is an obstacle to his total possession of Celina and his power over her. Certainly, the tension between John and Odigo illustrates the concept that there is no real and deep personal satisfaction to the ego when there is a parity of power. It is only when one can demonstrate a power exceeding that of the other that satisfaction is guaranteed.

John considers Odigo's clandestine lovemaking an intrusion into his territory—a shaking of his possession of, and a shaking of his power over, Celina. It is for him a humiliation, and he reacts violently: "He felt cheated. He felt used" (*Cyclist,* 126). He sustains the gathering storm of hurt, jealousy, and anger in him, and it explodes soon after Celina returns from the beach: "All his emotions boiled to a raging point and he reacted in the only way he knew. Two fast slaps executed almost like a chop across the face sent Celina sprawling across the table. He grabbed her by the hair and threw her forcefully across the room. . . . She had never seen him look so violent" (*Cyclist,* 125). In defense of herself,

Celina grabs the kerosene lamp in their bedroom and throws it against John's face, drawing blood. Near naked, she escapes to Odigo at the beach for protection. But there is no protection for her in the face of John's uncontrollable rage. Their tragic deaths and the madness of Celina are a result of the inability of John or Odigo to give up Celina to the other.

Viewed against the backdrop of the Nigerian civil war, perhaps Phil-Ebosie is interested in pointing out in *The Cyclist* that wars are man-made. Furthermore, peace is impossible when elements opposed to it are dominant in man's mind as evidenced in Odigo and John. *The Cyclist* is a true illustration of the view that world peace must begin with the individual.

Although Zoro is an entertainer—a calling that many Africans would regard as not mentally or intellectually rigorous—he looks more responsible and intellectually and spiritually stronger than Odigo and John. Odigo exercises no restraint in leaving his wife to join the army, and John exercises no caution in marrying a girl who he himself knows is already married and not divorced. It is true he presumed Odigo dead, but one should not marry someone unless one is sure she is free. Unlike Odigo and John, Zoro knows marriage is responsibility and commitment and draws back from it until circumstances are favorable. He sees his relationship with his cycle in terms of what his relationship with his wife would be like—one of inseparability of mind and spirit. Undoubtedly, such a relationship augurs well for a good marriage foundation, which can withstand any crisis.

Odigo and John are not emotionally mature enough for marriage, yet they go into it. Their love and marital affairs have a shaky foundation that cannot resist shock or stress. In moments of crisis their love and marriages collapse. The author intends the relationship between Zoro and his cycle to serve as the standard to which Odigo, Celina, and the rest of the village should aspire. The thrust of the novel, then, is that whether in times of peace or war, patience, caution, reason, and maturity need to be exercised before one goes into marriage.

Child of War

Unlike *The Cyclist*, which deals with the effect of war on an African home, on human relationships, and on the larger African community, Alexander Kanengoni's *Vicious Circle* (1983) and Ben Chirasha's *Child of*

War (1985) deal with Zimbabwean war of liberation from colonial domination. For a long time in Rhodesia (now Zimbabwe) literature was expected to enforce discipline and peace. In *Decolonizing the Mind: The Politics and Language of African Literature* (1986) Ngugi wa Thiong'O states, "In Rhodesia the Literature Bureau would not publish an African novel which had any but religious themes and sociological themes which were free from politics. Retelling old fables and tales, yes. Reconstructions of pre-colonial magical and ritual practices, yes. Stories of characters who move from the darkness of the pre-colonial past to the light of the christian present, yes. But any discussion of or any sign of dissatisfaction with colonialism. No!"[2] Zimbabwe's fight for political independence, like that of Kenya, was bloody.

While *Child of War* deals with the actual fighting between the African guerrillas and the government forces shortly before political independence, *Vicious Circle* deals mainly with the early beginnings of the fight—when the storm of violence gathers. *Child of War,* where the storm of violence explodes, is a more accomplished youth novel than *Vicious Circle,* primarily because the point of view of the youngster, Hondo Tapera, is quite prominent. It is through him that we the readers get a picture of the war.

Narrated by a Zimbabwean youth, 13-year-old Hondo Tapera, the only child of a widowed mother, *Child of War* describes the effects of the Zimbabwean war of liberation on an idyllic village. The conflict provides the book with a historical reference point and a narrative anchor. Ruled by the village head Baba Zijena, this nameless, closely knit community is an agrarian one, with cattle raising also an important means of livelihood. It is important to note that Hondo is first seen as a cattle herd boy. The family bulls are "revered as the animal embodiment of our great ancestral spirit."[3] There is a strong emotional, traditional, and spiritual link between the peasants and the family bull. This tremendous significance of the bull compels Tapera, Hondo's father, to risk searching for him at the much-dreaded Taylor's farm.

Farmer Taylor is a hostile English settler with a very large, fertile farm:

> The name Taylor brought fear to every soul in the village. On hearing that name shouted, even old grandmothers took their ancient skirts up in their arms and scurried for safety, while brave men lay on the ground, hiding. . . . Every child knew him. We nicknamed him 'M'pengo [madman] because of his violent character. His farm was

large—*perhaps ten or fifteen times larger than our village.* The land was, oh, so much richer than ours . . . the stoneless soil crumbly black. (*War,* 11; my italics)

Farmer Taylor tolerates none of the village peasants on his rich farm, impounding any cattle that step onto his land. He scares young African peasants with his revolver when they climb over his fence to gather fruits and wild honey, clattering after them up the rocky slopes to their mothers' doorsteps, leaving only after shouting angry threats for a quarter of an hour and firing warning shots into the sky. He roughs up two teenage girls who come to his farm to collect firewood, and one of them he rapes. When the girl becomes pregnant and gives birth to a mixed-blood baby, the shamed and anguished parents pack up and leave their ancestral village for another.

Tapera goes to Taylor's farm not to trespass but to search for his bull. The spiritual significance of the bull is at the root of the rare courage that Tapera displays in going to Taylor's farm. Despite the objections of his wife and Hondo, Tapera remains adamant. He cannot bear the thought of losing the best—the family bull—of the seven or eight bulls they own. The tragic result is that Tapera is shot to death by farmer Taylor for "trespassing."

Through his continued cruelty, farmer Taylor plunges the peasants into sorrow and heartache. His killing of Tapera renders Hondo an orphan and Mia Hondo a widow. His seizing of the peasants' cattle makes them poorer. Farmer Taylor's behavior reflects some of the white colonists' racism, brutality, and exploitation. These fundamental issues cannot be resolved by peaceful dialogue or conciliation but must be fought out doggedly and unremittingly. *Child of War* is both a historical novel based on the Zimbabwean war of liberation and a social statement, showing the suffering and disintegration of solidarity among the peasants because of the long, drawn-out war.

It is in such a war-torn environment that Hondo emerges and operates as a child of war. Besides Taylor's cruelty, the obvious dichotomy between the African peasants' small village and Taylor's farm is noticed by young Hondo: "As a child I had often wondered why our cattle browsed on the barren slopes and why we wasted our time scratching the stony fields with our hoes instead of using the rich grass land on the other side of the fence" (*War,* 11). Although Hondo notices this difference, he is too young and inexperienced to correct the situation or to understand and analyze it. This confusion of the youth is given articulation and vitality by the commander of the guerrillas in one of the *pung-wes* (meetings) in the village:

> Our country is full of Farmer Taylors. . . . There are thousands and thousands of them who have swarmed over our land. They robbed our fathers of their land, took all the rich areas for themselves and left us with these rocky barren wastes which cannot yield enough food for our starving bellies. Look at Farmer Taylor's farm—how big and flat and rich it is. And look at the stony wastes we call our fields. Is this fair? How can this land that belonged to our forefathers be called Farmer Taylor's? Who did he buy it from if not from them? Did he and his friends not grab it from us at gunpoint? (*War*, 18)

I quote this passage in its entirety to bring out the difference between the youth's conception and reaction and the adults' conception and reaction to the Europeans' occupation of their land. Obviously Hondo's childhood is not a carefree state of existence. Innocent children like Hondo are involved in the Zimbabwean war. The Europeans' appropriation of his native land leads to agitation, which Hondo begins to experience early. Since *Child of War* dramatizes the events of the Zimbabwean people's relatively recent fight for independence, it is possible for it to be a catalog of political events. It is a credit to Ben Chirasha that he moderates a depressing series of political events by filtering them through the mind of the youth Hondo.

Hondo does not go into the liberation struggle on his own: he is drawn into it. While the fierce war of liberation rages throughout the country, Hondo only hears of it and anticipates it spilling over the borders of his village. But, at only 13, he does not act. Although he is very nervous in his first meeting with the guerrilla commander, he gives his full cooperation by showing the fighters, on demand, the way to Baba Zijena's house. Thus young Hondo enters the war to liberate his country from perpetual colonization.

The war suddenly envelops him when he is grazing his cattle. Indeed, to still have the time to graze cattle in a war-torn environment presupposes that some peace and tranquility still exist. This oasis of peace is associated with the boy and his grazing cattle, but the sudden appearance of two guerrillas shatters the scene: "Many cattle stopped grazing to watch the approaching strangers. I stood dumbfounded, aware of my tattered shorts and cracked herd boy's feet, clutching my useless, long whip" (*War*, 1). His long whip is now useless because he suddenly realizes that, in times of war, grazing cattle, if there are any to graze, is a luxury.

Hondo says, "I was not afraid, somehow. I had heard too much about the war to be afraid" (*War,* 1). Besides, all Hondo's neighbors anticipate the war's spilling over into their village, indicating that the community is not immune to violence.

Impressionistic youngsters and even simple adults are taught by authoritarian governments to hate rebels and revolutionaries and to inform on these people. Hondo himself may have been taught this way. Throughout *Child of War* the guerrillas are described in negative terms: terrorists, dogs, scoundrels, mongrels, and brutes. This is why the guerrilla commander is so interested in impressing on the young generation that he and his men are not terrorists but patriotic freedom fighters. The commander thoroughly questions Hondo to ascertain the boy's knowledge of the political situation and his emotional well-being. In fact, the first meeting between Hondo and the guerrilla commander is meant to mirror the suspicion and unease that seems to characterize human relationships during wars. It is only after the guerrilla commander is sure of Hondo's loyalty that he enlists him as a helper in the fight and makes his request to show him the way to the village head's compound.

Hondo represents very young teenagers who enter into bloody wars. As the village head, Baba Zijena, tells Hondo's widowed mother,

> It's the young people who are going to be fighting the war. We elders are going to be observers only. Observers of our own deaths, too. It has happened in every village where the war has penetrated. Soldiers have tried to kill the young men, the *mujibhas,* or attempted to drive them out of the countryside, so that the guerrillas cannot rely on their active support. (*War,* 29–30)

The thought of losing her only son to the war is unbearable for Hondo's mother. There is no escape for anyone. Baba Zijena himself is soon brutally killed for helping the guerrillas. Having been beaten unconscious, they tie his legs to a rope towed by a helicopter. The helicopter takes off, whipping his dangling, upside-down body into the air and flying so low that the grizzly white head is just a few feet above the villagers heads. This graphic description indicates the government soldiers' determination to ruthlessly crush the freedom fighters by all means. The final barbaric killing of Zijena is primarily to instill fear in the villagers, deterring them from seeking change.

Hondo's regular participation in the series of midnight *pungwes* conducted by the guerrillas in his village gradually transforms him into a bold young man. From the various songs and discussions in the *pungwes* it becomes obvious that liberation in colonial Southern Rhodesia becomes synonymous with the expulsion of the farmer Taylors, the end of the colonial administration, and the recovery of the lost lands.

The villagers believe that it is necessary to recover their lands and to regain their freedom, but there is no clear agreement about the means for achieving this end. Propelled into the war by the guerrillas, they are in fact psychologically and socially unprepared for it. The government soldiers' unleashing of violence on the villagers for participating in the killing and consumption of farmer Taylor's cows strikes fear among the villagers. When the guerrilla commander announces the capture of six of farmer Taylor's beasts for feasting, they are no longer excited because of the severe beatings many of them have received from government forces. But the commander appeals to their emotions by explaining their method of operation:

> I see you all are afraid tonight. . . . I know many among you are asking why the guerrillas were not there this morning when soldiers invaded the village. . . . [T]he answer is simple. This is a guerilla war—hide-and-seek, hit-and-run. We shall not stop singing, whatever the circumstances, until our country is free. And if we don't sing tonight, then we might as well pack up our guns and admit defeat. (*War*, 33–34)

While most of the villagers join in the war dance after this speech, some traitors are already conspiring in the village. Gwara does not attend this rally. Some of the villagers join the government soldiers to deal with the guerrillas and anyone who cooperated with them. The treacherous taking of Hondo and other village youths by an African soldier pretending to be a guerrilla, and their subsequent torture by government soldiers, is one of the saddest episodes in the novel. The soldiers who strongly believe that the youths have helped the guerrillas trick them into being captured and punished. Drenched with buckets of chilly water and burned with lighted cigarettes, Hondo is compelled to tell them "everything more than all they wanted to hear." He adds much primarily to get the burning cigarette off his skin.

Three youths die as a result of torture, and the survivors are later tied tightly to tree trunks—each young "prisoner" on his own, only to be rescued during the guerrillas' fierce attack on the government camp. Farmer Taylor is killed during this attack, and the soldiers' camp is completely destroyed. The office of the colonial district commissioner, who fled some days before the guerrillas' raid, is also destroyed. With the crumbling of the administrative machinery, the guerrillas take over control of the village.

Unlike some adults like Gwara, who betray their people, Hondo and the other youths do not. Their torture is a way of suffering for their homeland. Hondo's and Zindera's efforts to bring desperately needed drugs to guerrillas indicates their commitment to the liberation struggle. The cooperation Hondo receives during this mission—the mysterious old man who poses as his father when the soldiers question them, and the doctor and the nurse who provide the drugs—reflect the cooperation of majority of Africans in the liberation struggle in Zimbabwe.

But not much is devoted to illustrating a recognizable young character in Hondo. Apart from presenting him as a herd boy under the care of his widowed mother, the author does not take much pain to delve into his emotional makeup. The story centers on his trials and tribulations. He does not have any delusions of grandeur. Perhaps Hondo and the other youths are in the story primarily to show African youths the grim reality of war. The youths' participation in the liberation struggle— scouting the foot of the mountain, scouting the area around the village, keeping an eye on the township, and manning the roads passing through the village—makes them realize that in such times of crisis even youth does not exempt one from responsibility.

Child of War has the capacity to make the young conscious of the vandalism and emptiness of war. After the guerrillas' victory Hondo realizes that war is essentially destructive—in the loss of lives, the betrayals, the cruelty and heartlessness. At the guerrillas' graves in the mountains, he mourns and reflects: "Choking with grief, I picked up seven small stones and tossed them one by one onto the grave, paying silent tribute to the heroes who lay there in the earth. . . . All that mattered now was that whoever they were, they were buried in the soil they had fought to free" (*War,* 96–97). Despite the reconstruction—forming an African government, opening schools, and building dwellings—Hondo finds it difficult to wipe the ravages of the war from his memory: "Forgiving is easy, but forgetting is hard. I am sad that so many people died, but I will never forget how Farmer Taylor and the soldiers tyrannized us" (*War,* 99).

The author presents farmer Taylor as a stereotype of the high-handed colonist—more high-handed and more of a caricature than Mr. Howlands, the English farmer-settler in Ngugi wa Thiong'O's *Weep Not Child* (1964). Unlike Ngugi, who takes the reader into the mind of Howlands and exposes his thoughts in connection with his "ownership" of the cultivated fertile land, Ben Chirasha does not probe farmer Taylor's mind. He lets the child's point of view as reader and main character dictate the novel's action and form. The novel's inability to probe into farmer Taylor's character as well as into the character of the village elders and soldiers may be attributable to the first-person narrator. Because the narrator is a character in the story and not a peripheral observer, he has a limited viewpoint. Hondo lacks experience and sophistication to delve into the psychological complexity of humankind and to probe into why people behave as they do, and consequently he describes the characters superficially, as he sees them.

Child of War is a historical fiction about the Zimbabwean war of political independence from colonial domination. But Chirasha does not present mere history but rather some particular events—perhaps some part of his autobiography, since he grew up in Zimbabwe and went to school during the turbulent war years. A plausible way to present such historical events is to use the first-person narrative point of view for some immediacy and authenticity that can draw young readers into the narrative. *Child of War* makes the young reader think and reflect deeply on the grimness and inhumanity of war. The novel informs and at the same time challenges. As Jo Carr asserts, "A good nonfiction book, as it marshals facts, should create a challenge. It should encourage a child to think—to relate one fact to another and test a familiar idea against a new idea—until at last he or she is able to weave a pattern of increased understanding. What begins as idle curiosity should end as independent thinking."[4]

Viewed against this assertion, *Child of War* is quite a successful African youth novel. While narrating the actual events of the war, *Child of War* reflects also the why and how of these events and strives to bring the reader to what history is essentially about—human behavior. Chirasha concentrates on young Hondo, costumes him correctly as a young African herd boy against a background of war in a village in Zimbabwe, and gives him the thought and feeling expected of a 13-year-old while he allows the youth in him to dictate much of the form of the novel.

Conclusion

Taken together, *The Cyclist* and *Child of War* are a remarkable contribution to African war fiction. Despite the fact that the novels deal with actual historical events, they do not contain dates that some scholars believe can give historical authenticity to fiction. Dates, however, can also detract from the novel as a work of art. Be this as it may, the historical veracity of these two works cannot be questioned. The common artistic sensibility of these works is that children and youth cannot completely escape the ripples of war—either in domestic setting or in the larger society.

In *The Cyclist* tension and war rage in John and Celina's home. This domestic war between two young adults takes its toll on the seven-year-old Beaty, who is struck in the face by her enraged uncle. The ugly scenes of domestic violence caused by war—John's beating of Celina—seem to do untold damage to Beaty's emotional development. Similarly, in *Child of War* the peace and happiness of Hondo Tapera vanish, and he looks at the future with uncertainty. These novels show that during war—in a domestic setting or in the larger society—no one is free from its disturbing effects.

Chapter Seven

Reaching African Children and Youth and "Thinking Multicultural"

In those days even in the cities adults still had time to tell stories to their children. They did tell folk-tales, but many a time when they ran out of tales of old heroes they would gravitate to modern stories about the living. (*Naira,* 44)

In Africa, where a reading culture is yet to be entrenched, reaching the young population through the printed word is a crucial matter. If the printed word is to pique their interest and whet their reading appetite, it must be exciting and relevant to them in their sociocultural environment. African Children's and youth literature is not just for art for art's sake. It has a function. Modern African literature is the repository of the cultural life of the people and is a major source of education for the young everywhere and urban people who have lost touch with their roots.[1]

I have discussed here mainly a select body of major African children and youth novels. My selection is neither exhaustively complete nor absolutely definitive. The writers are still living, and other children's and youth works may be forthcoming from them. Undoubtedly, contemporary African writers have successfully expressed themselves to children and youth through the novel—the most flexible and versatile of all literary forms. But they have also expressed themselves, in a limited way, through other literary forms, such as drama, biography, autobiography, the short story, and the African school story. Although examples of these genres are too ephemeral to warrant the kind of in-depth analysis I have given the major youth novels discussed here, some points about them are worth mentioning.

Most of Efua Sutherland's children's literature is drama and verse, which makes her contribution especially important since little poetry and drama are written for children.[2] Her greatest influence is probably through the children's theater group she founded that performs plays throughout Ghana. Sutherland's play *Foriwa* (1967) is based on an African folk tale used to caution African girls in their relationships with strangers. But Sutherland gives the tale a different twist in her play because her intention is to stress the need to unite and work together and curb prejudice in multiethnic Ghana. In *Foriwa* the desire to educate children and young adults about the benefit of working together is vividly realized. Likewise, the desire to impress on the young African's mind the ugliness of curruption is visible in another play, Olu Olagoke's *The Incorruptible Judge* (1962), whose didactic element is crystal clear: do not give or accept bribes.

Such laudable and positive thinking in the aforementioned plays is continued in the lives of real people through biographies. Biographies serve the function of "myth building" and are used to extol the virtues that the nation hopes to inculcate in its young citizens. Consequently, the lives of great national heroes such as politicians, religious leaders, reformers, artists, and musicians have provided ready subjects for biographers in societies all over the world.[3] In Africa the multinational publishing company Longmans has come out with a biography series, "Makers of African History," and Oxford University Press has "Makers of Nigeria." Heinemann Publishers has the "African Historical Biographies" series. An indigenous publishing house, Onibonoje, has a series called "What Great Men Do." Most of the titles in these biographies are "single-feature biographies with one central subject whose life history is portrayed and the historical span covered by the titles is from the undated, preliterate era . . . to more recent figures of the early and middle twentieth century."[4]

The literary quality of biography writing in such series is very thin, however. It is formula writing. There is hardly any scope for a critical evaluation of the historical material available, as the expressed aim is to induce the child reader into emulating the particular person whose individuality is often hidden behind a whole cluster of stock phrases and stereotypes (Martini 1987, 41–42).

The title of Ezekiel Mpahlele's semibiographic short novel *Father Come Home* suggests a child's appeal to his father to come to him, and it also suggests the need for fathers to be around their children. Young Maredi has been separated for more than 16 years from his father, who works in the mines in a South African city, and his idealized father image is very remote from the reality of his actual father. When he finally meets his father after 18 years, the father-son relationship is awkward.

The children's autobiographical writer Mabel Segun states that for decades, as a result of colonization, Nigerian children have had to read imported books which were completely alien to their culture. As a result some of them are beginning to lose their personal identity and seem to be unaware of those African traditional values which held the society together. In my books I try to emphasize the importance of these values in a transitional society such as is depicted in *My Father's Daughter* or in a modern setting as in *Youth Day Parade*.[5]

It is this thinking that has guided her in her creative works for children. Her two autobiographies for children, *My Father's Daughter* (1965) and *My Mother's Daughter* (1987), deal with her growth in a rural village and her relationship with her father, the village pastor, who strongly influenced her to become a disciplined individual. Her *Youth Day Parade* (1984), like Sutherland's *Foriwa,* stresses the need for cooperation in a multiethnic society like Nigeria.

Related to this emphasis on positive attributes in the aforementioned plays and *Youth Day Parade* is the African's perception of school and the African school story. The African school is seen as the place where morals and discipline are instilled in the young, and quite a number of African school stories have been published, like Anezi Okoro's *One Week One Trouble* (1973) and *Double Trouble* (1989) and Barbara Kimenye's Moses stories. In Chinua Achebe's *Chike and the River* (1960) the school prinicipal scolds Ezekiel, who fraudulently offers nonexistent leopard skins to pen pals in Britain in exchange for money. The discovery of Ezekiel's fraud results in he and his associates being humiliated before the whole school. Contained in the principal's scolding of Ezekiel is the need for youths to love their country and never to disgrace it through fraudulent activities.

According to Nancy Schmidt, "There is no need for authors to describe what African school children know well from personal experience. They can easily read between the lines and fill in the background" (1981, 186). This in part explains the relative thinness of the African school story. Certainly African school stories do not proclaim any complex psychological theme or philosophical position. Yet for all their simplicity and apparent transparency they offer exciting reading for children and whet their appetite for more. Such literature, however, does not seem popular any more, which indicates the slow death of a genre.

Whether it is the old gifted but illiterate storyteller or the modern educated writer, novelist, playwright, or autobiographer, the desire is to educate the young population and pass on Africa's cherished ideals to them. Like African literature for adults, African literature for children and young adults also looks to oral traditions. Black Africa's multitudinous nonliterate communities have always used the spoken word as their means of expression and entertainment. In fact, "of the present generation of Africans only a minimal percentage can make any pretenisons to having a reading culture."[6] When Buchi Emecheta now writes or tells stories like old African storytellers or griots, her goal is to continue the sophisticated informal instructional paradigm of her ancestors. It is this informal method of instruction that African children grow up with. If the young population comes to see literary creations as stories or works they are familiar with and can relate to, then such novels couched in traditional African folk narrative are a step in the right direction. Literature, then, comes to touch young people's lives culturally, socially, and individually.

A major social problem in Africa today is youth crime—especially armed robbery—and various national leaders have proposed draconian steps (even the death penalty) to prevent it. But perhaps what is needed is tackling the problem at its root—and that root is the home. A decent home and a disciplined adult population can nurture young people to become mature, responsible, and humane young citizens. Traditional African values that are timeless—honesty, hard work, and integrity—are perhaps transmitted best to young people through the oral tradition. This special return to an oral mode of transmission of stories as seen in *Naira Power* and *A Kind of Marriage* is not merely a fleeting fancy but a continuation and purposeful revival of an art solidly grounded in African culture.

Against this backdrop, African writers for children and young adults focus on themes that are socioculturally relevant to young people. Some African adults voice concern that much African youth fiction tends to concentrate on the vices it wishes young people to avoid. But one should realize that this fiction extols virtue by displaying the tragic consequences of vice. The ignoble race for money, the momentous choice of a life partner, the virtues of courage, honesty, and diligence in various spheres of life are subjects at the heart of these writings rooted in African folk traditions. As demonstrated in *Naira Power* and *A Kind of Marriage,* the integration of the African oral tradition into the novel form shows a tremendous leap forward in African imaginative works of art.[7]

Beyond Africa's multicultural societies is a multicultural world that young Africans themselves need to know. President Spyros Kyprianou of Cyprus in his address to the nineteenth congress of the International

Board on Books for Young People in 1984 stated that "books for young people are the main cultural nourishment for our youth. For this reason, they must send messages and teachings of humanism and altruism, love for the lofty principles of freedom, justice and democracy, respect for moral values and longing for universal fraternization and peace in the world . . . providing good books to the children of the world is conducive to the creation of a better future for mankind." It is this desire for multicultural and international understanding that incited Jella Leppman in 1948 to found the International Youth Library in Munich, Germany, which today is the world's foremost library devoted to international children's and youth literature. It is to promote international understanding that a second one—the International Institute for Children's Literature— was established in Osaka, Japan.

America has been a multicultural society for a long time, yet its multicultural content in literature is thin. As far back as 1956, Charles Stephen Lewis found little delineating modern conditions in foreign lands in American high school literature books in his dissertation, "The Treatment of Foreign People and Cultures in American High School Literature Books" (University of Michigan). In 1979 John Donovan, the late executive director of the Children's Book Council, stated that

> for the last decade . . . there were years in which there were less than a dozen translated children's books published in the United States, and there has not been a year in which as many as 75 translations have appeared . . . an objective assessment of contemporary American children's reading would have to conclude that American children read a body of books that may be more parochial than those read by children anywhere in the developed world.[8]

It does not seem that the situation has changed. Recently John Daniel Stahl observed that

> internationalism is an important dimension of children's literature too often neglected in the United States. Whereas in most countries of the world a high proportion of children's literature consists of works from other cultures and nations, in the United States the proportion of works translated from other languages is negligible. British and American authors dominate the curricula; even Canadian authors are underrepresented. . . . The exclusion of works translated from other languages from the canon of children's literature as it is being defined in the United

States is a form of cultural poverty and testifies to a lack of imagination in an information-rich world.[9]

It is hoped that this study will invite Americans and other nationals to read African children's literature where the expression of African culture can be seen.[10] These works accurately and successfully portray African society and are a vital part of African culture, contributing toward a comprehensive picture of the African worldview. It is a part of African literary heritage and, by extension, part of the black world literary heritage. When African children's and youth literature is addressed vis-à-vis other cultures' children's literatures, we might glimpse the humanity shared in the "universal republic of childhood." When that is achieved we will perhaps come to appreciate what it means to be integral human beings in a multicultural global cummunity.

Notes and References

Preface

1. Gloria Dillsworth, "Children's and Youth Literature in Sierra Leone," in *African Youth Literature Today and Tomorrow*, ed. German Commission for UNESCO and International Youth Library (Bonn: German Commission for UNESCO; Munich: International Youth Library, 1988), 24.

2. "South African Children's Literature," *Multicultural Children's Literature* 4, no. 3 (n.d.): 1–21

3. As South Africa has joined as a new member of the International Board on Books for Young People (IBBY), *Bookbird*, IBBY's international periodical on books for children and young people, gives a "special insight" into South African children's literature in its May 1992 issue (vol. 30, no. 2). See André-Jeanne Tötemeyer's essay "Impact of African Mythology of South African Juvenile Literature" (9–16; Part 2 is in the September 1992 issue, no. 3, 10–15). See also Isobell Randall's essay, "Local Literature for Children in South Africa's 'Let's Give Them Books'" (5–8).

4. Lillian Smith, *The Unreluctant Years* (1953; Chicago: American Library Association, 1991), 11.

5. Anne Scott MacLeod, "International Research Society for Children's Literature (IRSCL)," in *Children's Literature Research: International Resources and Exchange* (First International Conference, 5–7 April 1988), ed. International Youth Library (Munich: K. G. Saur, 1991), 218; hereafter cited in text.

6. U. C. Knoepflmacher, Introduction to *Teaching Children's Literature: Issues, Pedagogy, Resources*, ed. Glenn Edward Sadler (New York: MLA, 1992), 2.

7. I discuss the various dimensions of didacticism in African children's literature in "Didacticism in Nigerian Youth Literature," *Journal of Reading* 29, no. 3 (1985): 266–68. African children's works are not simplistic sermons per se. "Instructional details" do not displace the reader's or listener's sustained interest in the tales and novels or their understanding of them as carefully crafted art works. Didactic elements are also embedded in quite a number of songs. In his article "The Role of Play Songs in the Moral, Social, and Emotional Development of African Children" (*Research in African Literatures* 20, no. 2 [1989]: 202–15) Abu Abarry draws attention to the educational, aesthetic, and recreational values of traditional African play songs among the Ga people of Ghana.

8. Chinua Achebe, "Chinua Achebe: At the Cross Roads," in *Pipers at the Gates of Dawn: The Wisdom of Children's Literature*, ed. Jonathan Scott (New York: Random House, 1981), 192.

9. Quoted in Roger Sutton, "Kind of Funny Dichotomy: A

Convesation with Robert Cormier," *School Library Journal* 37, no. 6 (June 1991): 7.

10. Eleanor Cameron, "Writing from Experience: Some Books Come Directly Out of Their Writers' Own Childhoods," *Five Owls* 5, no. 3 (January–February 1991): 47; hereafter cited in text.

11. Virginia Hamilton, "Hans Christian Andersen Award Speech," *USBBY Newsletter* 18, no. 2 (Fall 1992): 7.

12. Akinwumi Isola, "The African Writer's Tongue," *Research in African Literatures* 23, no. 1 (Spring 1992): 17; hereafter cited in text.

13. G. A. Gundu has addressed the children's literature of the Tiv-speaking people in the article "Tiv Children's Literature: Content and Narrative Forms," *Journal of African Children's Literature* 1 (1989).

Introduction: A Farewell to Neglect

1. A. W. Kayper Mensah and Horst Wolff, *Ghanaian Writing* (Tübingen, Germany: Erdman, 1972).

2. Martin Tucker, *Africa in Modern Literature: A Survey of Contemporary Writings* (New York: Ungar, 1967).

3. Shawn F. D. Hughes, "Others' Africas: Recent Critical Studies of African Literature," *Modern Fiction Studies* 37, no. 3 (1991): 631.

4. Adrianne Roscoe, *Mother Is Gold: A Study of West African Literature* (Cambridge: Cambridge University Press, 1991); hereafter cited in text.

5. Ernest Emenyonu, *Cyprian Ekwensi* (London: Evans, 1974); hereafter cited in text.

6. Henrietta Otokunefor and Obiageli Nwodo, eds., *Nigerian Female Writers: A Critical Perspective* (Lagos, Nigeria: Malthouse Press, 1989).

7. J. O. J. Nwachuku-Agbada, "Review of *Nigerian Female Writers: A Critical Perspective*," *Research in African Literatures* 21, no. 4 (1991): 158–59.

8. Osayimwense Osa, "Adolescent Literature in Contemporary Nigeria," *World Literature Written in English* 23, no. 1 (1984): 298–303; and "A Content Analysis of Fourteen Nigerian Young Adult Novels," Ed.D. diss., University of Houston, 1981.

9. Nancy J. Schmidt, *Children's Fiction about Africa in English* (New York: Conch Magazine, 1981), 1; hereafter cited in text.

10. I have used the terms "tribe" and "tribal backgrounds," "ethnic groups," and "communities" interchangeably in this study to differentiate the various ethnic groups from each other. I do not see use of the term "tribe" as derogatory or offensive.

11. Asenath Bole Odaga, *Literature for Children and Young People in Kenya* (Nairobi: Kenya Literature Bureau, 1985); Gulten Wagner, "Nigerian Children's Books: An Evaluation," *African Book Publishing Record* 2, no. 4 (1976): 231–36 (hereafter cited in text); Osayimwense Osa, *Nigerian Youth Literature* (Benin City: Paramount Publishers, 1987) (hereafter cited in text).

12. John Rowe Townsend, *Written for Children* (Boston: Horn Book, 1965).

13. Dorothy Broderick, *Image of the Black in Children's Fiction* (New York: Bowker, 1973).

14. My review of Schmidt's *Children's Fiction about Africa in English* is in *Research in African Literatures* 14, no. 2 (1983): 257–61.

15. This article is a condensed version of Wagner's M.L.S. thesis, "An Evaluation Study of Children's Books Published in Nigeria," University of Ibadan, 1975.

16. Osayimwense Osa, *Foundation: Essays in Children's Literature and Youth Literature* (Benin City: Paramount Publishers, 1987).

17. Francis Nyarko, "The Production and Distribution of Children's Literature in Africa: A Diagnostic Survey," in *Children's Book Production in Developing Countries,* IBBY Nineteenth Congress, Nicosia, Cyprus, 1984, 63.

18. Jay Heale and Annari van der Merwe, "South Africa Joins IBBY," *Bookbird,* no. 2 (1992).

19. Nancy J. Schmidt, "4th Zimbabwe International Book Fair, 1987: An Overview of Published African Children's Literature," *African Book Publishing Record* 13 (1987): 239.

20. Sophie Masson, "African Children's Literature," *Papers* 1, no. 2 (1990): 71–74; and "Notes on African Children's Literature," *Reading Time: The Journal of the Children's Book Council of Australia* 36, no. 1 (1992): 12.

21. Naomi Lewis, Preface to *Twentieth-Century Children's Writers,* 3d ed., ed. Tracy Chevalier (Chicago and London: St. James Press, 1989), 5.

22. UNESCO, *Priority Needs and Regional Cooperation concerning Youth in English-Speaking Africa,* prepared by Yash Tandon, July 1987, 7; hereafter cited in text.

23. Katherine Frank, "African Womanhood in the Novels of Buchi Emecheta," *World Literature Written in English* 21 (1982): 484; hereafter cited in text.

Chapter One

1. Nancy J. Schmidt, "The Africanization of Children's Literature in English-Speaking Sub-Saharan Africa," *Journal of African Children's Literature* 1 (1989): 18. Schmidt draws attention in this essay to Emenyonu's devotion of chapter 3 of his *Cyprian Ekwensi* to Ekwensi's children's fiction and my inclusion of the essay "Ekwensi's Juvenile Works" in *Foundation: Essays in Children's Literature and Youth Literature.*

2. Cyprian Ekwensi, "Stimulating and Moulding Junior Minds," in *Junior Literature in English,* ed. Solomon Unoh (Lagos: African Universities Press/Nigeria English Studies Association, 1981), 2: hereafter cited in text.

3. *West African Review,* January 1950, 19.

4. See Neil Skinner, "From Hausa to English: A Study in Paraphrase," *Research in African Literatures* 4 (1973): 154–64.

5. Hugh Keenan, "Joel Chandler Harris and the Legitimacy of the Reteller of Folk Tales," in *Sitting at the Feet of the Past,* ed. Gary D. Schmidt and Donald R. Hettinga (Westport, Conn.: Greenwood Press, 1992), 82.

6. John Buchan, "The Novel and the Fairy Tale," *Children and Literature: Views and Reviews,* ed. Virginia Haviland (Glenview, Ill.: Scott Foresman, 1973), 228.

7. Cyprian Ekwensi, *The Passport of Mallam Ilia* (Cambridge: Cambridge University Press, 1960), 13; hereafter cited in the text as *Passport.*

8. Cyprian Ekwensi, *Gone to Mecca* (Ibadan: Heinemann Educational Books Nigeria, 1991), 18–19; hereafter cited in the text as *Mecca.*

9. See Bernth Lindfors, "Cyprian Ekwensi: An African Popular Novelist," *African Literature Today* 3 (1969): 2–14.

10. *The Drummer Boy* (Cambridge: Cambridge University Press, 1960), 81.

11. Cyprian Ekwensi, "The Problem of Writing, Illustrating, and Publishing Adolescent/Teenage Literature for Children," *African Book Publishing Record* 14, no. 2 (1988): 96; hereafter cited in text.

Chapter Two

1. Ezekiel Mphahlele, *Father Come Home* (Johannesburg: Ravan Press, 1984), 31; hereafter cited in text as *Father.*

2. Chikwenye Okonjo Ogunyemi, "Buchi Emecheta: The Shaping of Self," *Komparatistische Hefte* 8 (1983): 70; hereafter cited in text.

3. Buchi Emecheta, *The Bride Price* (London: George Braziller, 1976), 30; hereafter cited in text as *Bride Price.*

4. Nancy Topping Bazin, "Feminism in the Literature of African Women," *Black Scholar* (Summer–Fall 1989): 8–9; hereafter cited in text.

5. Lauretta Ngcobo, "African Motherhood: Myth and Reality," in *Criticism and Ideology: Second African Writers Conference,* ed. Kirsten Holst Peterson (Uppsala: Scandinavian Institute of African Studies, 1986): 144; hereafter cited in text.

6. Mario Azevedo, *Africana Studies: A Survey of Africa and the African Diaspora* (Durham, N.C.: Carolina Academic Press, 1993), 368.

7. Rolf Solberg, "Buchi Emecheta: The Woman's Voice in the New Nigerian Novel," *English Studies* 3 (1983): 249.

8. Helen Chukwuma, "Postivism and the Female Crisis: The Novels of Buchi Emecheta," in *Nigerian Female Writers: A Critical Perspective,* ed. Henrietta Otokunefor and Obiageli Nwodo (Lagos: Malthouse Press 1989), 2; hereafter cited in text.

9. Cynthia Ward, "What They Told Buchi Emecheta: Oral Subjectivity and the Joys of 'Motherhood,'" *PMLA* 105, no. 1 (1990): 83; hereafter cited in text.

10. Ernest Emenyonu, "Technique and Language in Buchi Emecheta's *The Bride Price, The Slave Girl,* and *The Joys of Motherhood," Journal of Commonwealth Literature* 23, no. 1 (1988): 130; hereafter cited in text.

11. Interview with Buchi Emecheta, *Spare Rib* (n.d.); *In the Ditch* and *Second-Class Citizen* are titles of two of her works.

12. Buchi Emecheta, *Head above Water* (London and Nigeria: Ogwugwu Afo, 1986), 165; hereafter cited in text as *Head.*

13. Using *The Bride Price* and *The Summer of My German Soldier,* I discuss at length young adults' common need for love in "Adolescent Girls' Need for Love in Two Cultures—Nigeria and the United States," *English Journal* 72, no. 8 (1983): 35–37.

14. I discuss the nondidactic nature of *The Bride Price* in "Buchi Emecheta's *The Bride Price:* A Non-Didactic Nigerian Youth Novel," *Children's Literature in Education* 19, no. 3 (1988): 170–75.

15. Kirsten Holst Petersen, "Buchi Emecheta: Unorthodox Fictions about African Women," in *International Literature in English: Essays on the Major Writers,* ed. Robert L. Ross (New York and London: Garland, 1991), 286; hereafter cited in text.

16. As a British Council scholar visiting at the University of Stirling in 1986, I met Professor Ian Milligan of the English Department who generously gave me a copy of his *The Novel in English: An Introduction* (London and Basingstoke: Macmillan, 1983). I found the chapter "How the Story Gets Told" very helpful in my discussion of Emecheta's *The Bride Price.* I owe him many thanks for his friendship.

Chapter Three

1. Eckhard Breitinger, "Literature for Younger Readers and Education in Multicultural Contexts," *Educafrica: Bulletin of the UNESCO Regional Office for Education in Africa* 11 (1984): 173.

2. See Jurgen Martini, "Sex, Class, and Power: The Emergence of a Capitalist Youth Culture in Nigeria," *Journal of African Children's Literature* 1 (1989): 43–59; Wendy Griswold and Misty Bastian, "Continuities and Reconstructions in Cross-Cultural Literary Transmission: The Case of the Nigerian Romance Novel," *Poetics* 16 (1987): 327–51; Wendy Griswold, "Formulaic Fiction: The Author as Agent of Elective Affinity," *Comparative Social Research* 2 (1989): 75–130 (hereafter cited in text); and Virginia Coulon, "Onitsha Goes National: Nigerian Writing in Macmillan's Pacesetters Series," *Research in African Literatures* 18, no. 3 (1987): 304–19.

3. David Maillu, *For Mbatha and Rabeka* (London: Macmillan, 1980), 8; hereafter cited in text as *Mbatha.*

4. Jide Oguntoye, *Too Cold for Comfort* (London: Macmillan Pacesetters, 1980), 142; hereafter cited in text as *Too Cold.*

5. As popularly used in English-speaking Africa, *wonderful* means something unexpected or irrational, not something great or positive.

6. Buchi Emecheta, *A Kind of Marriage* (London: Macmillan, 1986), 31; hereafter cited in text as *Marriage*.

7. Michael D. Langone, "Social Influence: Ethical Considerations," *Cultic Studies Journal* 6, no. 1 (1989): 24.

8. Okello Oculli, "The Politics of Literature for Children in Africa," *Guardian* (Lagos), 30 November 1984, 9.

9. David Halperin, "Cults and Children: The Role of the Psychotherapist," *Cultic Studies Journal* 6, no. 1 (1989): 24

Chapter Four

1. Jack Zipes, "Second Thoughts on Socialization through Literature for Children," *The Lion and the Unicorn* 5 (1991): 19.

2. David Aronson, "Why Africa Stays Poor and Why It Doesn't Have To," *The Humanist: A Magazine of Critical Inquiry and Ethical Concern* (March–April 1993): 12.

3. Stephen Ekpenyong, "Social Inequalities, Collusion, and Armed Robbery in Nigerian Cities," *British Journal of Criminology* 29, no. 1 (1989): 21; hereafter cited in text.

4. I discuss *Director!* as a complex example of a didactic African youth novel in "Didacticism in Nigerian Young Adult Literature," *Journal of Reading* 29, no. 3 (1985): 266–68.

5. Buchi Emecheta, *Naira Power* (London: Macmillan, 1982), 3: hereafter cited in text as *Naira*.

6. Nancy Topping Bazin, "Feminist Perspectives in African Fiction: Bessie Head and Buchi Emecheta," *Black Scholar* (March–April 1986): 40.

Chapter Five

1. Ngugi wa Thiong'O, *Devil on the Cross* (London: Heinemann, 1982), 177.

2. Areo Agbo, *A Paradise for the Masses* (Lagos: Paperback Publishers, 1985), 4; hereafter cited in text as *Paradise*.

3. G. G. Dara, "Aborted Juvenile Utopia, " *Guardian* (Nigeria) 5, no. 3707 (7 March 1988): 13; hereafter cited in text.

Chapter Six

1. Philip Phil-Ebosie, *The Cyclist* (London: Macmillan, 1980), 126; hereafter cited in text as *Cyclist*.

2. Ngugi wa Thiong'O, *Decolonizing the Mind: The Politics and Language of African Literature* (London: Heinemann, 1986), 69–70.

3. Ben Chirasha, *Child of War* (London: Macmillan, 1985), 13; hereafter cited in text as *War*.

4. Jo Carr, *Beyond Fact: Nonfiction for Children and Young People* (Chicago: American Library Association, 1982), 4.

Chapter Seven

1. Tanure Ojaide, "Modern African Literature and Cultural Identity," *African Studies Review* 35, no. 3 (December 1992): 45.

2. Nancy J. Schmidt, "African Women Writers of Literature for Children," *World Literature Written in English* 17 (1987): 8.

3. Jurgen Martini, "The Author as *Sankofa* Bird: History in African Books for Children and Young People," *Matatu* 1 (1987): 41; hereafter cited in text.

4. Biola Odejide, "Biographies for Children in Nigeria," paper presented at the Ninth World Congress of the International Reading Association, Dublin, July 1992.

5. In *Twentieth-Century Children's Writers,* ed. Chevalier, 866.

6. S. I. A. Kotei, "Themes for Children's Literature in Ghana," *African Book Publishing Record* 4 (1978): 233.

7. Edward Sackey, "Oral Tradition and the African Novel," *Modern Fiction Studies* 37, no. 3 (1991): 405.

8. John Donovan, "The Civilize(d) Competition for English-Reading Young People," *School Library Journal* 25 (1979): 51–54.

9. John Daniel Stahl, "Canon Formation: A Historical and Psychological Perspective," in *Teaching Children's Literature,* ed. Sadler, 19.

10. For a concise discussion of the beginnings and development of African children's literature, see my essays "The Rise of African Children's Literature" (*The Reading Teacher* 38, no. 8 [1985]: 750–55) and "The Growth of African Children's Literature" (*The Reading Teacher* 41, no. 3 [1987]: 316–22).

Selected Bibliography

PRIMARY WORKS

Areo, Agbo. *A Paradise for the Masses*. Lagos: Paperback Publishers, 1985.

Chirasha, Ben. *Child of War* London: Macmillan, 1985.

Ekwensi, Cyprian. *The Passport of Mallam Ilia*. Cambridge: Cambridge University Press, 1960.

_____. *An African Night's Entertainment*. Lagos: African University Press, 1962.

_____. *Juju Rock*. Lagos: African Universities Press, 1966.

_____. *Gone to Mecca*. Ibadan: Heinemann Educational Books, 1991.

Emecheta, Buchi. *The Bride Price*. New York: George Braziller, 1976.

_____. *Naira Power*. London: Macmillan, 1982.

_____. *A Kind of Marriage*. London: Macmillan, 1986.

Maillu, David G. *For Mbatha and Rabeka*. London: Macmillan, 1980.

Oguntoye, Jide. *Too Cold for Comfort*. London: Macmillan, 1980.

Phil-Ebosie, Philip. *The Cyclist*. London: Macmillan, 1982.

SECONDARY WORKS

Interview

Cott, Jonathan. "Chinua Achebe: At the Crossroads." In *Pipers at the Gates of Dawn: The Wisdom of Children's Literature*, 161–92. New York: Random House, 1981. Cott's 1980 interview with Chinua Achebe in London focuses on his literature for children.

Books

Emecheta, Buchi. *Head above Water*. London and Nigeria: Ogwugwu Afo, 1986. Autobiographical work that sheds light on some aspects of her writings.

Emenyonu, Ernest. *Cyprian Ekwensi*. London: Evans, 1974. Study of Ekwensi that devotes a chapter to his literature for children.

German Commission for UNESCO and International Youth Library. *African Youth Literature Today and Tomorrow*. Bonn: German Commission for UNESCO; Munich: International Youth Library, 1988. Edited proceedings of a 1986 conference in Munich on African children's literature.

Odaga, Asenath. *Literature for Children and Young People in Kenya*. Nairobi: Kenya Literature Bureau, 1985. A study of children's literature—oral and written—of Kenya.

Osa, Osayimwense. *Nigerian Youth Literature*. Benin City: Paramount Publishers, 1987. A study of Nigerian youth fiction in English.

_____. *Foundation: Essays in Children's Literature and Youth Literature*. Benin City: Paramount Publishers, 1987. A collection of essays on children's literature in Africa.

Schmidt, Nancy J. *Children's Fiction about Africa in English*. New York: Conch Magazine, 1981. A study of African children's fiction and also a comparative study of African and Euro-American fiction for children.

Smith, Lillian. *The Unreluctant Years*. Chicago: American Library Association, 1953; revised, 1991. A critical study of children's literature.

Townsend, John Rowe. *Written for Children*. Boston: Horn Book, 1965. A study of children's literature in English.

Articles and Parts of Books

Aronson, David. "Why Africa Stays Poor and Why It Doesn't Have To." *The Humanist: A Magazine of Critical Inquiry and Ethical Concern* (March–April 1992): 9–14. Attributes Africa's poverty to the artificial creation of the states the people live in and points to the hardship poverty unleashes on people, especially children.

Bazin, Nancy Topping. "Feminist Perspectives in African Fiction." *Black Scholar* (March–April 1986): 34–60. A study of the feminism of Bessie Head and Buchi Emecheta.

_____. "Feminism in the Literature of African Women" *Black Scholar* (Summer–Fall 1989): 8–19. A study of feminist themes in the works of African women writers.

_____. "Weight of Custom, Signs of Change: Feminism in the Literature of African Women." *World Literature Written in English* 25, no. 2 (1985): 183–97. A study of the weight of African traditions, especially on women, and signs in the novels of Buchi Emecheta and Flora Nwapa from Nigeria, Bessie Head from Botswana, and Mariama Bâ from Senegal that couples are moving closer to egalitarian relationships.

Buchan, John. "The Novel and the Fairy Tale." In *Children and Literature: Views and Reviews,* edited by Virginia Haviland, 221–29. Glenview, Ill.: Scott Foresman, 1973. A study of the relationship between fairy tale and prose fiction.

Cameron, Eleanor. "Writing from Experience: Some Books Come Directly Out of Their Writers' own Childhoods." *Five Owls* 5, no. 3 (January–February 1991): 45–47. A writer's reflection on writing for young people.

Chukwuma, Helen. "Positivism and the Female Crisis: The Novels of Buchi Emecheta." In *Nigerian Female Writers: A Critical Perspective,* edited by

Henrietta Otokunefor and Obidgeli Nwodo, 2–18. Lagos: Malthouse Press, 1989. A study of Emecheta's enrichment of African literature with the African female point of view.

Dillsworth, Gloria. "Children's and Youth Literature in Sierra Leone." In *African Youth Literature: Today and Tomorrow*. Bonn: German Commission for UNESCO; Munich: International Youth Library, 1988. A survey of juvenile literature in Sierra Leone.

Donovan, John. "The Civilize(d) Competition for English-Reading Young People." *School Library Journal* 25 (1979): 51–54. A note on the reading of English-speaking young people compared with reading among young Americans.

Ekpenyong, Stephen. "Social Inequalities, Collusion, and Armed Robbery in Nigerian Cities." *British Journal of Criminology* 29, no. 1 (Winter 1989): 21–34. Thought-provoking essay suggesting that deemphasizing materialism as the prime value of society, together with the creation of a humane and disciplined society, may bring a reduction in armed robbery and related property offenses.

Ekwensi, Cyprian. "Stimulating and Moulding Junior Minds." In *Junior Literature in English*, edited by Solomon Unoh. Lagos: African Universities Press in Association with English Studies Association, 1981. Ekwensi's keynote address at the Nigeria English Studies Association conference; focuses on the utilitarian value of children's literature.

———. "The Problems of Writing, Illustrating and Publishing Adolescent/Teenage Literature for Children." *African Book Publishing Record* 14, no. 2 (1988): 95–97. Enumerates why writing and publishing for children has not been a priority with African writers.

Emenyonu, Ernest N. "Technique and Language in Buchi Emecheta's *The Bride Price, The Slave Girl*, and *The Joys of Motherhood*." *Journal of Commonwealth Literature* 23, no. 1 (1988): 131–41. A stylistic study of three of Emecheta's novels with particular reference to her use of language.

Frank, Katherine. "The Death of the Slave Girl: African Womanhood in the Novels of Buchi Emecheta." *World Literature Written in English* 21 (1982): 476–97. A study of the image of the African woman in Emecheta's novels.

Gundu, G. A. "Tiv-Written Children's Literature: Content and Narrative Forms." *Journal of African Children's Literature* 1 (1989): 79–91. A critique of African children's literature written in Tiv.

Hamilton, Virginia. "Hans Christian Andersen Award Speech." *USBBY Newsletter* 18, no. 2 (Fall 1992): 6–8. Text of Hamilton's acceptance speech.

Heale, Jay, and Annair van de Merwe. "South Africa Joins IBBY." *Bookbird* 30, no. 2 (May 1992). An update of children's literature status in South Africa.

Hughes, Shaun F. D. "Others' Africas: Recent Critical Studies of African Literature." *Modern Fiction Studies* 37, no. 3 (1991): 617–37. A critical review of recent scholarly studies in African literature.

Isola, Akinwumi. "The African Writer's Tongue." *Research in African Literatures* 23, no. 1 (1992): 17–26. A plea for African writers to use more of their indigenous tongues in writing.

Knoepflmacher, U. C. Introduction to *Teaching Children's Literature*, edited by Glenn Edward Sadler, 1–9. New York: MLA 1992. An introductory essay to scholarship in children's literature.

Kotei, S. I. A. "Themes for Children's Literature in Ghana." *African Book Publishing Record* 4 (1978): 233–39. A discussion of the prerequisites to reading-habit formation—folk tales, legends, drama for creativity and self-expression, and poetry for language development.

Lindfors, Bernth. "Cyprian Ekwensi: An African Popular Novelist." *African Literature Today* 1–4 (1969): 2–14. Criticism of some aspects of Ekwensi's literary works, including those for children.

Macleod, Anne Scott. "International Research Society for Children's Literature (IRSCL)." In *Children's Literature Research: International Resources and Exchange*, edited by the International Youth Library. Munich: K. G. Saur, 1991. A short historical overview of the International Research Society for Children's Literature from its beginning to the present.

Martini, Jurgen. "Sex, Class, and Power: The Emergence of a Capitalist Youth Culture in Nigeria." *Journal of African Children's Literature* 1 (1989): 43–59. A discussion of Nigerian youth novels that reflect the values of a capitalist society.

_____. "Linking Africa and the West: Buchi Emecheta." *Bayreuther Beitrage Zur Sprachwissenschraft* 7 (n.d.): 223–33. Discusses Emecehta's Westernized African approach to the role of women in African society.

_____. "The Author as *Sankofa* Bird: History in African Books for Children and Young People." *Matatu* 1, no. 1 (1987): 35–51. A study of the sense of history in African children's literature.

Masson, Sophie. "African Children's Literature." *Papers* 1, no. 2 (1990): 71–74. A study of the emerging children's literature of Africa.

_____. "Notes on African Children's Literature." *Reading Time: The Journal of the Children's Book Council of Australia* 36, no. 1 (1992): 12. A brief note on recent development in scholarship on African children's literature.

Ngcobo, Lauretta. "African Motherhood: Myth and Reality." In *Criticism and Ideology: Second African Writers Conference*, edited by Kirsten Holst Petersen. Uppsala: Scandinavian Institute of African Studies, 1988. A mythical and realistic depiction of African womanhood in literature.

Nyarko, Francis. "The Production and Distribution of Children's Literature in Africa: A Diagnostic Survey." In *Children's Book Production and Distribution in Developing Countries,* edited by Doros Theodoulou and Paulos Ioannides. Nineteenth Congress of the International Board on Books for

Young People, 9–14 October 1984. A survey of children's literature production and distribution in Africa.

Oculli, Okello. "The Politics of Literature for Children in Africa." *Guardian* (Lagos), 29 and 30 November 1984. A political dimension of children's literature.

Odejide, Biola. "Children's Biographies of Nigerian Figures: A Critical and Cultural Assessment." *Reading Teacher* 40, no. 7 (1987): 640–44. A study of biography for African children and discussion of how indigenous authors and publishers attempt to provide a literature that preserves cultural history while meeting literary needs.

_____. "Education as Quest: The Nigerian School Story." *Children's Literature in Education* 18, no. 2 (1987): 77–87. An examination of acquisition of Western education as a means of self-improvement and social mobility in the Nigerian school story.

Ogunyemi, Chikwenye O. "Buchi Emecheta: The Shaping of Self." *Komparatistische Hefte* 8 (1983): 63–80. A study of Emecheta's shaping of herself, which takes the form of 18 years' sojourn in Britain.

_____. "Womanism: The Dynamics of the Contemporary Black Female Novel in English." *Signs* 11 (1985): 63–80. Contrasts Buchi Emecheta's feminist stance in her novels with the womanist stance of other black women writers—African Americans.

Ojaide, Tanure. "Modern African Literature and Cultural Identity." *African Studies Review* 35, no. 3 (December 1992): 43–57. A study of the cultural distinctiveness of African literature.

Osa, Osayimwense. "Adolescent Literature in Contemporary Nigeria." *World Literature Written in English* 23 (1984): 298–303. A study of the evolution of adolescent literature in Nigeria and a discussion of its characteristics.

_____. "Adolescent Girls' Need for Love in Two Cultures: Nigeria and the United States." *English Journal* 72, no. 8 (1983): 35–37. Focuses on two female protagonists in two young adult novels, Buchi Emecheta's *The Bride Price* and Bette Greene's *The Summer of My German Soldier*, who suffer neglect from their parents and community and find love and happiness in the company of social outcasts.

_____. "The Rise of African Children's Literature." *Reading Teacher* 38, no. 8 (1985): 750–53. A survey of African children's literature from early times to the present.

_____. "The Growth of African Children's Literature." *Reading Teacher* 41, no. 3 (1987): 316–22. Discusses significant developments in African children's literature.

_____. "Didacticism in Nigerian Young Adult Literature." *Journal of Reading* 29, no. 3 (1985): 251–53. Discusses the didactic thrust—simple and complex—of selected young adult novels.

_____. "Buchi Emecheta's *The Bride Price*: A Nondidactic Nigerian Youth Novel." *Children's Literature in Education* 19, no. 3 (1988): 170–75.

Establishes the uniqueness of *The Bride Price* as a nondidactic work in African youth literature.

_____. "Touchstones in Nigerian Youth Literature." *ALAN Review* 15, no. 3 (1988): 56–58. A discussion of three outstanding young adult novels from Nigeria.

Petersen, Kirsten Holst. "Buchi Emecheta: Unorthodox Fictions about African Women." In *International Literature in English: Essays on the Major Writers*, edited by Robert L. Ross, 283–92. New York: Garland, 1991. A critique of Emecheta's novels.

Sackey, Edward. "Oral Tradition and the African Novel." *Modern Fiction Studies* 37, no. 3 (1991): 389–407. A discussion of the rootedness of contemporary African literature in the oral tradition.

Schmidt, Nancy J. "African Women Writers of Literature for Children." *World Literature Written in English* 17, no. 1 (1978): 7–21. A study of the achievement of female writers of African children's literature.

_____. "Children's Books by Well-Known African Authors." *World Literature Written in English* 18 (1979): 114–24. Discusses the often neglected works of some major African writers—children's books—and argues that much more needs to be known about these works.

_____. "4th Zimbabwe International Book Fair, 1987: An Overview of Published African Children's Literature." *African Book Publishing Record* 13 (1987): 237–39. A survey of published African children's literature.

_____. "The Africanization of Children's Literature in English-Speaking Sub-Saharan Africa." *Journal of African Children's Literature* 1 (1989): 7–19. Discusses the development of African children's literature from colonial times to the present.

Skinner, Neil. "From Hausa to English: A Study in Paraphrase." *Research in African Literatures* 4 (1973): 154–64. Establishes a very close connection between *Jikin Magayi* written in Hausa in 1934 and *An African Night's Entertainment*.

Solberg, Rolf. "Buchi Emecheta: The Woman's Voice in the New Nigerian Novel." *English Studies* 64 (1983): 247–62. A study of the new point of view of the African woman in Nigerian literature.

Stahl, John Daniel. "Canon Formation: A Historical and Psychological Perspective." In *Teaching Children's Literature: Issues, Pedagogy, Resources*, edited by Glenn Edward Sadler, 12–21. New York: MLA, 1992. Focuses on the problem of establishing a canon in children's literature.

Ward, Cynthia. "What They Told Buchi Emecheta: Oral Subjectivity and the Joys of 'Otherhood.'" *PMLA* 105, no. 1 (1990): 83–97. A study of Emecheta's works as a response to African tradition of storytelling.

Wagner, Gulten. "Nigerian Children's Books: An Evaluation." *African Book Publishing Record* 2 (1976): 231–36. A condensed version of Wagner's master's thesis, "An Evaluation Study of Children's Books Published in Nigeria," University of Ibadan, 1975.

Zipes, Jack. "Second Thoughts on Socialization through Literature." *Lion and the Unicorn* 5 (1981): 19–32. A study of children's literature as a sociopsychological agent legitimizing and subverting, with cop and criminal compelled by the same laws.

Reviews

Abarry, Abu. "Review of *The Journal of African Children's Literature* 1 1989." *Research in African Literatures* 22, no. 1 (1991): 148–51.

Dara, G. G. "Aborted Juvenile Utopia: Review of *A Paradise for the Masses*." *Guardian* (Lagos), 7 March 1988, 13.

Nwachukwu-Agbada, J. O. J. "*Nigerian Female Writers: A Critical Perspective*, edited by Henrietta Otokunefor and Obiageli Nwodo." *Research in African Literatures* 21, no. 4 (1990): 156–59.

Osa, Osayimwense. "Review of *Children's Fiction about Africa in English*, by Nancy J. Schmidt." *Research in African Literatures* 14, no. 2 (1983): 257–61.

———. "Review of *African Folktales for Children*." *Research in African Literatures* 18, no. 1 (1987): 91–93.

Schmidt, Nancy J. "Review of *Nigerian Youth Literature*, by Osayimwense Osa." *Research in African Literatures* 19, no. 3 (1988): 413–16.

Index

Achebe, Chinua, xi, xix, xxiii–xxiv, xxv
  WORKS
  Chike and the River (1960), 138
  No Longer at Ease (1960), 39–40
  Things Fall Apart, 90
  adventure stories, 20–21
Africa, civil disorganization in, 93–94;
  congestion in, 72, 78, 90–91; corruption in, 66–67, 69–70; cults of,
  55–56; food in, 126; Islam in, 79–80;
  juvenile literature in, ix; oral tradition
  in, ix, 1–3, 139; political division of
  tribes in, ix–x, 110; prostitution in,
  67, 73; robbery in, 66–67, 69–70,
  139; role of parents in, 87, 90; treatment of mentally ill in, 116–17
African juvenile literature, and autobiographies, 137–38; and biographies,
  137; black magic in, 41, 54, 60–61,
  76–77, 105–6; colonialism, 10, 11,
  127–35; communalism in, 3; as compared to that of America, xxvi; concept of childhood in, xxv; conferences
  about, xxi–xxiv; corruption in, 69–70,
  75–76, 86–92; courses on, xxiv; crime
  in, 66–73, 139; criticism of, xix–xxii,
  54–55; and cults, 50–56; 57; as
  didactic, xi, 21–22; drama and verse
  in, 136–37; family in, 47–48; as far-
  reaching, x–xi; and folk tale, x, 1–2;
  function of, 136; indigenous language
  in, xii; Islam in, 16–19, 23, 79–85;
  jealousy in, 112–15; love in, 47–50,
  112–15, 118–22; marriage in, 47–48,
  50–56, 115–18; materialism in, 7, 8,
  68–69, 73–75; as moral, xii; multiculturalism of, xiii, 54–55, 139–41; oral
  tradition in, ix, 1–3, 5–6, 7–8, 12, 22,
  64–65, 92, 139; organizations promoting, xxi–xxiv; periodicals concerning, xxiv; polygamy in, 33–35,
  56–65, 75–80, 85–86, 105–7; racism
  in, xxv–xxvi; rites of passage in,
  xxvi–xxvii; sex in, 40–41, 50–53,

77–79, 113–14, 126; situation in Africa
  regarding, ix–x, xiii; and stories about
  school, 138; symbolism in, 122–25;
  theme of power in, 125–27; vengeance
  in, 13–15; vigilante execution in,
  73–75, 86; war in, 125–27, 128–35;
  and women, 26–27, 31–36, 111
Areo, Agbo
  WORKS
  Director!, 66, 67–69, 75
  A Paradise for the Masses (1985), hatred
  of whites in, 103–4; and *magun*,
  xx, 105–6; plot of, 94–97; political activism in, 11, 100–109;
  polygamy in, 105–7
Armah, Kwei: *The Beautyful Ones Are Not
  Yet Born* (1968), 93
Aronson, David, 66–67
Asante tribe, x
Asare, Meshach: *The Brassman's Secret*
  (1981), x
autobiographies, 138
Azevedo, Mario, 33

Bastian, Misty, 54–55
Baule tribe, 33
Bazin, Nancy Topping, 32, 43, 92
Bemba tribe, 33
Biafra, 110
biographies, 137
black magic, 41, 54, 60–61, 76–77,
  105–6
Breitinger, Eckhard, xxiv–xxv, 47
bride price, 26–27, 111
Broderick, Dorothy, xxi

Cameron, Eleanor, xii
Carr, Jo, 134
Chirasha, Ben: *Child of War* (1985),
  127–35
Chukwuma, Helen, 43
colonialism, xii, 10, 11, 127–35
communalism, 3
Conrad, Joseph: *Lord Jim*, 65

159

Cormier, Robert, xii
Coulon, Virginia, 48, 54
crime, 66–73, 139
cults, 50–56, 57

Dankert, Birgit, xxiii
Dara, G. G., 107
Donovan, John, 140
dowry, 26–27, 111
drama, 136–37

Edo tribe, xii, 73
Ekpenyong, Stephen, 67
Ekwensi, Cyprian, xix, xxiii, xxv, 1–2,
   22–24
   WORKS
   An African Night's Entertainment
      (1962), x, 2–8, 13, 14–15, 19, 21, 69
   The Boa Suitor (1966), 47
   Burning Grass (1962), 1, 23
   The Drummer Boy (1960), 19, 21
   Gone to Mecca (1991), 15–19, 23
   Jagua Nana, 22
   Juju Rock (1966), 20–22
   "Motherless Baby" (1980), 19–20
   The Passport of Mallam Ilia (1960), 2,
      8–15, 18, 19; People of the City
      (1954), 1, 22
   Trouble in Form Six (1966), 19
   When Love Whispers (1948), 20, 22
Emecheta, Buchi, xxv, 25–26, 71–72,
   139
   WORKS
   The Bride Price (1976), autobiographical
      elements of, 36; conclusion of,
      41–46; feminism in, 31–33; non-
      comformity in, 37–39; the osu tradi-
      tion in, xx, 39–41, 45; polygamy in,
      33–35; sex in, 40–41; theme of
      maturation in, 35–37; traditional-
      ism in, 29–31, 41–46; as a youth
      novel, 27–29
   A Kind of Marriage (1986), xxv, 25,
      32, 48, 56–65, 92
   Naira Power (1982), background to,
      69–73; Islam in, 79–85; narration

in, 56, 63; parental duties in, 87,
   90; polygamy in, 75–79, 85–86;
   spiritualist in, 80–85; vigilante exe-
   cution in, 74–75, 86
   Nowhere to Play (1980), x
   Second Class Citizen (1975), 33
   The Slave Girl (1977), 25
   Titch the Cat (1979), x
Emenyonu, Ernest, xix, 23, 42
Ewe tribe, ix, 110

family, 47–48
Fayose, Osaze, xxi
feminism, 31–33
Fodio, Usman dan, 80
folk tale, x, 1–2
Frank, Katherine, 25
Fulani, Jihad, 80

Greene, Betty: Summer of My German
   Soldier, 39, 40
griots, ix
Griswold, Wendy, 48, 54–55
Gundu, G. A., xiii

hair plaiting, 113
hajj, 16–19, 84
Halperin, David, 55
Hamilton, Virginia, xiii
Hausa tribe, 7–8, 23, 79–80
Hillers, Elfriede, xxiii
Hughes, Shaun F. D., xix

Igbo tribe, xx, 27, 32–33
Innes, C. L., xix
Islam, 16–19, 23, 79–85
Isola, Akinwumi, xii–xiii

jealousy, 112–15
Jiki Magayi (East and Zaria; 1934),
   7–8
Jones, Jim, 55

Kanengoni, Alexander: Vicious Circle
   (1983), 127–28
Kimenye, Barbara, 138

Knoepflmacher, U. C., xi
Koresh, David, 55
Kyprianou, Spyros, 139–40

Langone, Michael, 54
Leppman, Jella, 140
Lewis, Charles Stephen, 140
love, 47–50, 112–15, 118–22

MacLeod, Anne Scott, x–xi, xx
magun, xx, 105–6
Maillu, David, xx; *For Mbatha and Rabeka* (1980), 48–50
marabout, 80–85
marriage, 7, 47–48, 50–56, 56–65, 115–22
Martini, Jurgen, xxiii, xxiv–v, 48, 54
Masson, Sophie, xxv
materialism, 7, 8, 68–69, 73–75
Mensah, A. W. Kayper, xix
menstruation, cycle of, and transition to womanhood, 36
mental illness, 116–17
Mpahlele, Ezekiel: *Father Come Home*, xxvi, 26, 137
multiculturalism, xii, 54–55, 139–41

naira, 70, 73
Nigeria, and African children's literature, ix, 22; anthem of, 93; authors of, xix, xxi; civil war in, 110; crime in, 66–70; Islam in, 79–80
Nwachuku-Agbada, J. O. J., xix
Nyarko, Francis, xxii

obas, 83
Odaga, Asenath, xxi
Odejide, Biola, xxi
Oguntoye, Jide: *Too Cold for Comfort* (1980), 48, 50–56
Ogunyemi, Chikwenye, 27, 42
Olagoke, Olu: *The Incorruptible Judge* (1962), 137
Onwu, Charry Ada, xix

Okoro, Anezi
  WORKS
  Double Trouble (1989), 138
  One Week One Trouble (1973), 138
oral tradition, ix, 1–3, 5–6, 7–8, 12, 22, 64–65, 92, 139
Osa, Osayimwense, xxi
Ossai, Anji, xix
osu, xx, 39–41, 45
Ovbiagele, Helen, xix

Pacesetters junior novel series, xxv
palm-wine tapping, 118, 121
Pellowski, Anne, xxiii
Peterson, Kirsten Holst, 43
Phil-Ebosie, Philip: *The Cyclist* (1982), characterization in, 118–22; jealousy in, 112–15; plot of, 111–12; symbolism in, 122–25; theme of power in, 125–27; theme of spousal obligation in, 115–18; theme of war in, 125–27, 134–35
polygamy, 30–31, 33–35, 56–65, 76–79, 80, 85–86, 105–7
power, 8, 125–27
proverbs, 6
prostitution, 67, 73

racism, xxv–xxvi
Roscoe, Adrian, xix
Ruprecht, Frank, xxiii

Schmidt, Nancy J., xx, xxi, xxiii, 138
Schultz, Joachim, xxiv–xxv
Segun, Mabel, 137–38
  WORKS
  My Father's Daughter (1965), 138
  My Mother's Daughter (1987), 138
  Youth Day Parade (1984), 138
sex, 40–41, 50–53, 77–79, 113–14, 126
shanci, 9–10, 13, 14, 15
Sierra Leone, ix
Solberg, Rolf, 33
South Africa, i, xxii
Stahl, John Daniel, 140–41

storytellers. *See* oral tradition
Streit, Gerda, xxiii
Sutherland, Efua, 136–37: *Foriwa*, xxvi,
137

Thiong'O, Ngugi wa, 110, 128
WORKS
Devil on the Cross (1982), 93–94
Petals of Blood (1977), 93
Weep Not Child (1964), 133
Tötemeyer, Andrée-Jeanne, ix
Townsend, John Rowe, xx–xxi,
xxv–xxvi
Tucker, Martin, xix

vengeance, 13–15

Wagner, Gulten, xxi
Ward, Cynthia, 35
witchcraft. *See* black magic
Wolff, Horst, xix
Wollof tribe, ix, 33, 110
women, 26–27, 31–36, 111

Yao tribe, 33
Yoruba tribe, ix, xx, 105–6

Zimbabwe, 127–28

The Author

Osayimwense Osa is associate professor of English at Clark Atlanta University, Atlanta, and former head of the Department of Languages and Literature at Bendel State University (now Edo State University), Ekpoma, Nigeria. Educated at Ahmadu Bello University, Nigeria, the University of New Brunswick, and the University of Houston, Professor Osa has taught in various universities on both sides of the Atlantic. In 1989 he established and is currently editor of the *Journal of African Children's Literature* (now the *Journal of African Children's and Youth Literature*) and is also the founding editor of *Ekpoma Journal of Languages and Literary Studies*. He is the author of *Nigerian Youth Literature* and *Foundation: Essays in Children's Literature and Youth Literature* and the editor of the essay collection *Youth Literature International: A Selection of Readings*. He has been a visiting scholar to the International Youth Library in Munich, Germany, and a fellow at the International Institute for Children's Literature, Osaka, Japan.

The Editor

Ruth K. MacDonald is associate dean of Bay Path College. She received her B.A. and M.A. in English from the University of Connecticut, her Ph.D. in English from Rutgers University, and her M.B.A. from the University of Texas at El Paso. She is author of the volumes on Louisa May Alcott, Beatrix Potter, and Dr. Seuss in Twayne's United States and English Authors Series and of the book *Literature for Children in England and America, 1646–1774* (1982).